Also by Caroline Dooner

The F*ck It Diet

TIRED AS F*CK

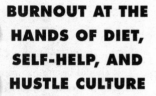

**BURNOUT AT THE
HANDS OF DIET,
SELF-HELP, AND
HUSTLE CULTURE**

CAROLINE DOONER

HARPER WAVE

An Imprint of HarperCollinsPublishers

TIRED AS F*CK. Copyright © 2022 by Caroline Dooner. All rights reserved. Printed in the United States of America. No part of this book may be used or reproduced in any manner whatsoever without written permission except in the case of brief quotations embodied in critical articles and reviews. For information, address HarperCollins Publishers, 195 Broadway, New York, NY 10007.

HarperCollins books may be purchased for educational, business, or sales promotional use. For information, please email the Special Markets Department at SPsales@harpercollins.com.

FIRST EDITION

Designed by Nancy Singer

Library of Congress Cataloging-in-Publication Data has been applied for.

ISBN 978-0-06-305297-0

22 23 24 25 26 LSC 10 9 8 7 6 5 4 3 2 1

For everyone who is tired

CONTENTS

INTRODUCTION: HOW TO BE FILLED WITH DREAD

A few years ago, I read *The Life-Changing Magic of Tidying Up* by Marie Kondo, and along with everyone else, I decided to declutter my entire apartment of everything that didn't "spark joy." I was feeling stuck, and I hoped that getting rid of my stuff would help me feel . . . *something*. Lighter? Freer? Clearer?

So I got rid of lumpy pillows stuffed in the back of the linen closet. They did not spark joy. I got rid of dresses that were supposed to make me look like a little princess for the musical theater auditions I still forced myself to go to. *Joyless*. I threw out my little box of mismatched buttons I'd collected over the years. I was never ever going to use them *because I am not a quirky seamstress*. Goodbye twelve tangled obsolete computer cords! Goodbye broken umbrellas! Goodbye to who I was before! *None of these things spark joy*. I decluttered and decluttered. I donated and threw out bags and bags of broken kitchen utensils and boots that had never fit, until I was left with a nearly bare apartment.

After a few days, once the temporary high of seeing thirty-five empty hangers in an empty closet wore off, I realized: oh . . . my stuff wasn't actually the big problem; my *life* doesn't spark joy. My life sparks dread. It exhausts me. And it has for a long time.

I was sick of *everything*. I was sick of auditioning for acting jobs. I was sick of a career that I needed to medicate myself for in order to calm down. I was sick of never feeling like I was doing enough or being productive enough or impressive enough or innovative enough. I was sick of online dating and the drain of bad first dates, and the *guilt* I felt for wanting to just stay home. And after fifteen years (more than half my life at that point) of self-help books, I was so *so* sick of trying to self-improve in one way or another.

I was exhausted, but I didn't feel like I *deserved* to be exhausted. Most people have way harder lives than me, and most people just push through—because they have to. So, what the hell was wrong with me? Was I weak? Lazy? My burnout seemed like some sort of personal failing. But no matter how ridiculous or weak I thought it looked on the outside, I couldn't deny it: I *was* exhausted. I *was* burnt out. And I could either keep going the way I was going and probably get even *more* tired, or do something about it.

The truth is, the exhaustion went beyond physical exhaustion (even though physical exhaustion was definitely part of it). The exhaustion was stemming from an even deeper place. I had been operating under so many beliefs that I had never consciously recognized. Beliefs about human worth tied to our productivity: *You must always be productive. You must always be improving. You can only relax once you reach your goal and become more impressive.* I never felt like I was allowed to just . . . be. And I didn't think I was allowed to accept myself the way I was, because the way I was *wasn't good enough. I was deeply flawed.* And I thought until I fixed all my flaws, I had to suffer. I was never able to enjoy and relax, not only because I'd chosen a life and career that was so nerve-racking to me, but also because I was constantly supposed to be self-improving and *getting somewhere else.* And because the goal-post is *always* moving, and I never actually *got there*, it never ended. I never felt calm. And it was frying my nerves.

Usually, when I started feeling this way, I looked for a self-help book to help me figure out what was wrong with me, and how to fix it. But this time, something inside me told me that instead of reading *another* self-help book that promised to heal me on a cellular level from the inside out, what I really needed was to *stop.* After more than a decade dedicated to rabid self-improvement, the answer for my exhaustion wasn't more self-improvement. It couldn't be. I'd already tried that over and over. I didn't want to be a project anymore. Honestly, I was too *tired* to be a never-ending project. Right now, the only answer that felt relieving to me was *rest. Rest* from self-improvement. Rest from the grind. And if *at all* possible, rest from my own cruel mind.

When you're burnt out, the answer isn't more pressure. It's less. I needed to, somehow, get off the hamster wheel I was on. I needed existential rest. I needed soul rest. I needed to opt out of the entire story I'd written for myself about what I was "supposed to be do-ing." We live in a culture that doesn't really *understand* or respect burnout. We all soak in this belief that exhaustion is weak and that we all need to just buck up and be a little bit less *lazy.* That's what I'd been trying to do. But it wasn't working for me. So, I needed to give myself permission to opt out of our entire culture that tells us we're never good enough and never doing enough. I needed to figure out if it was even possible to wake up every morning and *not* feel guilt or dread.

Four years *earlier*, I realized that dieting and trying to lose weight over and over again had run me ragged. Dieting messed me up physically and mentally and emotionally. So, I decided to stop dieting. I bought bigger pants. I deliberately unlearned most of our misguided cultural beliefs about food and weight and health. I examined some of the root causes of my body fixation—and it all eventually became *The F*ck It Diet* book.

My decision to opt out of our cultural diet mania completely changed my life, but after a few years I realized that I still had cultural expectations about *everything else,* not just food and weight. *Diet culture* pushes the belief that we should always be striving for *control* over food and over our bodies. It says that less food and being thinner is *always* better. But diet culture is actually just a subset of our culture at large that's obsessed with control, and hustling, and personal responsibility, and hyper-productivity. And when I addressed my relationship with food, I'd only actually addressed a small part of a bigger cultural paradigm that worships control and self-punishment. So, *now* I needed to say "f*ck it" to all the *other* cultural expectations that were still invisibly strangling me. I had to address hustle culture's hold over me, where every single fucking second of the day I expected myself to be working, hustling, and being productive. And the way I was deciding to opt out? I was going to rest. I was going to give myself a *significant healing period of rest*. And, just to be extra dramatic, I decided I was going to give myself *two full years* to rest. I wanted it to feel radical. And epic. And I felt like one year just wasn't going to be long enough.

Now, when I say *rest*, most people imagine that I'm saying either: rest from work, rest from physical activity, or good old-fashioned sleep. And while those things are great and important and *absolutely* a part of rest, I'm actually talking about something even bigger than just sitting still or lying down or doing less. I didn't want to approach rest as *just* an activity to check off my to-do list (though that's fine too!), I wanted to approach it as a sort of . . . way of life. I knew that just sitting around or forcing myself to lie down wasn't going to be enough. I had to release my stress over it. I had to release my resistance and guilt. I had to *radically allow* the act of rest. I needed *permission* to rest as an antidote to the anxiety and burnout I'd been experiencing for years.

I still had to work. I wasn't going to be just lying around for two years. So, my rest was about working through the beliefs I had around rest and relaxation in the first place. I needed to actually figure out how to operate in my life in a more restful *way*—long term. Not just with work, but with *everything*. With the way I talked to myself. With the expectations I put on myself. With the constant feeling that I was supposed to be *doing more*. I needed to give myself permission to chill out, even when I *was* working. I needed to untangle myself from the pressure I was constantly putting on myself. I needed to work on the guilt and antsy-ness that was programmed into my cells every time I *did* try to chill out. It didn't mean I wasn't going to work for two years—but I *was* going to stop pursuing a career that has chewed me up and spat me out. It didn't mean I wasn't going to exercise or get anything done or spend twenty hours a day in bed, but the *energy* I approached my life with was going to be very different. Hopefully. That was my goal at least. My new goal was rest, and radical *permission* to rest.

* * *

Years ago, while I was unlearning everything our culture teaches us about weight and health and food, I learned about the social determinants of health. And I was shocked. *Why* doesn't anybody seem to care about the social determinants of health?! No mainstream conversation is talking about it?! All we talk about is losing weight and eating "clean" and exercise and the newest fad diets. The mainstream dialogue never mentions the fact that chronic stress, poor sleep, poverty, racism, and all kinds of oppression *affect our health,* more than anything we eat.

Instead of giving people the well-rounded health care they need: sleep, support, access to doctors, trauma-informed therapy, a safe space to heal, and permission to rest, we are usually flippantly told to go on another diet and lose weight. Or go on a cleanse. Or intermittent fast. Or go keto. "Just lose weight! It's easy!" As if "lose weight" isn't already proven to backfire 95 percent of the time and lead to weight cycling, which often exacerbates chronic health issues. As if drinking celery juice or going keto weren't already accessible only to wealthy people, not to mention *completely* unhelpful for most people. No one is talking about the thing that matters even more: *Access to rest. Access to peace.*

This book is about my own experience in a culture that encourages productivity and "personal responsibility" at all costs. It ran me into the ground. And I'm sharing my story because I know I am not alone. You are not alone. So many of us are burning ourselves out trying to be the "best versions of ourselves." But what if the expectations we've taken on are unfair? What if the game is rigged? What if we are seeking something created by marketing companies and glorified by magazines and Instagram influencers? What if what we *think* is the best version of ourselves is actually an *impossible* version of ourselves? What if we'll be *exhausted* until we untangle ourselves from that pressure?

So many of us are impossibly hard on ourselves. So many of us are constantly seeking beauty and thinness through extreme dieting and searching for miracle cures through spiritual self-help. So many of us are seeking excellence and approval through soul-crushing workaholism. So many of us are trying to force ourselves into boxes we don't fit in and don't belong in. So many of us are trying to have it all and ignoring our body's signs of burnout.

That was my experience. And no matter what it looked like on the outside, stress and self-hatred were eroding me from the inside out.

In this book I'm going to tell you my story, and how I was *always convinced there was something horribly wrong with me*—and the exhausting things I did to try to fix myself. I'm not telling my story because I think it's the *most* dramatic or horrible or exhausting or interesting story ever. I really don't. But telling you some of my story will help me get to a common thread for so many of us: being *convinced* there is something wrong and broken inside us. These are the things that will continue to exhaust *all of us,* until we see them for what they are. So, I'm going to tell you about my perfectionism, my self-help obsession, my undiagnosed eating disorder, and how our culture applauded my extremism every step of the way. Everywhere I looked, it felt like I was being encouraged to *push even harder. Keep trying to improve!* And so—I did. There are so many ways we are *encouraged* to torture ourselves to become and stay impressive—and usually it doesn't fucking work. And it isn't fucking worth it.

And *then* I'm going to tell you how I broke my cycle of exhaustion. I mean . . . don't get me wrong, *I still get stressed. I still get tired.* But it's way better than it was, because I have a different relationship with rest and productivity. After years of running myself ragged, I finally learned how to prioritize my own peace. I want that for you too.

HOW TO NOT BE A
PSYCHOPATH

Last night in bed, I googled "Do sociopaths like dogs?" and I lay there reading the responses from self-identified sociopaths and psychopaths on Quora until after midnight. So, I'm very tired today—and angry with myself. But I learned *a lot*. I learned that, *yes*, sociopaths like owning dogs, because dogs are obedient and trusting and easily manipulated. Which is upsetting, because I was hoping that a dog could be my man filter so I don't accidentally end up marrying a murderer one day.

I learned a lot last night, actually. I learned the difference between *socio*paths and *psycho*paths. It's mostly a nature vs. nurture thing (at least according to what I read last night—I am in no way a psychopath expert). Apparently, sociopaths are made, and psychopaths are *born*. Psychopaths are literally born with a different brain—a smaller amygdala—and do not feel anxiety or fear. *Whaaaaat? No anxiety or fear?* They don't have the *capacity* to feel fear like most other humans. And they have no conscience. No little voice telling them that what they're doing is wrong. Obviously, that can create major problems, like serial killers and cult leaders and diabolical CEOs, but before thinking about the problems, I tried to imagine what it would feel like to not feel fear or anxiety. And I felt immediately jealous.

Can you imagine how freeing that would be? To walk around life like you're in a video game? To feel like a god among stupid humans? No doubt? No constant self-nagging and self-worry? No incessant voice in your head telling you you're *doing life wrong*? Wow. Not fair.

After a minute of imagining the fantasy freedom of psychopathy, I decided that even if I *had* a choice, no, I would not choose psychopathy. Psychopathy is *not* the answer to our exhaustion. I mean, maybe it actually is, but I know that we'd just be trading one problem for another, bigger problem.

But . . . no anxiety? I'd sleep like a baby. I mean . . . I'd sleep like a psychopath.

I didn't actually realize how much anxiety I had until a few years ago. I know . . . that seems like a hard thing to miss, but for so long, I really thought that this was *just what life was. Dread! All the time!* I thought that my constant feelings of dread were happening because I had things that I needed to *fix* and figure out and conquer, and that once I finally fixed and figured out and conquered them, all my feelings of general dread would go away. I didn't identify it as anxiety, I thought it was just the *reality* of having a million things about myself that I needed to improve. And I thought that once I *improved*, I wouldn't feel so scared and miserable anymore. In a way it's how so many of us are primed to think, hoping that the next product we buy, or the next program we complete, is going to finally fix our brokenness and make us peaceful and content.

I've now realized that some anxiety is normal and the result of being a non-psychopath human with a normal nervous system and a normal-sized amygdala. Some anxiety is chemical and genetic. Some is the result of unresolved trauma and the body being stuck in a "fight, flight, or freeze" state. And some is from *learned beliefs*.

My internal thermostat is always set to the "mildly anxious" setting, and sometimes it breaks and overheats into the "very anxious" setting, and I need to open the windows and let the air in and call the electrician. I'm guessing that for me, at least *part* of it is genetic, and unfortunately, it's just the way it is.

But a *lot* of my anxiety stemmed from believing that I was constantly supposed to be impressing people. And it started back in 1990, when my parents realized that I had a really good singing voice for a toddler. I don't know what that realization process was like, and I don't know what a good-singing toddler sounds like, but as far back as I can remember, I have been told I have an absolutely *amazing singing voice*. And as far back as I can remember, I have been singing for people, and have been *very stressed about it*.

"Caroline, you're such a good singer [for a three-year-old], will you stand up on this coffee table and sing a little song for all your aunts and uncles?"

"Yes! Do you want me to sing 'I'm a Little Dutch Girl'? Or 'How Are Things in Glocca Morra'?"

I felt a constant need to impress people. And *then* once they were impressed, it didn't get easier, because then I had to *keep* people impressed. The constant expectation of performing and *impressing* people started to stress me out.

I *did* love singing. But even more than that, I learned to love impressing people. And I became very, very stressed about my voice from a very young age. I was *very* critical of my singing from a young age because I wanted to live up to the hype! I didn't want to let my peeps down! I couldn't let down Great-Aunt Bernie! She just told everyone in the room how great I am!

What happens to a person's brain when they are constantly getting praise for something that stresses them out? This dynamic came to haunt me, and will haunt this very book, and it only got worse and worse the more people were part of the hype cycle, and the more high-stakes the performing venues became. This happens to a lot of us, I think. We're all so caught up being impressive or worth something and holding on to whatever praise we get that we don't often stop to consider whether it's actually worth it. Can't we just *live*?! Can't we just enjoy life's little pleasures without worrying that we are unimpressive?

So to any four-year-olds who are reading this book, here is my advice to you: do *not* take your singing voice too seriously, because your perfectionism might backfire on you with debilitating shakiness and performance anxiety, and the one thing you could have truly loved will come to haunt you and make you cry. And even at thirty-one, when you are singing at your best friend's wedding, instead of joy you will only feel terror. Instead, maybe just lurk in the background and become OK with simple joys and *not* being the center of attention. It is more peaceful there.

Anxiety is exhausting. It's depleting. It's distracting. And it affects your mind *and* your body. And, if you are not a psychopath, you probably have some anxiety. It's to be expected. The question I think we eventually have to ask ourselves is: How much of our anxiety is inherent and chemical and unavoidable, and how much of it is *learned* and accidentally perpetuated?

I eventually realized that at *least* a chunk of my anxiety was coming from learned beliefs and cultural pressures I'd taken on. A million little beliefs I never ever questioned. I just let them run my life and the way I felt. Beliefs like: "You should always be trying to manage your weight, or else you're irresponsible." "You can't trust *anything*, you have to tightly control everything or it'll all fall apart." "You'd better live up to the expectations people had of you in high school." (*Why?*) Decluttering a lot of my learned beliefs brought me a *lot* of peace, and I was finally able to access more calm because I wasn't being ruled by ridiculous things from my subconscious. But I want to be clear that it never "cured" my anxiety. I still have it. In fact, understanding that there are probably always going to be *unavoidable* factors that affect our anxiety can help us take some of the pressure off. It's OK to have anxiety! It's OK to get stressed. We're human. Life is scary. In fact, sometimes anxiety is intuition and your body communicating with you, which is another reason it is so important to learn how to feel and trust what's going on in your body. But it's *also* OK to try to manage your anxiety and support your mental health. The expectation that we can and should be completely curing ourselves of anxiety (or any other pain) with just a little self-help can become toxic in its own way. It's just setting us up to fail and—ironically—probably leading to more anxiety.

HOW TO BE CULT
SUSCEPTIBLE

I think a lot about cults. And extremism. And zealotry. I think a lot about the difference between *believing* in something (generally: positive) and dogmatic cult mentality (generally: negative). And the truth is that the line between the two is very fuzzy.

I have always been what you could call . . . *cult susceptible*. First of all, I'm extremely gullible. Second, I love getting approval from authority figures. Third, I have a frighteningly vivid imagination, where the line between reality and fantasy sometimes gets blurred. Fourth, I have *always* been seeking answers and meaning and healing and understanding. Fifth, I am open to believing in magical things we can't see.

So, I have *often* crossed the line over into dogmatic cult mentality, first with different religious beliefs, then with diets, and eventually: spiritual self-help. I never joined any *actual cult* cults (that I know of . . .), but I sought miracle cures with a desperate and frenzied cult mentality.

Now, I don't want to be flippant about cults. There is a difference between *destructive* cults and cult *mentality*. Destructive cults use deception and deliberate mind-control techniques to cause *harm*. Cult *mentality* is also a big part of destructive cults, but cult mentality is actually a very common phenomenon beyond formal cults. Cult mentality is the kind of extremism that has people believing "our way is the one true way." It's the rejection of any uncertainty and any doubt, and the conviction that you and your community are *the good ones*. And the scary part is that this extremist way of thinking *is not* reserved for actual cults. No. It's the way humans relate to *everything*. Religion, diets, CrossFit, politics, our countries . . . and even medicine and science. We *love* to buy into an ideology and make it our worldview. It's simpler that way. We *love* to give over all our power and autonomy to a guru or belief system or diet or self-help methodology or health practice. We are all looking for meaning, belonging, and a feeling of safety, and sometimes it just feels easier to let someone else tell us what to think and what to do. Sometimes it just feels easier to believe that we've found something that will save us.

It's hardwired into us to seek community and belonging and meaning. We are seeking the safety of a tribe. We are seeking the safety of a shared worldview. And this is totally warranted. *We need connection. We aren't meant to do this life thing all alone.* And in modern society, when the majority of our social interactions are online, and we are doing even *more* remotely post-COVID, we are craving that connection even more. Unfortunately, it can backfire on us and lead to an "us versus them" mentality, which is a huge component of cult mentality. "We are right. They are wrong." Our extremist thinking is just a coping mechanism. Black-and-white thinking *feels easier* than being open to nuance, and doubt, and how complicated life really is.

It's easy to see extremism in relation to spirituality, but people can have a cultlike mentality about *anything*—including science. It's called scientism, where scientific beliefs are seen as immune to scrutiny or inquiry. A lot of times, scientific theories and current medicine and current research are considered absolute, without remembering that our understanding of what we call science changes and evolves as we learn more. There is always more to learn in science. It is not static—and it never has been. In an article in *Quartz* called "Be Careful, Your Love of Science Looks a Lot Like Religion," author Jamie Holmes wrote, "faith in science can serve the same mentally-stabilizing function as religious beliefs." We do it with a lot of things. In fact, you could replace the word "science" in that article title with "diets," or "health," or "work," because we can have a dogmatic, cultlike relationship with *anything*. And a lot of us do.

A lot of cults, and culty groups, and culty ideologies, actually start out with some really great, noble ideas, but that doesn't take away from the fact that extremism usually becomes a runaway train. Even the current trend of "keeping people accountable" on social media, though well intentioned, often slips into a cultlike ideology and mob mentality. Because once you're not allowed to question something, and are encouraged to punish and excommunicate people, and are peer pressured to follow along for fear of retaliation, I mean . . . that sounds a lot like how cults operate to me. My point is: *no* group is immune to cult mentality, no matter what the initial intent of the group is. It is human nature. The mentality of "this way is the one true way" is dangerous because it doesn't allow you to think for yourself or allow for nuance. It's a big reason that self-help has a dark side. It's the reason that people claiming to have the *one true cure* can take advantage of sick or desperate people. It's the reason that multilevel marketing exists, and why so many people buy in and pay the initiation fees, and keep going even though they've gone into debt buying the essential oils. It's the reason why Scientology exists. It's the reason why there has historically been so much abuse of power in religions. And it's the reason why so many of us treat our diets like a religion. In so many ways, dieting *is* our new religion. It fills the same role that religion used to. It's the way we try to stay safe, pure, and moral.

The same assurance that religions give people, diets give people too. It takes out the guesswork. It gives you a simple worldview. There are rules to follow. There are activities to take part in. There are community members to connect with. There is a path. There is a goal. And the *promise* is that if we follow the rules, we will be saved. Either by absolving us of our sins and getting us into heaven, *or,* with diets, by keeping illness at bay and, usually, the unspoken promise: making you *hot.*

The *problem* is that this way of thinking also sets people up to be manipulated and exploited. When your group positions itself as having all the solutions, and sets up the "us vs. *them*" dynamic, you're always at risk of losing the safety of the group. You're always at risk of being "othered." You've been given community and acceptance and endowed with purity for following the rules and being a good member, but you have to keep following the rules to keep up your status. That's how cults work. It's how the more dogmatic and culty religions work. And it's how the more dogmatic and culty *diets* work. And it's how our culture at large works. We have to stay impressive. We have to keep up the hustle. We have to lose weight. We have to keep up with social media, post things that make us look *cool*, make that money, get that promotion, and work through the weekend. And then keep doing it! Maybe forever! *And it's exhausting.*

HOW TO SECURE
A MIRACLE TOOTH

When I was eight, my mouth x-rays came back showing that in *nine places* where there were supposed to be adult teeth waiting in the gums (to eventually come down and push out the baby teeth), there were nine *missing* teeth. Nine. And most of the ones that *were* there were small and in the wrong places. Some were actually in a position to push out *two* baby teeth, but only replace it with one, small adult tooth.

Missing nine adult teeth is missing . . . a lot of teeth. But back then, I wasn't particularly concerned. I had baby teeth, so . . . *calm down everyone, please. It's going to be fine!* When my mom tried to explain it all to me in the car after the dentist appointment where they showed her the x-rays, all she ended up doing was crying. I remember telling her everything was going to be OK. I figured it *would* be OK because I could just keep my tiny teeth forever. (Sorry . . . no.)

My mom was trying to understand *why* this had happened. *Why?! Where did I go wrong?!* The thing she landed on was: *calcium*. I'd been diagnosed lactose intolerant by a doctor when

I was two. Also . . . I'm *not* actually lactose intolerant, even though my mom actually is. I think I just had a stomach bug at the time. Either way, our family had been essentially dairy-free for my entire childhood. (Except for my dad buying himself his own skim milk. Rebel.)

She realized: "It *must* be *calcium! Caroline must be calcium deficient.* Calcium = Bones = Teeth! UGH!" So, my mom became obsessed with having me take calcium supplements. It's important to note that tooth buds develop in the womb—so *logic* (and science) would tell you that this had nothing to do with my childhood calcium intake. And my mom had basically lived on skim milk while she was pregnant with me, before she (actually) developed lactose intolerance. A doctor recently told me that a mother's lead exposure can affect the development of tooth buds in utero. I cannot confirm this is true, *but* if it is, it makes way more sense, and also potentially explains a host of other things . . . but back then, calcium intake was the thing she could control, and try to control it she did.

My parents knew that my toothlessness meant I was either going to be mostly toothless my whole life, *or* I was going to have to get lots of mouth surgeries done at some point— probably in my teens or twenties once I looked like an adult but still had a mouth half-filled with baby teeth. But before we got there, not only was my mom going to bribe me to take calcium, she was going to try to appeal to the Lord above, who had smitten me with semi-toothlessness, and ask for a tooth miracle.

My mom decided to take a bottle of liquid calcium to church, and instead of eating the eucharist ("the body of Christ/ cracker"), she covertly shoved it into the bottle of calcium and brought it home to me. This would be our miracle elixir. This would be the focus of our prayer. She would spoon-feed me this now-holy calcium once a day, while we prayed for miracle teeth.

(You're not supposed to use "the body of Christ" like holy water, but she had to do what she had to do for her miracle/spell/prayer.)

My mom grew up in the 1960s, hoping she was maybe a witch like Samantha Stephens from *Bewitched*. I think Catholicism gave her the feeling that she could do white magic and call it holiness. So, she drew a cross in Sharpie on the calcium bottle's label. And every day, for a couple of weeks, she would sit me down, pray about teeth, and feed me liquid calcium from a spoon. Then, of course, life got in the way, and we stopped the holy sacrament of calcium. And we did this off and on for months.

I hated this whole thing. I thought it was weird. The calcium tasted bad. I would be happily living my life with my tiny teeth, avoiding my homework and making Kid Pix on the family computer, and she would interrupt me and tell me we had to go pray and take calcium because we had already forgotten every day this week so far.

She needed my dedication, because without it, we just kept dropping the ball. So, she bribed me with guinea pigs if I promised to remember to take the magical calcium every day for one month. So, I got serious, and we performed the holy sacrament of calcium every day for a month, and I got two guinea pigs that I didn't pay enough attention to, and to this day I still have nightmares that I go down into my parents' basement and there are hundreds of pets that I forgot about that have been slowly starving for the past twenty years.

The next time I went to the orthodontist, they took new x-rays. They were going to try to make a plan to move forward with my jacked-up mouth, because, beyond aesthetics, missing that many adult teeth is a legitimate functional problem. Baby teeth have little roots and do not last forever, and they do not fit into a normal adult jaw bite. And I *needed* teeth in order to do my favorite childhood activity: eat snacks.

But the second x-ray they got back showed there was a *new* tooth in the gums that didn't exist in the x-rays from the year before. They compared the two images and were genuinely stumped. It wasn't actually possible to have a tooth appear at nine years old because, again, the tooth buds form before you're born, and they are already fully formed in childhood. The dentists brushed it off as an error in the first x-ray and told my mom the tooth couldn't possibly be *normal*, so they would have to operate and remove it from my gums. (If you think about it, that logic doesn't add up. Why are you removing it if it was just a tooth that was missed in the first x-ray?) They cut open my gums and removed what was a *perfect and normal* canine tooth.

I currently have a dental bridge in my mouth where that perfect canine tooth could have been. My mom was in the room while it happened, looked at the dentist, and said, "What is wrong with that tooth?" And he said, "I . . . don't know. Nothing."

God's Holy Calcium gave us a miracle tooth and we trampled all over his magic. We literally pulled out the miracle and we threw it in the trash.

Is this weird? Yes. Absolutely. Was there *really* a tooth miracle? You can decide for yourself. Is this just our lead poisoning leading to toothlessness *and* delusions? Honestly, it's very possible. But this whole experience was very formative for me. It set up very early that when things go wrong in your body, it's because you did something wrong! We *must* have caused it! And that we should *always* be trying to fix our bodies and exert control over our circumstances. Now, there's nothing wrong with problem solving. There's nothing wrong with trying to improve your situation. But trying to anxiously exert *control* over my body with magical thinking is something I really ran with in the years following.

The other dynamic that it set up was: dentists? X-rays? Unreliable. Praying over a bottle of calcium and asking for the impossible? More reliable than dentists and modern medicine. Even though I thought the calcium ritual was annoying and weird, it maybe . . . *worked?* Maybe? And because of that, I subconsciously filed away "prayer" and "seeking outright miracles" as a legitimate avenue for getting what I wanted.

HOW TO EMAIL GOD

A few years after the miracle tooth saga, my mom set up an AOL email account where she could send all her prayers. She was looking for something that would help her with prayer organization. I mean, hey, maybe if she'd had more *organization*, we wouldn't have dropped the ball on calcium, and I'd have a mouth full of beautiful, miracle teeth.

The logical solution? She made an email account for *God*, and then she sent her prayers to the email address. She told me I could send prayers to God's email too, but I never did because I didn't trust that my mom wasn't checking the account.

To be clear, my issue with cult mentality, or prayer, or magical thinking, is *not* actually about believing in things that seem ridiculous or out there. I *love* believing in seemingly ridiculous, out-there things. My issue is with the *certainty* that people start to have about their beliefs, and then imposing that certainty on other people.

I have always had an on-again, off-again relationship with God/the Universe/spirituality—however you want to imagine it. I go through phases. And I have lots of God trust issues. But really, I think that's OK. I think doubt is healthy. I'm more wary of people who are 100 percent sure about invisible things.

I believe in some sort of God, I just have *a lot of questions*. So, if I *were* to send God an email today, this is probably what I'd write:

To: GodEmailOfficial@aol.com
Subject: Hello! Questions!

Hi God,

Uh . . . How are you?

I have been trying to get in touch throughout the years, but I haven't heard back. Actually, I might've heard back, but I have a hard time confirming if it's you or not. Which is a problem. Can we clear up the communication issues? In general? A *lot* of people are saying a *lot* of things that you apparently want or think. And it's creating DRAMA down here.

Also, my first draft of this email was nine pages long, but I cut it down because I didn't want to overwhelm you. I have a *lot* of questions. In no particular order, these are just a few things I would love to understand more, to start:

1. Invisibility.
I'm extremely frustrated about the invisibility factor. Why is there so much secrecy? Why are we expected to have faith in something that is impossible to prove? It is asking too much of me. And it is asking too much of humans. It is asking us both to suffer and have

jobs we hate and be exhausted and get sore throats and lose people we love—and *also* be faced with this constant existential drama of being expected to believe in something that we may be fully insane to believe in.

I just . . . I just don't think this setup is fair. And I would like to hear you address this.

2. Are You . . . the Universe?

Like . . . what am I supposed to be imagining when I imagine you? You're not actually a bearded man on a cloud but more like . . . formless? Genderless? Should you go by they/them and not he? Real question. And are you everywhere? Are you sparkles? Are you the sun? WHAT is up? I'm confused.

Also, what do you *want*? Like, what do you want and also what is the point? Of all of this?

3. Is Science Spirituality?

Is it one and the same? Like, a tree growing from a seed is science *and* magic. (That's smart, I know. I think I heard someone say that before, though, so it's not my idea.)

OK, that's it for now . . . I have a *lot* more questions (and lots of requests), but I'll write my requests in a follow-up email. Thank you for listening.

Honestly, please respond.

With gratitude (I promise!),
Caroline (Dooner)

* * *

I don't know exactly what I believe, but I *do* believe that there is something out there, nudging us toward truth. And what I've also learned is we can't *hear it* when we are busy, exhausted, and distracted by the stupid trappings of modern life.

I think we are all intuitive. And I think if we were given the permission to trust our gut, and the *space* to trust our gut, we'd spend less time trying to conform and fit in, and more time doing what fulfills us. We'd spend less time fighting who we really are, and more time being who we really are. But we *aren't* taught to trust our gut, we are taught to follow the rules. And the more people who start trusting their gut, the less people would follow the rules, and the more people would break free.

In the cult NXIVM, part of the cult brainwashing was getting people to *distrust* any negative emotion they had. If they had a negative emotion, or a bad feeling, it was *their fault*. It was a sign they had to do more work on themselves, emotionally and spiritually. It was a sign that they weren't doing enough work on themselves. It was a sign that they needed the cult even more. That meant that whenever they felt like something was off with the rules or the teachings, they'd already been programmed *not* to trust themselves. It was a *them* problem. They were taught to actively *distrust* their gut.

This is a more extreme version of what we are all programmed to do. We assume that society is right, and we are wrong. The business we work for is right, and we are wrong. Our family, religion, diet, political party is right, and we just need to follow. A lot of us suppress who we really are, what we really want to do, and how we really want to express ourselves so we can fit in with the group. We want that safety and approval. *And of course we do.* It can be dangerous to be different. People are still physically attacked for being different. The high rate of abuse and violence toward trans and nonbinary people is just one example of the risk it sometimes takes to just be who you are. People whose truths don't line up with the group they're affiliated with have to make a calculated risk to listen to their gut and have a chance at happiness, or bury it and stay safe but betray themselves.

One of the things that keeps us from trusting our gut is that we *have no time to hear it in the first place.* And even when we *do* have time, we are filling that time *constantly.* Especially now with smartphones and social media, we are on our phones *nonstop.* There is always a TV show to watch. A notification to read. A podcast to listen to. Believe me, I'm no monk. I haven't mastered this *at all.* All I know is that when I deliberately take the time to do less, and fight my urge to fill up every single second of free time with a distraction, I hear myself more. I am more in touch with my gut. I can sense that force out there, or maybe inside, nudging me toward truth.

But usually, I don't feel it. Usually I'm scrolling my phone, and I hear nothing at all.

HOW TO
BECOME OBSESSED
WITH FOOD

"Umm . . . do you feed your child?"

". . . Oh, no—yes, yes of course. I'm so sorry . . . Did she eat all of your food??!"

My mom was picking me up after a kindergarten playdate, and I'd just eaten my weight in snacks and packets of Easy Bake Oven powder, and the friend's mom was . . . concerned. Or at least thought it was worth pointing out that something wasn't normal about the way I ate their food.

I was a tiny little waif-child, obsessed with gorging on other people's snacks. And then asking them for *more* snacks. *And yes,* I *know* that all kids love snacks. But I really was next level. It was my sport. It was my passion. It was my obsession. And when I went over to friends' houses, all I wanted to do was eat snacks, because I *finally* had access to the resources to focus on my passion. I finally had access to *cool snacks*. At home, all we had was, like . . . apple slices and almond butter.

And this kindergarten friend, on this particular playdate, had an Easy Bake Oven. Which, to me, was *the pinnacle of luxury and happiness.* Just sitting there in her family room was a little plastic oven and little packets of sweet powder that would make *tiny doll-size cakes?!?!* I didn't even have the patience to wait for the little cakes to bake, I just ripped open bag after bag and ate the powder while the playdate mom said, "*Wait, wait!* Caroline, we are supposed to . . . Wait! . . . We need to mix it with . . . water and put it in the—" She was eventually able to wrangle me, and we *did* make one tiny cake. And it was shit, actually.

I looked skinny enough, and was obsessed enough with food, that this mother thought there was a *possibility* that I was starved at home? Maybe? I could, and would, eat snacks for hours at a time if I was given the chance, which was either funny or concerning to people. I tried to lean into the *comedy* of it to distract people, and to encourage people to give me more food, for *more* comedy. *Ha ha! See me eat this entire twelve-ounce filet mignon! Ha ha! Yes, I'm five!* It was like another kind of entertainment. Yes! I can stand on the table and sing *annnnd* I will eat this entire bag of cookies! But I wasn't eating for attention. I was eating because it was my passion. And more important: I felt like I was *very* denied cool snacks, and this might be my only chance.

In my mom's defense, we really were *not* underfed. I mean, yes, we rarely had cookies in the house to leave out for Santa Claus on Christmas Eve, which really stressed me out. (*What are we going to leave him, RAISINS?!*) But we weren't underfed. We ate a lot of rice and beans and meat and quinoa pasta and casseroles and salmon and potatoes and broccoli. And Cheerios and almond butter and jelly . . . like, we *ate*. I was never starving. I just *hated* our snacks.

My dad had fewer food rules for us than my mom did, and he would make us French toast with white bread and scrapple on Saturday mornings. On special occasions, he would take us to our favorite diner for pancakes. The place looked straight out of a movie set from the 1980s, and I would gorge on the pancakes because *YES! THIS IS MY CHANCE AND CAN WE PLEASE BUY GUM AT THE CASH REGISTER TOO.*

My mom *even* took us to McDonald's sometimes. We usually weren't allowed to get the Happy Meal with the toy because they were "more expensive" (were they? My mom probably just didn't want extra crappy plastic toys lying around). But even though I was *not* starved, and not actually denied anything, I still *felt* very denied. And that was the whole reason I was obsessed with food: I *felt* denied. Even if I wasn't.

My mom wasn't doing anything that unusual. Food rules and judgment with kids are very common in our culture. She was doing what she assumed was best for us. She wanted to teach us good nutrition. She wanted to give us a good, *fiber-filled* jump-start. So, she bought the health-food-store version of everything. She talked about "healthy foods" and "junk foods," and our access to the junk food was limited, especially at home and in our lunchboxes. And when we *did* get "junk food" or a McDonald's run, it was with lots of moralizing over how *this was junk food* and *sugar is bad for your teeth*. And an eye roll about how obsessed we were. "My *God*, you guys are *so* obsessed with food . . ."

And we were. My brother and I *really* were. We were absolutely *obsessed* with snacks. We were obsessed with *other* people's snacks. We were obsessed with learning the best ways to manipulate people into *giving* us cool snacks. And I became a very skilled but annoying cafeteria beggar. It didn't always work, but *I may as well try, right*?!

It was also very clear to me that I could and would eat more than most people I knew. I remember someone in the cafeteria said, "I ate sooo many cookies last night. I ate *three*!" And I thought . . . *Wait. Three? That's . . . nothing.* Eating was a sport to me, and because I was always so thin throughout my childhood, it felt like a sport without consequence.

My obsession with snacks made my mom double down on the food rules. *What is wrong with my kids?* And honestly, if I were my mom, with the same beliefs my mom had about food and health, I would have done the exact same thing.

It took me decades to learn that food scarcity *causes* food fixation. And it actually feels like a food addiction. It's supposed to; it's plain survival instinct. Our bodies are wired to fixate on food when they're experiencing *any sort* of food insecurity. Food scarcity—like a famine *or* having trouble putting food on the table—makes people obsessed with food, until the threat of famine passes, but it can linger too. So, anyone who grew up in a low-income household and experienced any food insecurity will most likely feel a little "addicted to food." It's *not* a food addiction, but until the trauma of scarcity is dealt with, it will probably feel like one.

The less psychologically understood piece is that even *perceived* food scarcity will do the same thing, which is what was happening with me. I was never, ever starving. (Even though I was *sick of* carrots. Sick of them!) But something in me felt extremely denied access to Goldfish, and so I obsessed. I binged. And I assumed I was addicted to food.

My school friends whose kitchens were stocked with all the snacks I never had in my house didn't really seem to *care* about the snacks. They ate them, yeah, but then they could take them or leave them. Whereas I wanted to sit in their kitchen for the entire five-hour playdate eating fruit gushers, they wanted to stop eating snacks and *play*. And I noticed it, because *I* had to try to convince them to stay in the kitchen to eat as many snacks as possible. It became crystal clear to me that I was obsessed with snacks, and they weren't.

Having rules and judgments around food will make kids feel more obsessed with food. It'll make them feel out of control around forbidden foods. In fact, girls who diet are twelve times more likely to binge, which only sets up a diet/binge cycle. Having rules and judgments around food will make *adults* obsess over food too. It's a pretty consistent phenomenon. And think about how many people that is. *Most* adults judge the way they eat. I'm not saying that this is the *only* factor that affects people's relationships with food, because it's not. But it's a pretty big factor. Being denied, or even *feeling* denied, causes food fixation, even if you are plenty-fed, and even if you are imposing the restriction on yourself, like: a diet.

Thanks to our diet *culture* (our culture that's generally pretty fixated on weight and judgmental about food), more kids *and* adults have disordered eating than we may think. To our bodies, our constant attempts to diet actually feel like nonstop semi-famines. Yeah, I know that sounds extreme, but that's what's going on in our bodies *physically*. The diet/binge cycle is actually a famine cycle, and by fixating us on food and wiring us to binge in response to restriction or arbitrary food rules, our bodies are safeguarding against famine and future famines (future diets). It's actually a state of crisis. Our bodies are conserving energy, lowering our metabolism, and elevating our hunger hormones, and wiring us to binge. And do you know what living in a state of semi-famine for years on end does to us? It exhausts us. Physically, *and* also emotionally and mentally. Think about it . . . we live in a culture that demonizes *eating*. *Eating!!!! Survival 101!* And we are afraid of it. We're all walking around frustrated with ourselves for being hungry or for eating a snack. How fucking backward is that? We also live in a culture that demonizes *resting* and relaxing! We feel guilty for eating and resting, two of the most basic, fundamental building blocks of life. And then we wonder why we're all unsettled and anxious and burnt out and obsessed with food.

We deserve better than this. We deserve naps and snacks.

HOW TO START
PANICKING ABOUT
YOUR FACE

Eighth grade was the year when I realized I was possibly ugly. And possibly even *very* ugly. I'd been *really* excited to become a teenager, because, according to my sources (TV) and my one pretty second cousin: *teenagers were pretty*. And *I* wanted to be pretty.

I was very specifically excited to have boobs and *braces*, because I thought they were the markers of teenagerdom, and therefore the markers of beauty. (I know that no one else in the world thinks braces are pretty, but my pretty teenage second cousin made them work, so I was a fan.)

Now, there actually *are* some teenagers who seamlessly evolve into beautiful, confident, smooth-skinned creatures. It's what I expected to happen to me. And I was *really looking forward to it*. But instead, becoming a teenager was an absolute horror show. Nothing prepared me. Nobody knows how to introduce you to your new face and your new skin and your new body that's now covered in purple stretch marks, or help you deal with your boobs that fit no bras. I'd never seen a stretch mark on TV. I truly thought I was the only person covered in purple stripes.

My face changed from a small child-face with a mouth full of tiny teeth and missing teeth to a bigger, oilier, acne-covered, adult-looking face, with a mouth still full of tiny teeth and missing teeth. And, in eighth grade, I had to wear a plastic retainer with two fake canine teeth in it that I had to pop out in the school cafeteria to eat my lunch. One of those fake canine teeth would have been my miracle tooth if they hadn't ripped the miracle from my gums. They became dental bridges in high school (and are still bridges in my mouth right now).

Very plainly, I felt absolutely hideous. And grotesque. And beyond just acne, I noticed that my pores had become significantly bigger than anyone's I'd ever seen. I'd truly never seen pores that big before. But OK! No problem! *No problem.* I am a problem *solver.* I will just . . . get the stuff in the pores *out.* I will operate on my pores to save my nose from itself. But after I did my emergency excavation, I was left with huge holes on my nose. *Actual* holes. Holes that you could . . . put the tip of a sharpened pencil into. *Holes.*

For a few days after each personal pore surgery I performed, I would have a nose with pencil-tip-sized holes all over it, and then, as if I'd never done anything at all, they would fill up again, just as big and dark and scary as before. I'd stare at other people's faces and think, *How is yours so SMOOTH?!?* Squeezing my pores clearly wasn't working, and I tried quite a few more times, just in case this was an "if at first you don't succeed" kind of thing. I would watch in horror as my skin went through the same process each time: a nose covered in actual holes, and then, *poof*, filled up again.

So it was time for Doctor Google, who was just starting his career. I dialed up on the family computer and typed: "how to make pores smaller." And I quickly learned that there *is no way* to make pores smaller. It cannot happen. It does not happen. And, in fact, not only is there no way to make pores smaller, but some articles even said that squeezing or excavating your pores will eventually make the pores even bigger, because it will stretch them out. At the same time, *other* articles said that it's *not* squeezing and excavating your pores that will make them even bigger, because the pores will just keep filling up, and that will eventually stretch them out too. So . . . basically, no matter what I did, not only were they never going to get smaller, but they were going to become even bigger. And do you know what? The internet was right—they have not shrunk. They are still the same way. Maybe bigger. Hard to say.

Another thing that spun out of control quickly was my ability to fit into *any* bra. I had to keep going back to Victoria's Secret with my mom every month because I kept growing out of the bras we had just bought. Finally, the girl who worked there told us: "You should probably shop somewhere else where they have abnormal sizes." My mom snapped, "Don't say that?! Abnormal?? Why would you say that?"

That's how it feels for a lot of us, though. Our bodies are weird and wrong for not fitting the standard sizes. Less than a hundred years ago, everyone had clothes tailored to their unique body proportions. They didn't have to walk into a store and be expected to fit the exact proportions of mannequins. Now we all have this assumption that our bodies are just . . . *wrong. Wrong wrong wrong.*

Anyway, this was definitely *not* the "boobs and braces" fantasy I'd had. This quickly became the nightmare version. "You want braces? How about years of mouth surgeries instead?! You want boobs? Ha Ha Ha. HERE YOU GO! HAVE FUN NOT HAVING FUN! NO SPAGHETTI STRAPS FOR YOU, MY FRIENNNNNND." Also . . . what . . . is happening with my face?! Is this going to be my face for the rest of my life? Am I going to be covered in purple stretch marks for the rest of my life?!

Once I officially looked like an adult with huge boobs but jacked-up tiny baby teeth and holes in my nose, but I *still* hadn't gotten a normal period a year later, that's when my mom had my doctor to do a hormonal panel and an ovarian ultrasound, and I was diagnosed with PCOS.

HOW TO FOCUS
ON THE WRONG CURE

PCOS is polycystic ovarian syndrome, and it's a hormonal syndrome that I've heard "they" are apparently renaming so it won't include the terms "polycystic" or "ovaries" because it's actually a misnomer. Basically, they don't *really* understand PCOS.

Why don't researchers fully understand PCOS? Probably, at least partially, because it's a woman's health issue, and research is still behind on things related only to women. The symptoms of PCOS are *supposed* to be: weight gain, acne, "cysts" on the ovaries (but not *actual* cysts, they're actually just egg follicles . . . isn't that confusing?), hormonal imbalance, slightly high testosterone, which can lead to excess dark hair, *and* sometimes hair loss on your head, infertility, *and* it's also associated with almost every health problem you can think of. It's associated with type 2 diabetes, because insulin resistance is either a *cause* of PCOS or a *side effect*? I don't think they really know. *And* you don't have to have all the symptoms to be diagnosed with it, either! Fun. It's *so fun*.

The standard treatment includes a *hyper*-focus on weight,

weight loss, and food, which usually just makes people more erratic around food. The reason for the hyper-focus on weight and food is that the syndrome is associated with insulin resistance. But get this: in 1992, an expert panel evaluating the success of weight loss interventions concluded that 90 to 95 percent of people regain the weight they lose, *no matter what*. A study in 2007 found that it's not a question of whether people regain the weight they lost, they *do*, it's just a question of how quickly they gain it back. And not only do people regain the weight they lost, but 23 percent of people gain *more* weight than they lost. And a study in 2006 found that weight cycling (gaining weight and losing weight over and over, which is exactly what happens with diets) *exacerbates* insulin resistance, among other problems. So, the craziest part about this whole weight loss *thing* is that dieting, and the erratic eating and weight cycling that dieting *causes*, all make insulin resistance, and therefore PCOS symptoms, *worse*. Of course, I didn't know that then, because for some reason this connection between dieting, weight gain, and insulin resistance never makes it into the mainstream conversation about dieting and health.

I've also recently heard that no teenager should be diagnosed with PCOS, because a lot of the symptoms are things that teenagers can grow out of. But, *instead*, I was casually told to go on a low-fat diet, exercise, and keep my weight down for the rest of my life. Simple!

First of all, a low-fat diet is now fully outdated. That advice was a remnant of the 1980s and '90s when everyone thought that "fat made you fat," and it was also *just* as the world and all the diet books were pivoting to low-carb. So, *first* let's just take stock of the fact that a doctor was giving me diet advice based on, essentially, a passing fad, because the advice for PCOS soon became all about low-carb (another fad).

Let's talk more about insulin resistance. Not only can dieting make insulin resistance worse, especially if you aren't eating enough carbs or enough food, or if you're going from diet to binge to diet to binge in a never-ending yo-yo, but there are also *lots of other things that affect insulin sensitivity.* Stress! Lack of sleep! Certain vitamin or mineral deficiencies, like vitamin D and magnesium! *And did I mention stress?* Plus a host of other factors as well . . . so, *why* is everyone focusing on dieting and weight loss, when dieting is linked to *more* weight gain? When intentional weight loss is actually proven to backfire the majority of the time? When methods for voluntary weight loss lead to people gaining *more* weight than they started with, as well as weight cycling and exacerbated insulin resistance? My doctors told me to diet and to focus on weight and food, instead of sleep or stress or anything else that could have actually improved my little high school nervous system and my stressy little life.

This is a huge problem. We are told to starve ourselves in order to heal, when the actual core problem is *stress*, and dieting *increases* stress. How the hell are we supposed to navigate that? We are told to blame ourselves and use our willpower to overcome our health problems, when the real problem is the dynamic we're in in the first place.

When they told me to diet at fourteen, it felt like they were telling me that my skin, pores, face holes and cystic acne, weight, huge boobs, stretch marks, and chubby cheeks—and my new oiliness and ugliness—were all *caused* by my eating. They were caused by *my choices* and my inability to get control over myself. This was my fault, wasn't it? *I mean, I **do** have a food addiction, don't I?* Based on what they said, it sounded like food and weight were the causes, and dieting and weight loss were the cures. And it seemed crystal clear that my health and my ugliness were just going to get *worse* if I didn't do something about it.

So, I decided that I was going to heal myself with food and weight loss. And if weight gain is a symptom (or a cause?) of PCOS, I was going to get *ahead* of it by losing weight and staying skinny. *I don't care if PCOS is supposed to be incurable. I choose magical thinking.* I chose to believe that if I just tried hard enough, I could heal myself.

This isn't the beginning of some triumphant story of unlikely and miraculous healing. All this did was set me up for a ten-year eating disorder that was never diagnosed, and even *more* health problems caused by my erratic and restrictive eating, that I blamed on me not eating *well* enough or not being *thin* enough. It set up a singular focus on total-health-and-healing that took over my life and kept me from relaxing and enjoying the health I *did* have. Fun!

Most people who treat eating disorders will tell you: "For the love of God PLEASE don't tell a teenager to diet, no matter what their weight is! Please don't tell a teenager to keep their weight down!" Because dieting is a *huge* predictor of disordered eating behavior. Oh, well! *Whoops!* At fourteen, I was told to diet, exercise, and keep my weight down. And dutifully and desperately, I listened.

I wanted to heal. I wanted to be responsible. I wanted to

stay impressive. But most of all, I wanted to be *beautiful*. Because *that* is what our culture told me was *the most important thing for a woman to be. Beautiful.* It was a nonnegotiable. And I was petrified of this diagnosis and all the symptoms. I was petrified by the idea of them spiraling and getting worse and worse *because* of food.

The thing that still blows my mind is why there was no understanding that it's a dangerous thing to tell a teenager to diet. *Why* is our understanding of health so limited and so black and white? Why didn't anyone tell me about the effects of chronic stress, or to focus on stress reduction and sleep, or y'know . . . *fun*? Why didn't anyone teach me about emotions and emotional resilience? Why didn't I go to fucking *therapy until I was twenty-eight*? Why didn't anyone tell me about diet culture or the *danger* of yo-yo dieting and weight cycling for insulin resistance, when it's well documented that dieting leads to all of those things?

The answer I have so far is that our culture is obsessed with weight. Really *truly* obsessed. And we are *blinded* by our obsession with weight. Our confirmation bias *keeps* us obsessed with weight, blaming it for every health problem under the sun, and considering weight loss a cure-all. It's our cult mentality. It's extremism. It's zealotry. We treat dieting and weight loss like a collective religion. We worship thinness and fitness. We equate weight with health. We equate weight with *character and morality and personal responsibility*, because we see our bodies as a simple and straightforward project, without understanding all the nuance that goes into our relationship with food and all the factors that affect our weight. There's also always been an underlying connection between religious purity, thinness, and food purity that still lingers today in the way we think about weight and inherent *goodness*. And there is such a widespread belief that we can all heal ourselves by taking that personal responsibility, training for a half-marathon, and cutting out _____ foods (literally take your pick! Carbs, meat, dairy, gluten, processed foods, whatever your religious diet sect believes in!).

We are in a diet dark age, where we demonize calories and weight gain without any understanding about how that is *also* harming us. We think it's a simple formula for health and happiness, instead of realizing that nothing is that simple, *and* that this mentality can and will end up destroying lots of people's physical and mental health. We treat diets and weight loss like the cure-all, when what we need is more awareness around the effects of chronic stress, as well as the social determinants of health (poverty, oppression, and marginalization).

Again, when I say cult mentality, I know it sounds extreme. Obviously, we're not in a *cult* cult on a commune with a leader who thinks he is the messiah and who tries to sleep with his members, but it's the cult *mentality*. The actual definition of a cult is: "a social group that is defined by its unusual religious, spiritual, or philosophical beliefs, or by its common interest in a particular personality, object, or goal." Particular interest in a particular goal. Hmm! Ding ding ding! Thinness. Purity. Health.

It's easy to identify a cult mentality if the ideology is unusual or foreign to you or when it's preaching about doomsday and the leader marries multiple teenage brides. But *what if* it's a widespread cultural ideology that we were all raised in? What *then*? In fact, the words "cult" and "culture" come from the same Latin word. Is our culture not a cult of its own? An informal, diet culture cult?

We are indoctrinated into this cult as soon as we're born. We grow up believing thin is good and pure and noble. We think it's a direct correlation of how responsible and controlled a person is, a sign they aren't consumed by life's pleasures . . . as if that's a bad thing.

And when we're presented with facts and studies that show:

Lots of people's weights are actually genetic!

We can actually improve our health without losing weight!

Focusing on weight may actually lead to poorer health outcomes!

Undereating isn't actually good for you, long-term!

Forcing weight loss is wired to backfire!

Chronic stress, stigma, and marginalization are worse for us than being a higher weight!

Weight stigma actually accounts for a lot of the poor health outcomes we associate with higher weight!

Even when we are given the proof and the studies, most of us can't process it, because it goes against our *core beliefs*. It is at odds with our belief system, and so we write it off as nonsense. It's not nonsense, it's just at odds with what we've all been taught.

It's at odds with our culture. It's at odds with our cult mentality. The cult of thinness. The cult of health and personal responsibility, where "no excuses" is our mantra. Lots of us are not formally religious, but religious undertones are still behind the way we relate to our bodies, which have made us obsessed with purity, especially the purity of women.

Let's go through some of the *specific* markers of cult mentality . . .

First, there's the indoctrination and brainwashing that happens nonstop with magazines, photoshopped images, and the constant message that we are gross and ugly and need to improve and lose weight. We are broken down: *I am ugly and gross.* We are given the solution: *beauty and health and happiness.*

With cults there is also usually a noble or spiritual cause that everyone buys into to make it all feel worthwhile. In our case . . . *health.* And when anyone comes at our toxic obsession with achieving beauty, we pivot to health. *No no no, I only really care about health.* Hmmmmm, sure, Jan. Did you know that starving yourself isn't great for you? Did you know that working out for two and a half hours a day is often the sign of an eating disorder? (Sometimes called "exercise bulimia" or "anorexia athletica.")

Did you know that one of the *very* common cult practices to break members down is to starve and exhaust people into submission, so it muddles people's minds and they don't have the energy to fight back or critically think? Yeah. *Yeah.*

Also, one of the reasons people don't *leave* cults, or any cult-like group, is that they've bought in so much and for so long. They usually have *already* spent a fortune, and years and years of their life, and so people start to only see what they want to see. They only see things that will support the choices they've already made. The more you've already sacrificed, the more difficult it is to admit that you've made a mistake and that your cult is taking advantage of you.

Then there's isolation from people who *aren't* in the cult. Anyone who doesn't understand or agree with your diet or exercise plan is uneducated and trying to derail your success! A "suppressive," as they call them in Scientology.

Then there's the dependency on the cult's rules. *All* decision making is taken away, and you follow the rules, trusting that it's leading to something noble and healing and worthwhile. And if it *isn't* working for you, it's *your* fault. And if you leave the cult, you're *really* screwed, because then you'll *never* be saved. Because remember?! Your *health*. This is the way to heal yourself. If you leave, you're abandoning your health!

Dieting is the cult I accidentally joined at fourteen. You always start off thinking you're doing something good for yourself. You think you've found *the way. The path. You've been saved.* No one says, "I'm joining a cult!" They say, "I've found something that is finally going to help!"

Most people I knew were already members of the diet cult. My parents, my doctors, my friends, every magazine, every message board . . . it was like finding your people. *We are all passionate about health and food and exercise and beauty. We are the responsible ones! We get it!* I'd already been indoctrinated throughout my childhood . . . I was primed. I didn't want to be *ugly*. I didn't want to gain more weight. I didn't want to get fat shamed and dehumanized like I'd seen happen *over and over and over again,* in real life, in ads, and in TV shows and movies. I saw a cruel society, and I wanted to protect myself. I didn't want to be excommunicated from society.

I was ready to move to the commune and put in the work. And everywhere I looked, and everyone I ever talked to, *confirmed* the belief that dieting was a very good idea. It would keep me safe. It would make me healthy. It would make me beautiful and loved and accepted. And that's what I wanted.

If you try to break out of the diet cult, a lot of people in your life will think you've lost your mind. They'll think you're irresponsible. Maybe even dangerous. You're *hurting* yourself. You're hurting your *health.* And there's a lot of policing each other too: "You've gained weight, and I'm just really worried about your health!" "Lemme give you a tip! Stop eating in the mornings! It's really worked for me." (You'll *also* be shamed for openly caring *too* much about food and weight. I don't think "fit" shaming is comparable to fat shaming at all, but it's still a way to trap you. You're damned if you do, damned if you don't.)

If we *really* want to talk about health? Like, really *really*? Health is *so* impacted by stress. And our culture focuses on dieting and weight loss and *personal responsibility* when that often just continues the cycle of stress in the first place.

Health is also very impacted by socioeconomic factors: social power, marginalization, and stigma. Meaning, if you struggle to pay your bills, that's a chronic stress that *affects your health.* If you are the recipient of nonstop racism or microaggressions or xenophobia, that affects your health too.

On top of *all of that,* a lot of stress comes from our constant attempts to fit in, and the constant work and worry we have to put in to stay an upstanding member of society. We end up punishing ourselves and putting ourselves through a lot of self-flagellation just to fit in. But obsession with health and beauty is not actually good for us.

And it's fucking exhausting.

HOW TO LET EVERYONE KNOW YOU SUCK

I was *ready* to put in the work to lose weight, but there was another problem: I also hated my face. In fact, I wanted a completely new face. Specifically: I wanted a nose job. I figured my parents wouldn't let me get one, because every time I brought it up to my mom, she said I was being absurd. "Don't be silly. Remember when Mrs. Angstadt said you looked like Audrey Hepburn??"

"Pff. That's when I was twelve, mom. *Look at me now.*"

My mom was not on board with me getting plastic surgery at fourteen, but I had a plan. I was going to do it once I was an adult. Really. Once I was in charge of my own life, either in college or after college, when I . . . somehow had money, I was going to get a nose job. And it was going to fix everything.

I was starting to feel trapped in ugliness, so having a plan to one day take control of the situation, and buy myself a prettier face, calmed me down. *At least I won't have to stay like this forever.* So, I started praying for a nose job. "Please please please God, let me get a nose job, either very soon, *or* if not soon, then once I can pay for it myself. Please." Y'know, because a higher power *definitely* wants to make sure we are all very pretty. And if it takes cutting your face open, then so be it.

I think I would have been obsessed with beauty, and being beautiful, no matter what, just because of the culture that we live in. *However,* a PCOS diagnosis just made beauty feel so much more elusive. Whether you have all the symptoms or not, the diagnosis feels foreboding. *Especially* as a teenager. Oh? Do you want clear skin? No, sorry. Maybe never! Oh! Do you want to be thin? No, you probably just can't. Do you want to maybe be a bearded woman? No? Oh, well, you *might* be! Just give it time! Whether it's fair or not, a very particular kind of beauty and femininity is a very powerful social currency, and I was panicked to lose that social currency before I even got it.

It's uncommon to be diagnosed with PCOS as a teenager. Most people don't find out they have PCOS until they're in their twenties or thirties because they're having trouble getting pregnant. *Then* they get diagnosed. PCOS does *not* mean that you won't be able to get pregnant, just that it can make it more challenging, but infertility was not even close to my concern back then. I was fourteen. Also, my aunt had PCOS and had four children. She was also *very* thin, and was a runner and avid exerciser, so that sort of hammered it down more for me: if I can just *become very good at weight control,* everything will work out. I really only cared about the superficial symptoms. I thought: *If you're healthy, you're pretty. So, if I can become healthy, I will become beautiful.*

On top of my fears about being ugly, I also constantly had to *get up in front of people and fucking sing.* I sang at random second cousins' weddings and great uncles' funerals, and with my music school, where I somehow had started taking freaking opera voice lessons as a twelve-year-old. I sang in child classical voice competitions. I went to Paris and Monaco with my Russian music school to sing with world-class cellists. I sang and performed at my school where everyone hyped up my singing. I was constantly in situations where I was being looked at while performing, and it made me extremely nervous.

My issue, I thought, was that I sounded exactly like a Disney princess, but I didn't *look* like one. Disney princesses do not have these pores, or these stretch marks, or . . . no teeth. They don't have boobs that are too big to fit into any dresses. The fact that I was getting cast as the princess-ingenue pretty-little-woman in the school plays didn't end up making me feel more confident, it only magnified how ugly I felt. It *magnified* my fear of gaining weight. It magnified how much I hated my face, because now everyone else was going to realize that they hated my face too.

But still, everyone around told me, "Doons, you're going to be on Broadway." I *am? LOOK AT ME?!* It honestly just felt *stupid* to want to be an actor when I felt so, so ugly.

No matter how often I performed, my performance anxiety wasn't getting better. And each performance was giving people an opportunity to notice how very *not* beautiful I was. This was something that I felt I needed to *get ahead* of, like, *Hello, everyone. Don't worry. I know I'm ugly! I can see my skin! I can see my nose! I can see my tiny teeth! I get it—and I am working on it.*

My philosophy was: tell everyone how terrible and ugly you think you are *before they* judge you for being ugly and terrible. I wanted people to know that *I knew* I wasn't that great, rather than have them think that I thought I was really amazing and impressed with myself. I thought that this was just what life was. *I have to show you how much I disapprove of myself. I have to show you how disgusted I am with myself, until I somehow improve—or die.*

I thought it was all going to, hopefully, just be a temporary period of trial and strife and ugliness and complaining, because once I figured it out and became permanently beautiful, *then* I could stop complaining. Like a movie. The beginning is hard, and by the end, everything is figured out. Once I was beautiful, there would be nothing to complain about anymore.

I complained *a lot* about how ugly and lazy I was—to my mom, to my friends, in my diary. I thought my open disapproval would inspire me to do something about it. I'm pretty sure it ended up taking a toll on my best friend, Annie, who developed her own eating disorder and lost a lot of weight, really quickly. Instead of this waking me up, I actually felt jealous. Instead of being concerned, *I wanted it too.* I also didn't think that *I* had an eating disorder (I did). *I just needed to stop bingeing and stick to a diet, for God's sake!*

Once Annie started getting help, she had a talk with me where she asked me to stop obsessively talking about food and weight. This was the first time I ever considered that my very open, incessant, and *vocal* self-criticism was maybe . . . not so fun to be around. I'd been trying to protect myself from judgment from *other* people by openly judging myself *first.* And why wouldn't I? I read *People* magazine! I read *Us Weekly*! I knew how cruel we all were. I knew how everyone was just *waiting* to rip celebrities apart for gaining weight. I learned how *embarrassing* it was supposed to be to struggle with food and weight. I was no fool. In my tiny, non-famous way, I was using my open self-disgust as a way to try to get ahead of the story. I'd rip myself apart *first* before all you high schoolers had a chance to.

But that method clearly wasn't working. It was backfiring and causing people close to me to be even *more* annoyed with me and my food and body issues. So, I decided I needed to become the new, normal, *chill* Caroline. I was going to become *so chill* that I never even thought about food and, therefore, barely needed to eat. I was going to try to eat the smallest amount possible, for the rest of my life, but I was going to be *normal* about it. Like, I was going to eat *whatever*, but just . . . barely any of it. Y'know, like a normal person!

I was going to completely internalize my disordered eating. I was going to project *chillness*, even if it was a lie. Even if I was still overthinking every little bite, I was going to make it *seem* like I was extremely normal with food (even though I didn't even know *what* being normal with food actually *was*). This is also something expected of us in our society. Work extremely hard, but make it look easy and effortless. Work nonstop on your body, on your career, on your relationships, with your kids if you're a parent, but make it look *easy. Work hard and then work hard making it not look hard.* Which is, of course, actually making you work *harder.*

This specific attempt of mine to "barely eat but be chill about it" backfired so badly that I ended up bingeing on Cosi S'mores and going into hypoglycemic shock and lying on the floor before my theater camp's production of *Seussical* the musical, completely unable to move until the resident camp nurse put peanuts in my mouth and waited for my blood sugar to normalize. How *chill*.

OK, I guess this isn't going to work. I guess I should go back to formal dieting. I just won't talk about it as much.

HOW TO TRY EVERY DIET

One of the symptoms of my PCOS was that I rarely, if ever, got my period. Or . . . was that a symptom of me constantly dieting? What a good question that was *never* presented to me! I had no idea that constant, obsessive dieting could *also* mess up your hormones and make you lose your period. So, I was actually screwing myself over with the dieting that was supposed to be helping me. And there was no way to tell what was causing what. But I didn't know that.

My first formal diets were low-carb diets. First, I tried Atkins. That worked for a few months. I lost weight at first, until I started bingeing again. Then I tried the South Beach diet, which was low-carb *and* low-fat.

South Beach had "phases," and in later phases you were supposed to add in like a cup of whole grains or berries a day, but I never got to that part because I *kept blowing it* a few weeks in and having to start all over again in phase one with no carbs. When I started the South Beach diet, I *also* lost lots of weight—at first. Then I started bingeing again.

It always seemed like I *just* had to do it all again, but this time, *be better*. The diets clearly worked, right? I just needed to be better with my willpower. *I just needed to become very thin again, and then keep it up forever.* And once I did that, hopefully I'd fit into a normal-sized bra. *Then* I could wear normal clothes. Then voilà! It's straightforward. It's *healthy*, Caroline. And everyone apparently does it! I just needed to fucking *do it and then keep doing it.*

If I could lose weight and stop bingeing, it would hopefully balance my hormones and heal my skin too. And then after I got some good teeth and maybe some plastic surgery, I'd be beautiful. It seemed clear that beauty was the answer for everything: the answer for my day-to-day happiness, the answer for acting, and the answer for my performance anxiety. Because once I am beautiful, then I won't feel anxious about . . . anything! Everything will become a breeze.

Once I started exercising to try to lose weight, I would be alone running on the side of the road, and men riding by in trucks would honk and yell sexually explicit things out the window. I can't even remember what they yelled, because it was so jarring I don't think I let myself remember. Usually, there were *two* people in the truck when it happened. This probably does not need to be said, but: This is not flattery. This is *menacing*. It's a power dynamic. And to me, I blamed this all on my boobs. *Ugh, if I didn't have boobs, this wouldn't be happening.* Of course, that's not fully true, but it's what I thought. My next thought was, if I were *thin*, my boobs would be smaller, and this wouldn't be happening to me. Therefore, it felt *very* legitimate that losing weight would make me *safe*. It would make me *respected*. And what a fucked-up thing for a fifteen-year-old to grapple with: that thinness equals safety and respect, and fatness or boobs equals not. What I learned is that as soon as you start to look like a woman, you are immediately objectified. What's hard to articulate is how *terrifying* it can be to feel like your body is an object for other people to consume and comment on. You don't have any control over it anymore—so you try to exert the control you can: *dieting*.

I thought that once I lost weight, not only would I be safe, but I would *also* all of a sudden start emulating a sort of . . . woolen skirt, leather riding boots, skinny legs, shiny hair, smooth skin, normal teeth vibe. Like . . . a model who is also a socialite from the 1960s in London? This is what I was subconsciously going for. I wanted to look and feel *elite*. It existed in magazines. It existed on TV. And therefore, before I had any sort of critical thinking about models, ads, and airbrushing, and aspirational, whitewashed elitist marketing, it felt *tangible*, if *only* I stuck to my diet, lost weight again, and kept it off forever.

This was all before iPhones and Instagram and social media influencers. That would have *definitely* just amped this up even more. All I had was *Marie Claire* magazine and Google image search (where I would type in: "Catherine Zeta-Jones diet").

I guess, in a way, I also hoped that becoming beautiful was the way to feel the numb confidence of a psychopath. No more fear. No more doubt. Only beauty. Only teatime. Only shopping for a new pair of boots for my skinny little calves. That was really what I was searching for: numbness. Confidence. I just wanted to look like one of the models from the J.Crew catalogue with the tiny, tan legs and wispy blond hair. It's a really *great* thing I never did cocaine because I've heard that it would *also* give me what I was looking for: energy, blind confidence, and no appetite.

At the beginning of every new diet I tried, there was euphoria and extreme hopefulness, and riding that hope helped me stay militant enough to stick to it perfectly. Then, when my body started fighting back a few months in, finding and starting a brand-*new* diet, with new rules, and new promises, rebooted that euphoria and diet-rule perfectionism. For a bit. But the more diets you go on, the harder and harder it becomes. Because your body knows the drill at this point: this is *war*.

After I failed on the Atkins and the South Beach diets over and over again, I moved on to other, similar diets, hoping they would heal whatever was broken inside me. Maybe *they* would heal my food addiction. My understanding was that my hormonal issues were part of the reason for my food addiction. It was . . . some hormonal *something*, and *that* was the root cause of my health problems *and* my food addiction. I felt like if I could just heal my *hormones*, then my food addiction and ugliness problems would go away. That's what we are told over and over again with diets: You're broken. You have a problem. You have a weakness, and this diet is amazing and it's going to heal you. Then when you can't do it, it's all blamed on your willpower, instead of where the fault really lies: *the diets*. (If you have insulin resistance, that can absolutely affect your blood sugar, appetite, and ability to feel full. I've learned it's better to focus on sensitizing your cells to insulin with drugs or supplements, and supportive lifestyle interventions like sleep, *not* on dramatically cutting carbs or calories.)

One diet I tried was called the Rosedale diet. It was focused on "the science of leptin," and it was essentially just a low-carb diet, but with lots of fish and fish oils and vegetables and . . . other arbitrary diet rules. "Heal by eating *the right oils*," which happened to be fish oils. I remember that cashews were also allowed, in limited quantities, but I eventually started eating around 3,000 calories of cashews in one sitting. First, because I was starving, and second, it was the only slightly snack-y thing I was allowed. Third, *when you diet, your body goes nuts around food. (No. Pun. Intended. I never intend puns!)* This diet promised to heal my food addiction and bingeing through the *science of leptin*, and it did *not*.

The next diet was one of the most exciting (and the second-cultiest) diets to come my way. It was called the *Weigh Down diet*. My mom and I did this one together. It was all about appealing to *God* to help you not overeat. So, it finally brought overt religion/morality/prayer into the picture. Until now, these two parts of my life were separate. Now, dieting and religion were *together. On my plate.*

The rules? You were allowed to put all the things you wanted to eat in each meal onto *one* plate. It all had to fit on one plate. Which sounds relatively . . . reasonable. Then you *pray*. I'd say something like, "God, please help me to not be a glutton." Then you eat everything very slowly, constantly checking in with your hunger, and with God, to see if you are full. You are only allowed to eat three meals a day, and each meal fills one plate (filled with whatever food you chose), and you *have* to eat it slowly (and prayerfully, I guess). You are *not* allowed to eat in between mealtime plates. If you get hungry in between, you are just supposed to revel in the fact that your body is eating itself as a snack, and also *maybe* you are being filled with the grace of the Lord, who is thanking you for having self-control, and rewarding you with health and beauty.

Say you're still hungry when you've finished everything on your plate? Well, tough titties! You *can't* have more than what you put on your plate. But you *can* put *anything* on your plate *before* the meal starts. Brownies! Pasta! Bread! So, in many ways, this felt like a very exciting future for me. It made me feel like I could *maybe* live a balanced life, where I ate anything I wanted. But it *also* appealed to our strange relationship with God, who *finally* was going to intervene and save me from myself. But, of course, this one blew up in my face too, after a few weeks. *I can't freaking hear God. I'm literally just hungry. And my hunger is LOUDER than God.*

The more I dieted, the harder dieting became, but I didn't see the connection; I truly thought I was a lost cause. A little teenage glutton who needed spiritual healing, better willpower and control, and maybe *another* newer, doctor-approved fad diet. I *kept* trying. I kept trying to harness that devotion from my very first Atkins diet, but one little slipup in my resolve and I'd eat the entire jar of almond butter, or six low-carb protein bars, or, if I was *really* off the deep end: all the orange cranberry cookies in the package. And then I'd sometimes force myself to go for a very uncomfortable run.

I also had a few-month stint where I swallowed thirty supplements a day, all researched by my mom from PCOS forums. I'd swallow supplements by the handful in between classes at school. And unless it was a coincidence, I *actually got my period* during those few months on all those supplements. But then life got in the way. I tried to restock each supplement each time it ran out but I was taking around twelve different ones, and who knew which supplements actually were working and which weren't?

After a few solid years of failed dieting, and only getting my period a handful of times over the course of four years, I was panicked. It wasn't working. I wasn't *healing*. I was starving all the time, which couldn't be right. *Why* was I *so hungry? All the time?* I was eating exactly what they told me to in this revered diet book, but I was *so so so hungry.*

My mom was worried about my health and my self-admitted food addiction. She wanted to *help me.* After all, the doctor told me to diet, exercise, and not gain weight. We were simply listening and trying to be responsible.

In retrospect, all this focus on food and weight was horrible for my relationship with food, and if possible, even worse for my relationship with my mom. I know she just wanted to help and protect me, but it was all wayyyy too much focus on what I ate, what I weighed, and my skin. We were tracking my symptoms and kept trying to figure out what we needed to do. But I also felt like I was under a microscope. It was way too much focus on the *problems* with me and also, inherently, based on PCOS symptoms: what I looked like.

Then, the fact that I *couldn't* stick to a diet, and was constantly hungry, scared the hell out of both of us too. I felt extremely out of control. And it was ironic, because everything in my *being* was dedicated to exerting and maintaining extreme control over my eating. And it wasn't working. I was trying to control every single bite, but I was still binge eating all the time.

And because I wanted to conceal my inability to stick to a diet, I started bingeing in *secret* and hiding it from my mom, who would then watch me quickly gain thirty pounds back over the course of a few months while I was bingeing in secret but telling her I was sticking to the South Beach diet.

Neither of us understood that dieting literally sets up your body to binge. And that the bingeing was actually protective, and in the most basic sense, just trying to get my calorie levels back to normal. I didn't understand that the arbitrary number of calories I was trying to stick to was *way too low, even though every magazine was listing it as the ideal amount for women.* I didn't understand that restricting food or carbs wires our bodies to become more hungry, and our *brains* to fixate on food. Thinking about food nonstop wasn't a sign of deep moral failing, it was because of the diets I was constantly putting myself on. I also didn't realize that dieting and weight loss had no inherent ability to heal my hormones or skin. I didn't understand that the weight cycling I was doing, every few months, probably was actually the worst thing I could do for my health.

I didn't understand, so I kept dieting.

HOW TO BE EXTREMELY DRAMATIC

During my sophomore year of high school, I discovered a big lump on my thyroid, and for a few days, my doctor wasn't sure if it was cancerous or not. So, for those few days, I went off the South Beach diet and ate primarily Hershey's kisses and coffee cake, because I was *dying*, and there was no point trying to heal myself anymore. The cancer scare put me over the edge, and I felt too tired to go on dieting (for a few days).

They had just stuck a needle into my throat and drained the cyst of the fluid, and taken a biopsy to test for cancer or hormones and whatever else they were testing. I remember staring out of the car window as my mom drove me home, eating Hershey's kisses without blinking and throwing the silver wrappers in the little hand divot under the car window. I don't even know where the candy came from or why I had it on hand to cope with my imminent death.

I had been trying *so* hard to diet, and heal, and get some fucking control, but my body was betraying me. At this point, I felt like my body couldn't be trusted. There was just problem after problem after problem. Not only was I still covered in cystic acne, deep into what felt like an all-consuming food addiction where I was sure I could *never* trust my cravings or my hunger, and partway into painful implant teeth surgeries because my body decided to be born toothless, but *now* I probably had thyroid cancer. So, I just kept opening up Hershey's kisses and swallowing them. The irony is, of course, that the less I trusted my body, and the longer I remained at war with it, the harder it was on my health, and the worse things would continue to get.

It wasn't cancer. It was just a rude cyst that kept painfully filling back up with fluid every time they drained it, and it was producing thyroid hormone. They had no answers as to *why*. It was just one more thing to stress me out—and one more reason to distrust my body.

I've always been extremely dramatic. And, to be fair, some pretty dramatic things *were* happening, but I *really* leaned into it. Drama was my passion, after all. Stories have always been my favorite form of escapism. I can and will completely and absolutely lose myself in stories, in a way that might actually be troubling because of how much it takes over my mind. And then, I *majored* in it in college: BFA in Drama. So, this is my passion, my talent, and my vice. It improves my life. It ruins my life. Stories are wonderful and essential and human, but you can abuse wonderful things too.

Even though I was sure that I was hideous and had no business being cast as Cinderella, in the *dimmest* lighting in my bedroom, with lipstick and heavy eyeliner on, I thought I looked pretty good. I would sit on my bed, stare in the mirror, and act out dramatic scenarios. The more dramatic the better.

They usually involved me telling someone that I couldn't love them because I was dying. Or telling the father of my unborn child that even though we were teenagers, I was keeping the baby but moving to another town and working in a Victorian inn. I would perform a long, restrained monologue. I would move myself to tears. I would listen to the Bangles' song "Eternal Flame" while I blow-dried my hair and pretended I was burning at the stake. I would play my favorite song from the *Les Mis* cassette tape, "Javert's Suicide," over and over. This was how my brain worked. *Drama drama drama.*

Losing myself in stories was my "drug," so to speak. My overactive imagination and extreme ability to lose myself in my own mind was a coping mechanism. It was hyper-escapism. I would get *sloshed* on stories. And for me back then, my primary way of escaping was through thinking about Harry Potter. Yes. I spent all my free time at school and at home, from eighth grade on, on Harry Potter message boards talking about Harry Potter and his friends and reading Harry Potter fan fiction. I would immerse myself so fully that I didn't even really live in my life anymore. I would imagine I was living in a Harry Potter scenario *while* I was at school, or with friends, or at a family gathering. At the time, it felt like the *best* use of my overactive imagination. *This. This is living.* It was fun. It was *vivid*.

But it was actually a way to consistently check out of my *real* life, and primarily spend time in a fictional one. Why? I was overwhelmed. I didn't know how to cope or to process how scary everything was. To me, high school was a series of medical traumas, with no time or ability to process any of them. I rarely had a moment when there wasn't something scheduled. I rarely had a weekend when there wasn't some stressful performance or singing competition. That's the modern high school experience: hyper-scheduled within an inch of our lives. *Everything* is about impressing colleges. And apparently there is no way to impress a college unless you have literally no free time, ever. On top of that, I was panicked over my health, and my weight, and what seemed like a dangerous food addiction. I was afraid of my body. I was anxious about having to perform all the time. And I was really fucking tired. I needed a way to soothe myself, and this was one of the few ways I knew how.

Plus, when Harry would go through a very trying event, he got to convalesce in the hospital for, like, a week or two. He got to sleep it off. And people would come visit him and give him life advice, and candy, and time to process what had just happened. And then he got to go to a feast with his best friends and eat pies. I wanted that.

I craved comfort. I needed to *check out*. And look, I guess it's possible that *some* teenagers thrive on that kind of nonstop activity that's so common in high school, but I definitely did *not*. I emotionally imploded and crumpled in on myself. Also, I didn't party. I didn't do drugs. I didn't really date. I . . . went to play practice. I studied diet rules. And in my rare free time, I put off doing my homework and pretended I was in a wizarding war.

Stories and storytelling are healthy and important parts of the human experience. They can help us to process pain we don't know how to process by ourselves, and they can teach us to become more empathetic by seeing through other people's eyes and experiences. The ability to turn off your brain and distract yourself is really helpful. But any good thing can be taken too far. Anything can be used as a way to escape and distract. I was using *dieting and body obsession* as a way to numb and distract. And I was using escapism. Because I didn't know how to take care of myself *for real*. I didn't know how much I needed little creature comforts—and how healing those comforts could be. Things like: true downtime, therapy, more empathy and kindness toward myself and my body, and most importantly: *more food*. So, I relied on other coping mechanisms to get by. It's what so many of us are doing when we turn to lots of different vices: alcohol, drugs, toxic relationships, the diet/binge cycle, our phones—and on and on. The list of ways we numb ourselves is never-ending.

We all need comfort. We all need to soothe. And most of us just haven't been taught how to take care of ourselves.

HOW TO PRAY
FOR A NEW FACE

I'd been complaining about my nose for a few years. I spent my free time stomping around my house, moaning in misery when I looked at my face, and swearing to my mom that I *was* going to get a nose job one day, no matter what she thought. I'd see pictures of myself and rip them apart, and then spend hours on Google Images making myself depressed that I didn't look like Sienna Miller.

One day, after two years of complaining, my mom said in response, "OK, fine. Then let's do it this summer."

What.

"Wait . . . really?"

"Yes, if you hate your nose *so much* and are going to do this *anyway* when you're older, and you actually want to go into act-ing, then you just should do it before you get any real acting jobs, so nobody knows."

I was shocked. I was half . . . *thrilled*. This was my *dream*. My *prayer*. It was all coming true! But I was also . . . half horri-fied. "Wait, so you *do* think I need a nose job!"

"You know I don't think you *need* one, but I know how scrutinizing the performing industry is, and if you really *want* to be an actor, I understand that this could help."

So . . . we did it. *I* did. I got a nose job at sixteen, during the summer before my junior year. I don't remember exactly what I thought or did *between* this conversation and when the actual surgery took place. I don't even know how many months it was in between. It felt crazy. I was excited. I was scared. I was shocked that it was happening at all. But it's what I *wanted*. I had been *begging* for it. I'd been huffing and puffing around the house complaining about how ugly I was for years.

My mom recently said that she still thinks it's crazy that she let me get this surgery in high school, and that if I hadn't been so serious about acting, she would *never* have let me. I told her that it wasn't really up to her. I prayed and performed a miracle and forced her hand anyway. I used her own magical God tricks against her.

She also said that she and my dad were worried that if they *didn't* let me, and then I didn't succeed in acting, I'd blame my parents for not letting me get the surgery. And the truth is . . . I might have. If my parents had continued to say, *This is absurd, Caroline, you do not need this*, I wouldn't have agreed with them at all. I would have thought they were stupid, and had bad taste in faces, and that they were keeping me from my dreams by pretending I looked good when I clearly did not. And I probably would have gotten the surgery anyway when I was an adult, just like I was promising.

But *wow*. I mean . . . *I'd done it*. Look what praying for plastic surgery can do?! Have I performed a *miracle*? A plastic surgery miracle? A miracle where the *Lord* gives you the parental permission and money to cut part of your face off?

It wasn't a dramatic surgery. *It wasn't the super tiny flippy nose I wanted. It wasn't Catherine Zeta-Jones's nose.* It was so subtle that my siblings didn't notice. I mean, they were only fourteen (my brother) and seven (my sister). But my aunts and uncles also didn't notice (or did they?). My *mom's* parents didn't notice (or did they?). And the majority of people at my high school didn't notice. But my close friends noticed, and I denied it for a few years until I eventually just admitted it to them.

Also, after getting the surgery, I did *not* all of a sudden love myself. I didn't all of a sudden think I was gorgeous. I didn't think my face was perfect. I was not all of a sudden confident. But I guess *I* did think it was a *subtle* improvement, because I didn't notice my nose so much in pictures anymore. And I also quickly forgot that the surgery ever happened at all. It was so bizarre to me that my brain nearly erased that it ever happened from my memory.

That winter, about six months later, I was in rehearsal for Dance Motion, our school's winter dance "sport," and we were rehearsing "chaîné" turns down the aisles of the audience. It was an *audience entrance*, and we were all in a line throwing our arms out to get momentum for the turns, and the girl in front of me whacked my face, really hard. My nose made a loud *cracking* sound and immediately started gushing blood. When I looked in the mirror it was very obviously broken. My nose was completely out of place and off to the side. Oh. My. God. MY MIRACLE NOSE.

It wouldn't stop bleeding for ten more minutes, so I left

early. I sat in my car until it stopped bleeding and drove slowly home. My mom wasn't there when I got home, so I walked over to a mirror, and my nose was a whole quarter of an inch off center. *I . . . ruined it.* I stared in the mirror and tried to push my nose back into place and it *clicked* over. AGH! It MOVES! I had moved it closer to center, but it was still way off.

My mom saw it when she got home. "Oh, yeah. Wow. OK. It looks broken. We can go back to the doctor and see what they say . . ."

They had to put me under again to click my nose back into place. Which I also barely remember. But, ever since, it's never been centered. It looks broken, and in certain lights and certain angles, or when I wear sunglasses, you can see how broken it is. And I'd try to get it fixed again, but at *this* point I'm afraid to become like those people who keep trying to fix things on their face until they don't even have a human-looking face anymore.

Plastic surgery is a really great example of something that won't inherently fix how you feel about yourself. There were plenty of other places to focus my self-hatred on after the surgery. It didn't *actually . . . help me like myself.* And we live in a world where soooo many people are getting plastic surgery, especially actresses and models, and setting more and more impossible standards of what human bodies and faces look like, and lying about it. *Denying* it. Everyone is petrified to admit what it means about us that we *caved, and got it done,* but more petrified to *not get it done at all.* But the lying and denying just makes the expectations more and more impossible. I think that what's even *more* toxic than plastic surgery is getting plastic surgery and pretending you didn't. (Which . . . I did for years.)

And, if you don't address where the misery and self-hatred are coming from in the first place, and if you don't have mental health support to help you with perfectionism, and self-esteem, and how to make peace with your perceived imperfections, it will never be enough. There'll always be another surgery to get, another tweak to make, even *more* weight to lose, and you'll never feel better about yourself.

So, I would say . . . if you want plastic surgery, but you're not in therapy, go to therapy first.

HOW TO BE OBSESSED
WITH BEAUTY

When I was four, I told my dad that I didn't want him to put me to bed, I wanted my *mom* to put me to bed because she was prettier than him. According to a parenting book they were reading at the time, it was actually a "normal" developmental phase for four-year-olds. And they were thankful, because otherwise they'd have been like, *What on earth? Our sweet singing prodigy child is actually an asshole!?* But, either way, my parents started a mantra with me: "It's better to be nice than pretty." Now, you could pick that apart too. There are plenty of valid critiques on how little girls are raised to be nice, and agreeable, and not rock the boat, and little boys are raised to kick and punch and plan to be president. But, in *general*, I approve of what they were going for: *your character matters more than what you look like.* My mom told me that the first time she said it to me, I looked at her *so* confused. Like . . . *how could this be? How can prettiness not be the most important thing . . . ???*

Nice try, parents! The mantra *clearly* didn't work on me! It didn't work on me at all. Or, if it *did* for a few years, the mantra wore off by the time I was a teenager. By then, I was full-on *obsessed* with what I looked like.

I went to a secular, all-girls private school from first grade to twelfth grade that—*in theory*—was setting us on a path to do whatever we wanted. We were being primed to be confident, capable, and smart. We could and would be scientists and world leaders. In this environment, and with these resources, we could *transcend* a fixation on looks, couldn't we? Nope. All I cared about was whether I was pretty or not. Many, *many* girls in my school had very obvious eating disorders, and many others, like me, had less obvious ones.

As a society we are calling out harmful beauty standards more and more. There are more companies using models in different body sizes. There's slowly more diversity on TV and in major media outlets. We are *starting* to be more aware of Photoshop and absurd body and beauty ideals, and how harmful they can be, but there's *still* dissonance.

We *talk* about body positivity, we *talk* about being more than a body, but we still reward a narrowly defined beauty. We still hold people to impossible standards, even while saying that we don't. And it's important to note that beauty is inherently subjective, so when I talk about beauty, I mean: what our society has *deemed* beautiful. The beauty that I keep referring to in this book, and the beauty that I was obsessed with achieving, and a lot of the beauty we are all subconsciously going for, is based on Eurocentric beauty standards. And it's all a white, thin "ideal." In Tressie McMillan Cottom's book *Thick*, she talks about the beauty of whiteness as social capital. "Beauty isn't actually what you look like; beauty is the preferences that reproduce the social order." So, we're all trying to play this beauty game, not realizing that we are subconsciously clinging to *power*.

We are also primed to hate ourselves for not achieving this cultural standard. I wasn't even far off from the thin, Eurocentric ideal, but still, I hated myself, and as you can deduce: it's exponentially more toxic for people with more marginalized identities, who find themselves further and further from this cultural beauty ideal.

I felt like *being that kind of beautiful* was more important than anything else I could be or achieve, and it would also make everything else I became or achieved worth it, because I *saw* how it changed the way people were treated. I *saw* that all my favorite stories were about beautiful people, who all looked a certain way. I didn't need to be told, I *saw it everywhere*.

Women get slammed in the media for gaining weight or not looking young enough—"Why does she look so *haggard and ugly?*" As if it erases every important thing she ever said or did, and erases her humanity too. *What's the point if she isn't . . . hot?* And because I was so sheltered and privileged, and grew up in a relatively traditional and conservative household, I also naively thought sexism was a distant problem that mostly affected people in the olden days. Or that *sometimes* sexism still existed, but only around bad, powerful men. I didn't understand that it was the air we breathed, and that it shaped the way I saw myself. I didn't understand how much my obsession with beauty was a manifestation of sexism. Women *must* be beautiful, or else . . . what's the point? What *good* are they?

Every single story I ever saw in any TV show or any movie

was about a person who looked the way I wanted to look. Beautiful people *deserved* to have their stories told. Beautiful people deserved to be the lead in their own lives. Everyone else who doesn't fit that mold? Side character. Or straight-up villain. Our culture equates beauty with character and intelligence and worthiness, and I believed it.

Author and "story expert" Lani Diane Rich breaks down narrative theory in her podcast, and unpacks how to create a compelling story. She says, "Our stories are our culture." They hold a mirror up to our cultural values. You can learn so much about our culture by the stories that get written, produced, and *told*. They also *shape* our culture. What we see reflected in the stories we tell in movies and TV shows and in the news is a direct representation of what we value as a *culture*. And the stories and media we consume also brainwash us and either perpetuate our culture, or mold and shape it, for good or for bad. In a research article from 2010, it was found that constantly seeing images of "the thin beauty ideal featured in the media—and particularly in magazines, television shows, and commercials—increases body dissatisfaction, internalization of thin ideal, and disordered eating behaviors and beliefs." Meaning . . . just seeing only thin people *nonstop* in the media affects people's relationships with *food*, not just their bodies. Consuming the media that's been out there for the past century . . . affects our self-esteem and body image. And in this brave new online world, where we spend more hours online than we do sleeping, this brainwashing applies even more so to social media. Teen girls who use social media are way more likely than non-social-media-users to prioritize thinness and to engage in body surveillance. Even just using social media for thirty minutes a day can change the way we view our bodies.

I'd never heard anyone talk critically about our culture's obsession with beauty. Don't get me wrong, people *were* talking about it, but back in 2004, the conversation was *not* reaching me. Or not in the way I needed it. The power that beauty holds in our society went unchallenged, unquestioned, and unnamed. It went fully unexamined, and unexamined, and it was able to rule my life. I needed classes on this. Seminars. I needed to be *warned*. I needed it to be called out for what it was starting when I was young (good try, parents), and then even *more* when I was a teenager. I needed debriefings after every Disney movie. I needed people to share their stories with body dysmorphia and eating disorders, the same way we had D.A.R.E. meetings on drugs in fourth grade. I needed training on how the images you see in the media will brainwash you into believing that that's the only right way to look.

Would I have listened?!?! I don't know. Would it have necessarily saved me? Maybe not. But at *least* there would have been a chance that I would have recognized my thoughts and behaviors and self-loathing as *destructive*. Maybe I would have been able to identify my obsession with beauty as *a tricky, unhelpful thing that happens*, instead of a necessary and important part of my life.

The obsession with beauty and looks is not only the burden of women, at least not anymore. Men compare themselves to impossible standards too. And because of that, disordered eating is getting a *rebrand*, now that more men are jumping on the bandwagon. *When men do it*, it's called biohacking. It's a *science* for self-mastery, by treating your body like a piece of tech that needs to be updated to the newest operating system. But . . . it's really just disordered eating. And it's bad for us whichever way you slice it. It harms our brains. And it harms our relationship with ourselves.

The reason I'm focusing more on women is, *a*, I am one, and this is largely about my own experience. And *b*, women have had to be *literally* dependent on men, and dependent on *beauty* and staying attractive for survival since the very distant past, and it's still lingering. It's really interesting, because as women gain more power and mobility in society, men are starting to have more of a disordered relationship with their bodies. So, in a lot of ways, feeling the *need* to be attractive is actually about power dynamics and who holds the power in society. For instance, for women of color, beauty ideals go beyond just gender, because in a culture that has historically been run by white people, assimilating into the white, thin beauty ideal can also be a way of having more opportunity and social mobility (think about Black women being essentially *required* to relax their hair in order to hold a corporate job).

Looking at this past century, women couldn't even vote until 1920 (and in practice, even later for women of color). Women couldn't have a credit card in their name or sit on a jury in all fifty states until the 1970s. Women did not *have* power on their own, or access to well-paid jobs. So, the best way to *secure* power and safety was marriage . . . and culturally acceptable beauty.

In the book *Survival of the Prettiest*, Nancy Etcoff looks at many different studies over the past half-century about beauty and social mobility, and concludes that "better looking girls tend to 'marry up'"—more "beautiful" women end up marrying a man with a higher social status, education, and income than them. Being beautiful was (and in many cases, still is) a means for *social and financial* gain, *via* men. Meanwhile, a study from 1996 shows that women with greater *intelligence* have no advantage on the marriage market. And even without knowing those details, it was how my brain was wired in 2004. Prettiness was power. And I subconsciously saw myself as a person whose goal should be to, one day, be as beautiful a wife as possible.

Not only that, but beauty would keep me safe. It would help me be successful. It was a status symbol. A symbol that I'd conquered my health problems. A symbol that I really was allowed to become an actress. A symbol that I deserved a really *great life story*. And it was extremely toxic, because the way I *looked* was how I measured my success or failure. In this dynamic, women will continually rip themselves apart and starve themselves into dysfunction. This is not serving us.

So . . . what do we do about it? How do we deprogram ourselves from toxic beauty brainwashing? *Is* there a way to "not care about beauty"? The unfortunate part is that we *are* wired, even from when we are babies, to seek out symmetrical, *smooth* faces. You can argue that seeking out strength and youth is a biological advantage for procreation and safety. But beauty standards have also changed drastically over time depending on what we are *told* is beautiful. We can learn and unlearn *many* of our beliefs about beauty, the biggest one being that women's bodies and looks are the most important thing about them. Of course we will obsess over our looks if we believe that it's where we derive all our worth.

We also need our media and our stories to feature diverse bodies and diverse faces and diverse cultures and diverse races, because what we see *brainwashes us*. When all you see on your TV and in magazines are skinny white people, who all have similar faces, we subconsciously wonder what's wrong with us. We subconsciously learn that we do *not* look the way we are supposed to look. It causes stress and body shame and exacerbates the prevalence of disordered eating. But to see *yourself* represented on screen? In clothing ads? In commercials? In movies? Seeing different bodies and faces represented is legitimizing. It is healing. It *lessens* the shame we feel about our own bodies or faces. We need to believe that *the way we are is a valid way to be*. We need to feel that *people like me deserve to have their story told*.

If there had been diversity in the TV shows and movies I watched, maybe I would have looked at myself and thought: *My body is OK. My face is OK. I am a legitimate person in the world*. Instead of: *OMG, I am an ugly and unhealthy monster. In order to matter at all, I have to change*.

I don't fault anyone for wanting to fit in, or to be more conventionally beautiful. We are social creatures, we need people. So, fitting in feels like *safety* in a lot of instances. And beyond just the safety of community, we are often treated better when we are conventionally attractive. It's hard to stop caring when the benefits and consequences are so clear. But we *have* to diversify the images we see in the media. It has such a clear and direct correlation on the way we view ourselves. A study that was done in 2006 showed that by six years old, girls want a thinner figure, and it's highly influenced by *the images they see in the media*. And we need to see not just different body types and races, but middle-aged people's bodies and faces too. Let's *talk* about the expectations put on us to stay looking like a skinny little fifteen-year-old when we are fifty years old, because almost everyone on TV is the size of a toothpick, with faces that don't move.

I want to be clear: I am not above this. I am *not* immune to the pressure to be more beautiful. Not at all. I still feel it. Especially when I watch certain movies and TV shows, I hear a whisper in my head saying, *How can I figure out how to look like that?* The change now is that I can more easily snap out of it. And I'm not as harsh on myself as I was before. I've also been deeply miserable over chasing elusive standards of beauty, and I know that I don't want to feel that way again. Now, I know better. But it still creeps in, even when you know better.

HOW TO HAVE A
HORRIBLE TIME
IN FRANCE

The following school year, my new face and I went to France for two weeks with my high school. We spent a few days in Paris, did a week homestay in Nîmes, and then finished up with a few last days in Paris again.

To me, France was the *ideal place to finally miraculously heal from my binge eating.* Yes, I'd successfully prayed for a new face (*sort of, because now it was just a broken nose*), but my eating and weight yo-yoing was still a huge problem. And as far as I understood, the French had it figured out. They were thin. They ate cheese, they ate bread, and they were beautiful. I wanted that. I wanted bread *and* beauty. And I hoped my trip to France would be a chance to soak this in, to heal through osmosis, maybe pick up a smoking habit along the way, and return a healed, glowing, chill French person.

At the time, I was on metformin, a diabetes medicine that makes your cells more sensitive to insulin. This was during my attempt to do whatever the doctors told me to do. Drug me up. Heal me. Because it looked like my dieting wasn't working. (Though I was still planning on trying to make it work until the day I died, hungry and trying.)

Metformin was a *huge* pill that I was supposed to take with dinner, but at my first homestay night, I had to wait and take the pill in bed before I went to sleep with only a tiny cup of water. This was *FRANCE*. I couldn't take these American horse pills at dinner, *proving* to them everything they thought of us. I had to represent America well. I had to hide my food addiction. And I had to hide my drugs.

I went to bed feeling like the pill was stuck in my esophagus and woke up the next morning with full-blown burning, radiating pain right where my stomach meets my esophagus. Moving around hurt, and I couldn't lie down without being in extreme pain because stomach acid was rushing over the hole I burned into the bottom of my esophagus. I didn't really *know* what was happening, but I had an idea that the pill had gotten stuck and irritated my lower esophagus overnight. I just hoped it would go away over the course of the day, but it didn't. It just got worse. So, I had to try to explain what had happened in French to my homestay mom. . . . "Uhhhhh . . . le medecine de diabetes . . . uh . . ." How American of me.

Even though my *long-term goal* was to eat bread like the French, during the first week of this trip I had been eating *zero* carbs, but this was now a dire situation. The only thing that made me feel better was eating Kinder Chocolate. It gave me about seven seconds of temporary relief as it coated the hole that I'd burned, but for the next twenty seconds it made the pain even worse when it kicked up my stomach acid. I was in so much pain that I stayed home from the day when we got to go to school with my French homestay girl. I was alone in the French people's house watching *The Lion King* in French. "Hakuna Matata, mais quelle phrase magnifique."

I also remember sitting on the floor of my homestay bedroom, staring out the window, wondering if I was dying from metformin-induced stomach cancer, while I ate Kinder Chocolate bar after Kinder Chocolate bar. *This was my **one** chance to become French and to blend in with cool people who ate croissants and knew what the fuck they were doing. Instead, I'm sitting alone in a French bedroom listening to Keane's "Somewhere Only We Know" on my iPod, worrying that if I die young, I'll never get my chance to be in a famous love triangle.*

Nobody believed I was in actual pain or understood *what* I was talking about when I mentioned my diabetes medicine. I think they thought I was just homesick. "Avez-vous le diabète?" "Non, mais . . . mais j'ai les . . . autres problèmes. C'est difficile d'expliquer . . ." I have other problems. It's difficult to explain. Because I'm not fucking fluent in French.

The homestay mother eventually had to take me to the French doctor, who told me it was all in my head and caused by stress. I needed to calm down. The light in my eyes dimmed a little more. I mean, *you know* how much I believe health problems can be caused or exacerbated by stress. Yes, I *was* chronically stressed. But I still had a goddamn hole in my stomach.

At a certain point, I pushed through. I was miserable and in pain, but I hung out with the two French sisters I was staying with. I was sick of being sick and antisocial. I had to go with the flow once I decided I wasn't dying of stomach cancer. I even went with them to a "sud club" for their friend's sixteenth birthday party, where they literally rain down bubbles on your head while you dance, and where I had my very *first drink of my life*, le rhum et le Coke (wonderful for the hole in my stomach) and danced on *a French table*. The French parents totally condoned the sud club situation, and the older, college-age sister and her boyfriend drove us and chaperoned.

Then at the end of this weeklong homestay misery, Melinda, the English woman who had arranged our French homestay, scolded me on the bus in front of all my high school classmates. She was *very* angry and told me that I was *depressed* and that my *depression* had broken the *heart* of my homestay girl and made her *cry*. I apparently really let the homestay girl down, and therefore I should be ashamed of myself. She also told me that *her own son* had depression, so she could identify this *very* well in me, and that I *also* needed magnesium because that is what caused *her son's* depression. She was not nice about this. She was very angry with me about my magnesium deficiency and my depression.

Hey, I probably *did* need magnesium. And, fun fact, magnesium deficiency is also associated with insulin resistance. *But* I *also* needed to get the fuck away from Melinda. *Take some magnesium yourself, Melinda.*

HOW TO LOSE
FEELING IN HALF
OF YOUR FACE

I've been using the term "trauma" a lot, and before I learned what trauma actually *is*, I would have thought that throwing around that term was the definition of hyperbole. *OK, girl-who-loves-drama, calm down on claiming to be traumatized.* I used to think that trauma was reserved for truly horrible and textbook traumatic things: car crashes, violent attacks, overtly abusive relationships, losing family members at a young age, and, of course, war. It turns out that, while *yes*, those things are absolutely traumatic and can often lead to more complex manifestations of PTSD, trauma is less about *what happened* and more about *how your body processed it*. Or, rather, how your body *didn't* process it.

Trauma is the result of an *incomplete* fight-or-flight process and unprocessed energy stuck in your nervous system. And if you don't eventually process it while being *present* in your body, it will *keep* you in a fight or flight state and may become a more advanced manifestation of PTSD. The two books that completely changed the way I understand trauma, embodiment, and getting stuck in the fight or flight state are *Waking the Tiger* by psychologist and trauma researcher Peter A. Levine and *The Body Keeps the Score* by Bessel van der Kolk, a psychiatrist and trauma researcher. I recommend reading both of those books, because I'm never going to be able to explain the complexities of trauma as well as they do.

But the book *Waking the Tiger* helped me understand that *very* ordinary experiences can result in trauma, and those experiences can keep you stuck for a long time, sometimes for your whole life if they aren't dealt with. And being stuck in that fight or flight state will very quickly lead to physical and emotional symptoms, including exhaustion and burnout.

Here are *some* of the seemingly ordinary experiences that can be stored as trauma in the body and nervous system: an upsetting social interaction, a physical injury, witnessing violence, being bullied, certain medical and dental procedures, loss of a close family member, illnesses, a financial scare, and a stressful near-miss accident (even just *almost* getting in a car crash). Basically, nothing dramatic and horrible has to actually happen; it just has to be something you don't know how to process in the moment.

Trauma can manifest in a lot of different ways. Sometimes completely opposite ways. But some things that can signal you may have unprocessed trauma are if you are easily emotionally triggered by certain subjects, being in a state of high alert all the time, panic attacks, mental "spaciness," not remembering certain times in your life because you dissociated *during* the traumatic event or time, and not *wanting* to remember, as well as avoidance behavior.

Trauma is a contributing factor in a *lot* of physical and mental illnesses, including chronic exhaustion, because it keeps your body in a very stress-activated state for way longer than is ideal, and it also usually has people turning to coping mechanism after coping mechanism to try to avoid the discomfort of the unprocessed event. A scientific article from 2015 noted that if PTSD symptoms go unprocessed, they can eventually manifest as chronic fatigue, immune system problems, or endocrine problems, as well as lots of other anxious behaviors. Long story short: *unprocessed trauma is common, and trauma is a huge contributor to general exhaustion.*

When I learned that trauma was not reserved for violent attacks, I realized . . . oh . . . *I was traumatized by a lot of things in high school.* I remember *very* little. I was *rarely* present. And in order to process trauma, we have to be present. We have to "be in our bodies," feeling what it feels like *in* our bodies, and not dissociating into our minds or into Hogwarts. In *The Body Keeps the Score*, van der Kolk says that "trauma victims cannot recover until they befriend the sensations in their bodies." That was something I didn't know how to do for a really long time. It's something I didn't even know I *should* be doing for a really long time. High school was traumatizing to me at every turn: constant performing and constant health scares. Not to mention: living in a culture that makes you feel like you should be starving yourself in order to be accepted . . . that also results in unprocessed trauma for a lot of people. Believing that your body is unruly, untrustworthy, and inherently *wrong?* Traumatic. A *lot* of us have that trauma to unpack and process.

It turns out, my dental surgeries were also pretty traumatizing. And over the course of high school I probably had a dental surgery every few months, if not more often, and always with local anesthesia. Meaning my mouth was shot up with Novocain and I lay there *wiiiiide* awake for hours while they drilled into my jawbones. Eventually I started getting desensitized to Novocain and started getting feeling back in my mouth mid-surgery. And I had to yell with my throat closed, "Nnng! nnng!" so the dentist knew I was in pain and could give me more Novocain.

I had "temporary" veneers for *years* while they experimented with my "bite." Temporary veneers are not as sturdy as porcelain, and easier to drill and shave down to adjust the bite, but also easier to break. The temporary veneers had temporary glue, and the *one* day of my high school life that I let myself eat a bagel, it suctioned some of my veneers off.

My teeth fell out all the time. They *broke* all the time because of my nighttime stress teeth grinding. I'd taste the glue and know I was in for a very annoying two weeks. One time I used Krazy Glue to keep them in before my emergency dentist appointment. And no, this probably did not help my health, but what is a seventeen-year-old girl to do when she has broken teeth and her periodontist is in Europe!? WHAT WAS I SUPPOSED TO DO? *This* is why Harry Potter, and his friends, were *my friends.* I needed the escape. I *needed* my fantasies, otherwise I would crumble into a pile of ash, and the only thing remaining would be my fake, broken teeth.

After I had four dental implants drilled into my jawbone, one of them didn't heal correctly, and they had to redo the entire thing and re-drill into my jawbone. I'd been getting injected with Novocain, dealing with dental glues, and healing from major mouth surgeries for years, and taking *lots* of antibiotics every time I had a surgery. And this time, my mom and I decided I'd had *enough* antibiotics. The world was finally learning that overusing antibiotics wasn't great for you, or your gut, and creates superstrains of bacteria, so my mom and I decided I *wasn't* going to preventatively take them this time. I was just going to heal the old-fashioned way: kill or be killed.

Of course, *this* was the time my jaw got infected and swelled up so much that half of my face went numb and I thought it was the beginning of facial paralysis. *Oh, God, now I'll never be beautiful.* But once my face was swollen and numb for a few days, and it looked like I was leaning toward the "be killed" side of the plan, I panicked and took the antibiotics and I got feeling back in my face after a few days.

I want to be *very* clear that in no way do I think my life was harder or more traumatizing than anyone else's. Even with all my stress and inability to cope, it was probably still easier than most people's. So many people are faced with so much more: poverty, racism, and other forms of discrimination and oppression, and those are all traumas that can take a toll on the body and mind. My goal is to just illustrate how *common* it is to become burnt out and stuck in fight or flight mode. It doesn't take much. As a society, we don't really understand that *most of us* are operating with some level of unprocessed trauma, and I want to reassure you that what you feel is valid.

It's also experiences like mine that are, on the surface . . . not *that* big of a deal. *Big whoop! Your parents could afford to buy you nice teeth so you didn't become a toothless adult. And they had to redo one of the surgeries. It's not fun but . . . it's no use whining over.* That's how I felt back then too. This was just what life was. I didn't *like* it, but people had it way worse. I just had to tense up my entire body for years at a time and get through it.

That's what we *often* do to get through things that overwhelm us. Buck up, suck it up, and tense up your entire body for years at a time. The only problem is that eventually, this alone will lead to exhaustion, and it's not sustainable. Eventually, there will be some not-so-fun trauma to unpack and process.

HOW TO BE AN
ACTUAL CHEESE GRATER
IN A MUSICAL

During the fall and winter of my senior year of high school, on top of everything else, I now had a full-time job in a professional production of *Beauty and the Beast* in Philadelphia. I was an understudy and chair-mover, dressed in full townsperson garb with a huge red curly wig and bonnet. And I barely slept.

Every morning I would go to a cappella practice before school, then I'd go to my first few classes, and then before lunch I'd drive one hour into the city to rehearse. Once the show was open, I'd drive one hour into the city after my school day ended, park in a parking garage, and after the show ended at 11 p.m., I'd drive one hour back. Every day I'd almost fall asleep backstage while I was waiting for my big chair-move as we transitioned from the forest to the Beast's castle.

This is a year that I had all my tiny meals and tiny snacks timed out. I'd get home at midnight, eat a Luna bar, and lie in bed with restless legs syndrome that I'm convinced the birth control pill Yaz gave me. (Yaz was once considered "the most complained-about drug on the internet," according to the internet.)

I was *extremely* restrictive with my food during this period, *and* I was trying to go for a run every day during every small break I got during rehearsals, but I was so deeply exhausted that I could never make it past twenty-two minutes. But every day I would still force myself to run anyway, and I became very confused when my endurance never improved, even though I was forcing myself to run six days a week. I just assumed I was straight-up lazy, and I had to keep pushing harder. This "laziness" assumption is a manifestation of toxic diet culture and toxic self-improvement culture. We are primed to believe we are lazy, and if we just go on *this plan*, or buy *this product*, or push a little harder, we can *fix it*. But what if we are putting impossible expectations on ourselves? What if we are expecting ourselves to *do too much* and *have it all* and *wear the latest trends* on our *teeny tiny body* in a way that just isn't actually sustainable without having physical or mental consequences? We're constantly treating ourselves like machines, but even phones need to fucking recharge.

I was so busy and so tired this year that for a few-month stretch, I had no time or energy to cheat or binge on my new diet. I was just surviving. During rehearsal breaks, I would run, eat my tiny meal, and teach myself AP Environmental Science in the green room because I wasn't able to go to class. And to this day, this is the thinnest I've ever been. And I got . . . soooo many compliments. *From everyone.* Classmates. My family. Other, older actresses in *Beauty and the Beast*. I had been yo-yoing hard-core, up and down, over the past four years, but *finallyyyyy* I was on a plan that "worked"! And a plan that would hopefully work forever! *I did it I did it I did it.*

I also really believed I was eating whatever I wanted. *All I had to do* was measure out a certain ratio of carbs to protein, keep most things very low-fat, and *not* go over the allotted amount of carbs in any three-hour time period. I ate every three-ish hours. I mean, look how *free I am!* I can eat eleven chocolate chips! I even let myself order apple pie and eat the apples and one bite of crust! Wow. This is *livingggggggggg.* I genuinely believed I was on a *LiFeStYlE pLaN* that was going to work for me for the rest of my life. It probably lasted eight months, because eventually I started eating two whole dark chocolate bars in one sitting without blinking my eyes. And that's how it goes, my friends.

That fall, while I was very thin, I auditioned for another professional theater in the city for a musical that would be happening late spring until July. And I got the part as the "beautiful" virgin courtesan, who'd been sold to a Roman war hero, Miles Gloriosus, in the raucous musical farce *A Funny Thing Happened on the Way to the Forum.* I *just* realized that it was essentially a musical about sex trafficking, and I was the sex slave! *Hilarious!* It was a cast full of local Philadelphia stars—*and me.*

The problem was, in between my auditions in November and the actual rehearsals in April, my diet stopped working. I started gaining weight and my face broke out in cystic acne again. Maybe it's because I finally had a moment to breathe, and in that moment I couldn't keep being so hungry without eating more than eleven chocolate chips. My resolve was slipping. I couldn't ignore that I was starving. I would *still* go for a run every day, and my body *still* wouldn't let me run over twenty-two minutes. I couldn't do it. I would end up bent over about to pass out every time. *What is wrong with me?*

January to April were the months in between *Beauty and the Beast* and *A Funny Thing Happened on the Way to the Forum*, and besides going to school, I also had to audition for college theater programs. My big question: *Am I good enough or pretty enough or thin enough to actually go into this and major in this in college?* was answered, I guess, when I became temporarily really skinny and started getting professional acting jobs during high school. *OK, so I guess I should?*

Right after *Beauty and the Beast* closed, in the two weeks before my college auditions started, I had a big dental surgery. I had two bridges in my mouth (one of them was where the miracle tooth had been), and above the bridges; because there were no roots, the gums looked sunken in. So, I had a *gum graft.* I had gums cut and grafted off the top of the roof of my mouth (yes, fully awake), and mixed with some sort of animal bone-meal (*whyyyy*), which was then stuffed into the gums over my two dental bridges so the gums didn't look sunken in.

Not only was this procedure a horror, but my main perio-dontist who did *most* of my mouth surgeries was really angry that it was done improperly by this other dentist who did the graft. Apparently, this other guy did it in a way that was *more* painful, harder to recover from, and also less effective? All I know is that right after I got the surgery, my mom read that the bonemeal they used had been *recalled* because some of it was contaminated with mad cow disease. I, personally, did not have the wherewithal to process this. I couldn't even speak. My mouth was still numb, way longer than it was supposed to be, otherwise we wouldn't have planned the surgery so close to my college auditions. Even *worse*, animal bonemeal was actually falling out from the hole in my gums. And I had to audition for NYU in five days and I couldn't practice my song or monologue because my mouth was numb. I just shut down and pretended this wasn't happening, and my mom bore the brunt of the stress. She said that when she read about the mad cow disease, her hands started shaking and didn't stop shaking for months.

This gum graft and animal bone procedure never properly healed, or ever did what it was supposed to do: make the gums look less sunken in. And worse, gravelly animal bones were falling out of a hole at the top of my gums for a few *years*. I'm guessing I never got mad cow disease, so that's a plus. And a day before we left for my college auditions, I got feeling back in my mouth and was able to speak again.

This whole year, I was in a state of fight or flight. It was just about survival. I was underfed, underslept, and bonemeal was falling out of a hole in my gums. Every day was *just* about getting to the next exhausting day where I continued to undereat and undersleep. The irony is, I thought this would be good for my physical health? Somehow? At some point? If I could stay thin for long enough? But it just added to compounding exhaustion and chronic health issues that eventually only extreme rest could heal.

HOW TO NOT KNOW
YOU HAVE AN
EATING DISORDER

If someone sat me down and had said, Caroline, I think you might have an eating disorder, or disordered eating in the very least, I would have thought, *No, no, you don't know what you're talking about. My problems are food- and weight-related, and I'm going to figure it all out.*

Lack of fluency around eating disorders is a major problem. We don't seem to understand how rampant they are, and how easily disguised they can be as "a passion for healthy living." We don't understand how many times we praise or envy someone for having disordered habits or a full-blown eating disorder. For instance, are you praising them for being "so good" at sticking to Whole30 for the last three years? Or are you praising an eating disorder? Disordered habits are so normalized and glorified in our culture that most eating disorders fly under the radar.

Why? First, because we value thinness and fitness over mental health. Or we assume that thinness and fitness *is* mental health, and don't understand the nuance between what is self-care and what is a dangerous coping mechanism. This is a huge problem in the health and mental health world, and it's one of the most toxic manifestations of diet culture. Because dieting and exercising are generally seen as good, they're often prescribed as a cure for anything and everything under the sun, without doing any screening for eating disorders, and without understanding how often people take a diet and quickly turn it into disordered eating. The difference between disordered eating and an eating disorder is essentially just severity, but the line is blurry. Eating disorders are a mental health condition, but they are often diagnosed by weight, which actually is a mistake.

The biggest myth about eating disorders is that your habits are only a problem if you are extremely thin, and that's just . . . not true. Many people who are starving or anorexic do not look emaciated or even very thin, and because of this, so many eating disorders go undiagnosed. And worse, many eating disorders are encouraged and praised. Jennifer Gaudiani, MD, wrote in her book *Sick Enough*, "Starvation can occur in people of any body shape and size. It doesn't just happen in people with lower body weight, although society and the medical profession may not understand this fact." In fact, after everything I've learned, and all the tens of thousands of people I've heard from about their experience, I'd go as far as to say that a lot of fat people have anorexia, but because of medical weight stigma, it's rarely treated. ("Fat" is the preferred term of fat activists and anyone reclaiming the stigmatizing term. Not everyone wants to be called fat because it's become such a loaded word and commonly used as an insult. But when I use the term "fat" in this book, it's in the spirit of fat activists who want to neutral-ize the word. It's a body type, not an insult.) Fat people who have anorexia are often praised for their undereating and eating disorder behaviors, because our medical field still pushes and encourages weight loss at all costs. Atypical anorexia is what they call it when you have the behaviors of anorexia but aren't underweight. But it's not atypical at all, it's just undiagnosed. And anorexia and undereating will wreak havoc on your physi-cal and mental health no matter what your weight is.

This myth about eating disorders and body size exists and persists because of another myth: the myth that weight is always a matter of calories in vs. calories out. We assume this because we can usually lose weight and keep it off at the beginning of a diet or exercise regimen. And therefore, it seems like proof that body weight is just a simple math equation. We cut back on calories, and we lose weight. Voilà! It's math! However, we don't consider that the eventual regain, or food obsession, or bingeing are all still part of the equation, and all because of the way we are wired. Our bodies slow down and fixate us on food. Our bodies burn less the less we eat, in order to purposely hold on to weight so we don't diiiiiieeeeee. A 2012 scientific arti-cle, "An Inconvenient Truth about Obesity," discusses the vari-ous mechanisms in the body that will protect the highest adult weight in response to dieting. Another article in 2013 discusses how calorie restriction makes food extra appealing, increases the brain's chemical reward for eating food, and makes us more fixated on food. Our body fights back. And I'd say anecdotally that the more we diet, the more quickly our body seems to fight back.

Our bodies have a general weight range where they feel safest, and our hypothalamus adjusts our metabolism to generally keep us in our range. For some people, that's on the thinner side, for some people that's on the fatter side. Your weight set range isn't wrong, it's where your body wants to be. It's also the weight where, with sustainable healthy habits like joyful exercise and a nourishing, varied diet, and a good relationship with food, your body would be healthiest. Because, it turns out, health habits have more of an impact on your health than your weight does.

Lots of people hear about weight set range and assume that the point is to figure out how to have a lower or thinner weight set range. But that's misunderstanding the message. That's a prime example of the narrative that thin is always best (you know, our cult brainwashing). Your range is where your body wants to be. So, if you are engaging in disordered behaviors, undereating, overexercising, constantly hungry, or overthinking your food or calories or carbs, but you still aren't thin, that's an example of a restrictive eating disorder that is encouraged, simply because you don't "look sick." And so many people are doing this. So many people, in every size body from thin to fat, are chronically undereating, or chronically yo-yo dieting, chronically bingeing in response to all of this, and then beating themselves up with compensatory restriction or compulsive exercise. And because they don't look emaciated, their habits are overlooked or praised. So, a humongous issue in recognizing and treating eating disorders is size discrimination and a poor understanding of how weight, weight loss, and starvation actually works. People in larger bodies who need treatment for chronic dieting or undereating or anorexia will usually only be treated for bingeing or overeating. If they say they don't actually eat much, they are often not believed. We need a more nuanced understanding of how bingeing or overeating is very often a symptom of dieting, undereating, or weight stigma.

Another big problem in eating disorder fluency is the assumption that it's a problem that primarily affects thin, affluent white women. Yeah, there are a lot of thin, affluent white women with disordered eating or eating disorders, but people of color are actually more likely to have eating disorders, and less likely to be diagnosed and receive help. That belief that it's a thin white women's problem actually affects who gets diagnosed and who believes they should seek help in the first place. There's discrimination in the eating disorder field. Clinicians are less likely to recommend that Black women receive professional help for the same disordered eating behaviors that white women have.

I talked with Christyna Johnson, MS, RDN, a registered dietitian who specializes in eating disorders, and the only Black dietitian in the Dallas, Texas, area. She said that "there are simply not enough specialized eating disorder treatment providers that hold the same marginalizations as the people they provide lifesaving services to. Clients oftentimes do not feel safe to show up as their full selves." Plainly . . . our culture and medical field have a weight stigma problem and a systemic racism problem. She said, "In order to accurately treat and prevent eating disorders in people of color, we must understand the ways that white supremacy and anti-blackness show up through every stage of the treatment process."

The higher prevalence of eating disorders is partially because of the compounding traumas of racism. Christyna went on to say: "In marginalized communities in the US, eating disorders serve as a protection from systems of oppression and can also help someone assimilate into an oppressive culture to create a sense of safety in an otherwise threatening environment." This is the tip of the iceberg of a way bigger conversation on the insidious nature of white supremacy, how it shows up in health care, and the ripple effects it has on health and mental health.

One of the diagnostic tools used to screen for eating disorders is BMI, which is inherently flawed and discriminatory all by itself. BMI is based on a formula that was made by a mathematician (not a doctor or even a medical scientist), based on a bell curve of white men in the 1800s. It was never meant to diagnose anything; it was never even based on health. The cutoff numbers are not only arbitrary but were also arbitrarily changed by the NIH and CDC in 1998 so the cutoffs would be in easy multiples of five. This is one of the reasons we saw an increase in so-called obesity. Our bodies didn't change—the cutoff numbers did. But what this also means is that different ethnicities and races are meant to all fit into a random math formula based on white men, without taking into account body diversity, or the fact that these cutoffs are made up. You fucks! So, as an example, Black women are expected to lose weight to fit a graph made for white men in the 1800s, told to lose weight, and voilà: disordered eating.

So, what this all meant for me, was that I was in the demographic that was more likely to be diagnosed with an eating disorder, and more likely to be treated. I was thin. I was white.

(I mean, I still am white.) I had ample access to medical care. I went to the doctor all the time. But, because I wasn't emaciated, and because I would have described myself as someone who couldn't stop eating food, I didn't even know to be concerned. And, therefore, it flew under the radar.

But even if my disordered eating had been diagnosed, the majority of eating disorder treatment and medical care would still be steeped in diet culture and fat-phobia. Ah, it looks like you have an eating disorder! You shouldn't eat so little, but as you are recovering, you should also not eat too much. And don't gain too much weight. That approach and perspective leaves a lot of people stuck somewhere in a quasi-recovery, afraid to really eat and gain the weight their body needs to gain after restriction. And it's still making assumptions about what your body is supposed to look like in order to be healthy, which is a big part of the problem to begin with. Micromanaging weight is not the answer, and it's especially not the answer when we are dealing with eating disorders and disordered eating.

Another common disorder that people consider "healthy living" is an obsession with exercise. Obsession with exercise is actually an eating disorder called exercise bulimia or anorexia athletica. Anyone who gets stressed when they have to skip a workout, plans their entire life or vacation around when they can exercise, or uses exercise to "counteract" eating, or who only lets themselves eat certain things if they've exercised . . . that's an eating disorder. And it's one that we don't consider a disorder because we consider exercise healthy. So, we think it's OK if people become obsessive about it, because what a healthy thing to be obsessed over! Nooooo! Just because exercise is good for you doesn't mean overexercising is good for you! It's not. It can cause mood swings, depression, anxiety, lowered immunity, strain on your heart, injury, and trouble sleeping. Couple overexercising with undereating or chronic yo-yo dieting? Holy stress hormones. Bob Harper, *Biggest Loser* trainer, had a heart attack midworkout, and I will never let people forget this.

Honestly, most people who are obsessed with health, dieting, or exercise have some version of disordered eating or an eating disorder. And that's a lot of us. An unhealthy obsession with dieting and exercise is more rampant than we think, especially in a society that constantly demonizes food and weight. And while exercise is great for us when we are well fed and rested, so many of us exercise with one priority: weight. Not strength, not health, not feeling alive, but weight loss, weight management, and fear of future weight gain. Most exercise classes and gyms are marketed to get at this deep-seated fear of weight gain, because they know what'll get you running like a hamster on a hamster wheel.

As a culture, we focus so much on the horrors of eating too much and exercising too little that we aren't aware that the opposite is just as bad if not worse. And now that I've seen how rampant our cultural disordered eating is, I can't unsee it.

HOW TO HAVE NO BLOOD

During the last semester of high school, in the two months before the start of rehearsals for the sex slavery musical, I did a lot of weird things to try to heal my skin. I mean, they cast a *very* thin, clear-skinned girl to play their beautiful virgin sex slave, and I couldn't let them down.

On a message board for PCOS, my mom and I learned that there was a special flour made of ground buckwheat groats that was supposed to help, because they had a certain B vitamin in them—*apparently*. So, we ordered the special flour, and I made a freezerful of no-sugar buckwheat muffins and ate two a day. I cut out dairy. I went back on metformin (the insulin resistance medication that burned a hole in my stomach). I went on and off different birth control pills. I kept trying to run—and *still* had to keep stopping at twenty-two minutes. I went to a place and got a colonic, which was supposed to clear out my colon, which would heal my skin *and* maybe my hormones too. (I remember the woman who owned that place sat me down in her office and told me she could teach me a method to mind-over-matter dental surgery pain so I didn't need to get Novocain anymore during my dental surgeries. *Uhhh, what?*)

Nothing worked. So, all I remember about the rehearsal process for *A Funny Thing Happened on the Way to the Forum* was that I was *extremely* stressed over extremely cystic skin, and extremely stressed that I'd gained weight and didn't fit into my skinny-bras anymore. Then, somehow during the rehearsal process, I put myself on another, different crash diet again.

If you ask my *mom* about this time, she will tell you that she did a novena (a Catholic ritualistic prayer involving the rosary and the number nine?) and implored St. Thérèse to miraculously heal my skin, and because my cystic acne *did* clear up just in time for the day when they took promotional photos . . . she is annoyed that this miracle story is not the *central* story in this book, but I told her she would have to write her own book about her miracles.

So, yes, my skin *did* miraculously clear up just in time for the photos and the run of the sex slave show. They got their clear-skinned, skinny sex slave virgin, and it *may* have been because of a miracle. Maybe.

But the world wasn't finished stressing me out, because the morning of opening night, I woke up to find that I had broken my entire unit of front bottom teeth temporary veneers off in my sleep. Meaning, a whole chunk of connected bottom teeth broke off, and I woke up and spat the chunk of teeth into my hand. If you want to know what my teeth looked like, you can just google "Gollum" or "the goblins who work in Gringotts" and see for yourself. I had to be at the final rehearsal in the city in three hours, so I had to put an emergency call in to my dentist, who *thankfully* left his golf game early to glue my teeth back on. But if he hadn't been available, I would have resorted to Krazy Glue again. *I would have.*

Getting to be an actress was my dream. And now, I was *doing it.* I had everything I thought I'd wanted: I was skinny, I was acting, I was cast as "the beautiful young thing," but was I enjoying any of this? No. Not at all. All I knew was that my diet wasn't quite as effective anymore, I was gaining weight, and my temporary teeth were breaking in the middle of the night because I was grinding them in my sleep thanks to my deep, existential overwhelm. I was dieting, running, going to school, making up classes and taking AP tests, and again, driving one hour to the city, and one hour back at midnight only to lie in bed, unable to sleep, all so I could star in a comedy about sex slavery.

Just after the show closed, for my last month and a half before college, I went to get my pre-college doctor's checkup. A few days later my doctor called me and said I needed to *immediately* get retested, because the blood test showed that my hemoglobin was so low that it was probably a mistake. Apparently, it would be almost impossible to still be walking around if it really was that low. *Oh, great. Another problem.* I remember when I went back to get retested, my doctor looked at me and said: ". . . SIT DOWN! For God's sake, you shouldn't be standing." I thought, *Well, I just ran for twenty-two minutes this morning.*

They retested, and yes, it really was that low. I had *half* the hemoglobin I was supposed to, and I needed to get a blood transfusion if the levels didn't come up within a month with iron supplementation. They didn't know *why* I was anemic. They ran a lot of tests. They did a colonoscopy and a colon biopsy to test for celiac disease. *Nothing.* No explanation.

Not only had I spent the whole year *standing*, and walking around, and barely sleeping, and graduating high school, and being a full-time blond sex slave in a musical comedy who had to walk out on a slanted roof in the middle of the show—I had been forcing myself to run almost every day. *This* explained why I had never been able to run more than twenty-two minutes without feeling like I was going to die.

Turns out I was not lazy after all, just very ill.

HOW TO COPE WHEN YOUR PARENT HAS CANCER

During the one-and-a-half-month break between the end of the show and the start of my freshman year as a musical theater student at NYU, I read an article about Katharine McPhee, who had just been on *American Idol*. The article was about her eating disorder, and about how she *healed* by learning to eat normally. In the article, she cited the book *Intuitive Eating*, and how much it helped her. I was . . . fascinated.

Before that point, I had never, ever considered that I had an issue with dieting. But something in this article resonated with me, so I immediately read the book and I realized: *Wow . . . I need to do this. I need to normalize my relationship to food.* (Unfortunately, this was *not* actually the epiphany that led to The F*ck It Diet. That was still six years away.)

After I read *Intuitive Eating*, I was inspired for about a week and a half. I needed to sit my mom down and tell her that I was going to *stop* dieting. I was going to try to eat all the foods that I was so scared of, foods we both believed were bad for my health (because: carbs! Weight gain! Hormones! Insulin resistance!) and I was going to try to learn to eat *intuitively*.

My mom and I both believed I had a food addiction, because as far as we both could tell, I did. I was obsessed with food, and I couldn't control myself around it for long. I mean, I'd been obsessed with food since I was a child! I binged *all the time*. I ate until I was ill. All I did was think about food and *talk* about food. I felt hungry all the time. I *acted* like an addict, lying about whether I was on my diet or not, and hiding my bingeing. I was unable to get a handle on my issues with food, no matter what I did or how important it was to me. And it was VERY IMPORTANT TO ME.

In some ways, because my food addiction felt so dire, and the stakes felt so high, I really felt like I was trying to save my life. *And I still couldn't do it*—and it had gotten worse and worse every year. *Now* I had no *blood*, no energy, and no natural period, my face was covered in cysts (except when my mother was performing miracles, apparently), my thyroid nodule kept filling back up, and I kept breaking my teeth in the middle of the night.

Exhaustion is also arguably a side effect of PCOS, or any chronic illness, *and* it's a side effect of dangerously low hemoglobin. But it is also a side effect of chronic dieting and disordered eating, so I was just *extra* tired, all the time. But again, I had no context. I still thought this was my temporary period of strife, and that eventually, I *too* would get to lie in the hospital ward of Hogwarts and convalesce, and people would bring me candy and gossip and I'd say: *No, no, I don't like carbs.*

I sat my mom down and said, "Mom, I am reading this book, *Intuitive Eating*, and I actually think I have a problem with dieting that I need to heal. So, I am going to follow this book, and eat some of the things that are supposed to be 'bad' for me . . . and see if it helps."

She sounded exhausted too, and she softly said, "OK . . . OK, do whatever you need. The only thing is that I might be going in the opposite direction and eating *more* strictly because . . . I have cancer."

What.

". . . What?"

"I found out a month ago that I have lymphoma, but I didn't want to stress you out while you were still doing the show."

My mom had temporarily decided to try vegetarianism to see if it could cure her Hodgkin's lymphoma, and she hadn't decided yet about chemo. She told me she'd just read a book about vegetarianism and cancer, and that she could lend it to me if I was curious. I told her that I'd read it, but that I'd *never* give up chicken. (Also! Remember! I was just about to learn to be *intuitive*.)

Finding a diet that would heal her (and me) was, at this point, a part of our family culture. It was our worldview: "We are sick because we are not eating the right diet." When you believe that it's at least partially *diet* that made you sick, *of course* you will try to change your diet to try to heal yourself before taking the mainstream treatment, which, for cancer, is medical poison. I get why, if you believe something else will help, you'll try that first. I'm not necessarily condoning it, I just . . . get it. In reality, remember how her hands started shaking from stress of my possible mad cow disease implanted into my gums? Well, it all led here. Cancer. *Stress* was the thing that put her over the edge.

So, the next day I read the book about vegetarianism and cancer, and the day after *that* I was a vegetarian. The next week I was vegan. *Maybe I can do this . . . intuitively?* (No. I couldn't.) My mom was raw vegan, and I was regular vegan. I think *technically*, these days, what we were doing is called "plant-based" and the term "vegan" is reserved for when you are doing it for the animals. We were not doing it for the animals. We were doing it for ourselves. Either way: we were not eating *any* meat or dairy.

At the end of July, we flew to Phoenix, Arizona, for one night so I could see a specialist who'd inject my thyroid nodule with ethanol to try to dissolve it. It had been filling up with fluid over and over again for the past few years, and every time it filled up, not only was it painful, but you could see it sticking out of my neck when I swallowed. The endocrinologist who had been testing my thyroid nodule, and draining it every time it filled up with fluid, had finally recommended the Phoenix doctor, who was the only one in the country who did the ethanol-injection thing.

Because my mom was raw vegan, she brought two suitcases: one with her clothes, and one with organic lettuce, tomatoes, and almonds. It was food for her to eat, but *I* was so hungry at the airport that I ate all the tomatoes from her suitcase. When we got to the hotel, we finished off the rest of the lettuce and almonds. My mom had just had a biopsy of her lymph node on her neck to confirm that her cancer was Hodgkin's, so she was walking around the entire trip with a white bandage taped to her neck.

This was also a week that there was a lot of news coverage about a serial killer sniper who was active in Phoenix. So, we flew into a 105-degree city, where there was an active serial killer on the loose (actually *two*, they were caught about a week after our trip) who had been randomly shooting people from their car. Eight people had been killed and a lot more wounded. There was *no one* on the street. No one. Because nobody wanted to be sniped? Or maybe because it was 105 degrees and horrible out? Both were good reasons not to walk around.

After my quick and freaky procedure, where the doctor stuck a needle into my throat and injected it with alcohol, we had four hours before we needed to be back at the airport. We had already checked out of our hotel, we were starving, and we had checked the Happy Cow website before we left to find vegetarian restaurants in Phoenix. We'd printed out MapQuest directions from the doctor's office to the restaurant. On the map it didn't look that far, but in reality, it was a forty-minute, 105-degree walk, through deserted streets where there were two serial killers on the loose. We were pulling our suitcases behind us, both with white bandages on our necks, on a quest to get to one of the few vegetarian restaurants we could find in Phoenix.

This was 2006. There were no Google Maps apps on our Nokia phones. Halfway through the walk we wished we had gotten a cab at the doctor's office, but . . . how could we now? There was no Uber or Lyft. We didn't have the internet on our phones. We didn't know the number for the cab company. And we *could* have stopped on a corner to call the operator, I *guess*, but the longer we stood still, the more of a sniper target we would be. We had to keep rolling our suitcases and keep moving forward.

We survived, and a week after our trip to Phoenix, and just three weeks before I left for NYU, I became raw vegan too. I was convinced that wheatgrass juice and smoothies, and all the enzymes I'd be ingesting by abstaining from cooked food, were going to give me my blood back and heal me of my health problems, my anemia, my sadness, my exhaustion, my earthly woes, and my ugliness.

When they retested my iron right before going away to college, after being raw vegan for a few weeks, the levels were a lot better. No blood transfusion for me. I felt *vindicated*. I thought it was because of my new, raw vegan way of life. MY GOJI BERRIES HEALED ME!! I'd also been taking iron supplements, daily wheatgrass, and all the rest, but I decided it was my extreme dieting that was healing me. And I was an immediate convert. The cultiest of all my culty diets was beginning. Goodbye low-carb, hello *enzymes and "living foods." I am here to be HEALED*.

My mom ended up doing chemo that year while I was away at college. My dad put his foot down and didn't want to lose his wife to a fad diet. Thankfully, her body fought back against her diet during chemo and she really craved salmon and meat and potatoes, and she listened to her body and never looked back. She is in remission, and is *not* a raw vegan.

HOW TO JOIN THE CULT
OF RAW VEGANISM

I, however, was a raw vegan for my entire first year of college. And according to everything I read about the raw vegan diet, it was only a matter of *time* before I finally healed myself on a cellular level.

The big difference between raw veganism and my high school diets before was that raw veganism *wasn't* low-carb. This diet had a totally different premise. Raw fruit sugar was *perfectly* fine. *Healing*, even! But if your food wasn't 100 percent *raw* and uncooked, that's where you'd run into problems. Didn't you *know?!* *Cooked food!* That's why we are all diseased! If you heat food over 118 degrees, it ruins the *enzymes*. Raw food is *live* food. Cooking food makes the food "dead." And dead food equals a (sooner) dead you. But, if you eat 100 percent raw food, the way your body is "*meant to eat*," you will spontaneously and miraculously heal, which, as you know, had been my goal for a while now.

The first night in my dorm, I had to leave the dorm orientation mixer early because I developed a very high fever. I went up to my new room to writhe and hallucinate in my new bed all night, with my new roommate Emily sleeping five feet away from me. It was awful, but I remember thinking: *Yes! Maybe this is my final detox before I become healthy.* It wasn't. I still had all my problems the next day. I still felt *not-that-great.* My skin was still . . . really bad. So, I kept going because it was only a matter of time before I was healed.

So much of the premise of raw veganism (and lots of other purity-based diets) is about detox. The idea is that it often gets *worse* before it gets better. So, my skin getting even more horrible was, according to the message boards, just a detox. And once my body *detoxed,* I would be healed.

The reason this concept worked on me is that it was based on something that resonated with me. The body "detoxing" is a real thing (think of a hangover). Better out than in! And there *are* many situations with healing where things feel like they are getting worse before they get better. One example is that when you stop dieting, you usually feel MORE out of control around food before it starts to feel more balanced. People re-feeding after extreme restriction or an eating disorder also often have really uncomfortable physical symptoms that make it seem like things are getting way worse, but it's just the body adjusting. That's all very normal and documented. And *trusting* your body is a really important part of the process. Another example is with our emotions. A lot of people feel a lot *more* emotional when they start therapy and begin working through the big things they haven't dealt with, before things start to feel better and more even-keeled.

So, the concept of detox on the raw vegan diet seemed legit

enough to me. But . . . the idea of *purity* is a fallacy—there is no "pure state" to get to. The body is detoxing all the time, and yes, sometimes you might feel it as a headache, but there is no *static* state of purity. I would say that a good rule of thumb is: How *obsessed* are you with the idea of detox? How scared does it make you of the world around you? How miserable are you letting yourself feel and writing it all off as detox?

I was labeling all my discomfort and broken-out skin and diarrhea as *detox*. And I spent my energy trying to make sure my diet was 100 percent raw, which left me starving, so I would binge on whatever higher-calorie 100 percent raw food I could get my tired and hungry little hands on, which was usually boxes and boxes of dates. Or bags and bags of dehydrated snacks from health food stores. But according to all these raw food gurus and bloggers, I was *just around the corner* from health. Yes, my skin was genuinely horrible. Worse than ever. But health and beauty were *coming*. Once I detoxed everything, they were coming.

Not only was I in NYC with tons of weird, niche food options, but my freshman dorm just happened to be three blocks from one of the swankiest raw food restaurants *in the worllllld*. It was owned by a beautiful couple: Sarma and Matthew. I'd read their "cook"book over the summer, which was pretty much just pictures of them being hot and using a blender, next to a page with a smoothie recipe with blue algae in it, and their book was the one that convinced me to go *100 percent raw*. They were beautiful. They were in love. They were raw food chefs and their tagline was "get the glow." Going raw would make me *glow*—and I wanted to glow.

Sarma was selling a lifestyle. She was selling a *feeling* of absolute health, beauty, *purity*, and *NYC . . . swankiness*. You could hang out in a twinkly, dimly lit bar in the most expensive city in the world, drinking a raw vegan sake martini in a spaghetti strap dress, and still be following a perfect diet and getting healthier by the day. The glossy pictures in their book were *what I wanted*. I wanted to be healthy. I wanted to be skinny. I wanted to be beautiful. I wanted to sit in their swanky bar, be in love with a hot chef, and drink pure organic wine! *Or whatever! Just give it to me! I want this life!*

I read their book back in August, after our trip to Phoenix, and I saw they had a restaurant in NYC and looked up their restaurant address and realized that it was . . . three blocks from the dorm I was moving into in two weeks. *Are you kidding me?* I decided it was destiny. *Hello, God, is this you? Has every step along the way led me here? Have you been listening and answering my prayers all alonggggg? Is it your will that I should be eating only raw, living foods? Thy will be done. Please make me hotter. Thank you.* I remember sitting on my mom's bed while she lay there, exhausted from cancer, and telling her that *this* was destiny. I was being put on the *path* to heal my body and soul through raw veganism.

I only ever went to the actual Pure Food and Wine restaurant one time when my mom was visiting for my nineteenth birthday, because it was an extremely expensive restaurant for celebrities and idiots. But the spot I would frequent almost daily was Pure Juice and Takeaway, their little hole-in-the-wall around the corner. Yes, they called it a "takeaway bar," and let me just remind you that no one in America says "takeaway," they say takeout. So, that was their attempt to be extra swanky and European. *It's takeout, but it's very fancy.*

The "Takeaway" was tiny and smelled like parsley, but it was filled with expensive dehydrated treats and had three tiny little tables where you could eat. Gisele Bündchen would go in there to get green juice. Y'know, a normal college hangout! I would buy their salads and their dehydrated crackers and their coconut macaroons and their cashew-nut-cream-based ice cream. I spent so much money on food. So much of my *parents'* money, which was a privilege all by itself: the privilege to be absolutely ridiculous with my food. It's interesting how so many of these extreme diets are only available to people with money, anyway. You pay exorbitant prices for low-calorie food that you can't even digest, and it's like you never even ate anything at all. And while I am sure my dad was *not* happy about it at all, he was back in Pennsylvania taking care of my two younger siblings and my mother who was going through chemo. He had enough to deal with for the time being, without trying to teach me a well-needed lesson in budgeting and not spending all his money essentially being a diet cult member.

I was extremely insecure about my skin this entire year. I was also extremely insecure about *looking* so unhealthy, while also being the girl obsessed with health and health food. And I also remember the first day of class at my musical theater conservatory at NYU, our program head, an ex–Broadway dancer, told us that the city air was a lot more toxic than normal air. She said that our bodies might have to get used to the air pollution. And *this* put me over the edge. I was *already* freaked out by toxins, both in my body and outside my body. *I'm already detox-*

ing all my toxins and my face is a fucking mess and I'm literally at this program to look and sing pretty oh nooooo. How much more of detoxing toxins can I take!?

What I was experiencing at this point was orthorexia nervosa, which is an obsession with the purity and health of food, and fear of toxins. It was the strongest manifestation of my eating disorder. I'd had orthorexia for a while even though I had no clue, but this period was my most *extreme* orthorexia. It took over my entire mind. It's what made this diet the most culty of them all—my *extremism*. There were so many, many things in the world to be extremely afraid of, but thankfully *This. Diet. Was. Going. To. Cure. Me.*

That year, my friend Sandy *also* decided to go on a raw vegan diet. She told me, "Yeah, I read a book about raw veganism, but you can still eat goat cheese and stuff sometimes. So, I just do it when I can, but when I go home to visit my family I still eat the pasta my mom makes for dinner." What? I told her she was *not* really a raw vegan.

What was this *chill* mentality?! What was this "eh, I do it sometimes but it's no big thing" thing? That approach to dieting was so foreign to me and my extremist brain. I wouldn't have even known *how* to do that if I'd tried. No, I was the kind of person who went all in and lost her mind in the process. And the reason is desperation. I *desperately wanted to heal*.

After about three months on the regular raw vegan diet, which is already extremely restrictive, I decided that something was very wrong. I was not glowing. I was not healthy. My body was barely digesting food. My face was covered from top to bottom in acne. I was losing hair by the handful in the shower.

For a while, I thought this was a detox. My body was purging the old to make room for the new. But eventually it became clear: this was not working. I was *not healed*. Or, seemingly, even healing at all. So, I took to the message boards:

My skin is still bad three months in—is this still detox? Or is something else going on?

What I heard back from the other members of my cult was that I should try to cut out sugar. Meaning, on top of everything else I couldn't eat, I also couldn't eat fruit. Which left me eating primarily: salads, vegetables, nuts, seeds, avocado, coconut, coconut oil, and expensive dehydrated nut crackers. And I am honestly not sure how I did it, but I *did*, for about a month. And, at the end of a month, when my skin was just as bad as it was before, I took to the message boards again:

I have been 100 percent raw vegan for four months at this point, and this past month I cut out all sugar in an attempt to heal my skin. And my acne is STILL really, really bad. What's going on?!?!

And what I heard back *this* time was that maybe I actually should be going in the opposite direction and eating *only* fruit, and *no* fat.

Really? . . . OK! Here I go! I was going to join a tiny little *more* extremist sect. This was called: being a fruitarian. Or LFRV (low-fat raw vegan). Or 80/10/10, where 80 percent of your calories were carbs (fruit), and 10 percent was fat, and 10 percent was protein. Which meant I ate only salads with orange juice as dressing, and lots of fruit, and like a quarter of an avocado sometimes.

I ate low-fat raw vegan for three months. *Three months*. At Christmas I brought a papaya, and sat down at the table while everyone was eating Christmas dinner with a half of a papaya on a plate, took a spoon to it, and that's all I ate. My aunt asked me, ". . . so, how long are you going to do this for?" and I said, "Oh! This isn't temporary. I'm going to eat this way forever. . . . I feel great!" And I scooped another bite of papaya into my mouth.

I didn't feel great, but I had to convince myself I did. I had to convince myself that this wasn't all wasted obsession and money and time. I had to look for the positives! *I think my nails might be thicker than they were? Maybe?* I had to buy in, because it took a *lot* of energy to exist this way. It took a lot of energy to convince myself that this was worth it and good for me, and that it was going to end up rewarding me. I was . . . delusional.

You know who else may have been delusional? Our good friend Sarma. My beautiful, skinny, blond, tan idol and owner of Pure Food and Wine and Pure Juice and Takeaway. I looked her up a few years ago, while I was writing *The F*ck It Diet*. And lo! By that point she had already been dubbed the "Vegan Bernie Madoff." She broke up with Matthew and then got into a relationship with a manipulative, gambling, serial fraudster, and together they stole nearly one million dollars from restaurant investors and eventually they both went on the run before being caught. Her defense now is that she was manipulated and abused by the fraudster boyfriend. He made her feel crazy, using similar tactics that cult leaders use (see?). He told her that sending him money was part of a series of cosmic tests, and if she passed, she and her dog would become immortal. She believed him.

I was not that different. This is the kind of extreme thinking that had *me* surrendering so much of my life to the diet I was on. I trusted so deeply that it was the one true way, and that it would heal me if I just committed. I mean, was I not *also* believing that I was being put through a series of cosmic tests? And, if I hadn't had such horrible skin on the raw vegan diet, *who is to say* how long I would have continued it for? If I had been glowing the way she had been glowing, maybe I would have been able to buy in even harder, and even longer. Maybe I'd be writing a book on the glory of raw food right now. *Who knows.*

HOW TO MAKE A
VISION TIN

At a certain point I didn't know if I was going to the pure raw "takeaway" every day because my diet was so limited or because I had a crush on the guy who worked there, who was just *amazing* at working that cash register and that blender. What can I say, when your mother has cancer back in Pennsylvania, and you eat exclusively fruit all day, you distract yourself.

I assumed he must be as gung-ho about being 100 percent raw vegan as Sarma and I were, because he *worked* there. At a certain point, near the end of the school year, while I was buying some packages of raw dehydrated nut crackers, I told him that I had been completely 100 percent raw for eight months, but that I must not be doing it right because I wasn't feeling good, and my skin was still *horrible (don't look at meeeeee)*. He told me that he didn't necessarily think being 100 percent raw was a good idea.

What? I couldn't compute. It felt like . . . a priest was telling me that Jesus was just a guy with some good quotes. I stared at him with my jaw dropped, unable to process. But! It actually turned out to be a helpful perspective to get from someone "in the know," so, *thank you* hot smoothie priest, because not long after, I decided that raw veganism was ruining my life. Once again, I told myself that I needed to learn to eat "normally," though I didn't know exactly what that meant.

This is the point where I pivoted away from extreme diets and started applying a similar mentality to *other* forms of self-help. I was still informally dieting (not that I realized that back then), but I was still hoping that my *self-help* would cure my "food addiction." However, the focus shifted. Instead of realizing I had just been experiencing a very fruity eating disorder, I transferred the obsession from raw veganism to a new extreme ideology. Enter: *The Secret*.

The Secret was the new big thing—it was a *book* and a *documentary* (that I watched on my laptop in my dorm room) about the Law of Attraction and the power of positive thinking. The tagline is "*The Secret* has traveled through centuries . . . to reach you." *Fuck yes*. Wow. Wow wow. They really knew how to get through to my cult-susceptible mind. The secret of *The Secret* was that we all hold the ultimate power in our mindsssss and that we can attract anything we want through the power of quantum physics. Let me tell you, this information was . . . enthralling. It was *right* up my alley in the mystical, magical, prayer side, but it also gave me the hope that I was losing with diets. I needed hope. This gave me not *only* hope, but ultimate power over *everything in my life*.

The Secret teaches the Law of Attraction, so *The Secret* is like a branded version of what it's teaching. The Law of Attraction is baseball, and *The Secret* is MLB. Why the hell did I just use a sports reference? OK, *The Secret* is Kleenex, and the Law of Attraction is tissues. The two can be used interchangeably and are sort of the same thing, and sort of not. The Law of Attraction literally means that "like attracts like," so when you think positive thoughts, you attract positive things, and when you think negative thoughts, you attract negative things.

The concept of positive thinking was completely new to me. Up until this point, except for begging God for things, which wasn't necessarily *positive*, I didn't use any positive thinking. None. I thought life was a long, hard slog of trying to transform your ugliness into beauty through suffering. I was Little Miss Doom and Gloom. My method was to complain about how ugly I was, and then starve and obsess myself into the eventual transformation. I thought complaining was the safest mode. I thought positivity was . . . kind of . . . annoying.

Ha! Not anymore! I was a new woman. I was going to think and grow rich. I was going to think and grow healthy. I was going to say my mantras, think positive thoughts, and *turn this ship around*. After reading *The Secret*, it was clear to me that I was spending too much time and energy calling myself unhealthy. Dieting was . . . giving diets too much power. My *new* plan was to *manifest* my health and beauty with positive thoughts, instead of slaving over it by eating raw sprouts. I was going to use the Law of Attraction to manifest my dreams.

One of the first things I tried to manifest was to stop grinding my teeth at night, because during the second month at NYU, I woke up to a chunk of broken-off teeth *again*. I called my dentist back in Pennsylvania, and he recommended a peri-odontist in NYC who I made an emergency appointment with the following day. I skipped class and hid in my dorm for a day and a half, eating bananas from my closet with my back teeth, and the next day went to the appointment uptown, and this NYC dentist made new temporary teeth for me.

OK. I need to manifest calmness in my jaw! No, wait, I *want* to manifest calmness in my jaw. When you said your mantras, you weren't supposed to say anything desperate or anything in "the negative." Like you aren't supposed to say: *I* don't *grind my teeth.* Because that was still giving "energy" to the grinding. You were supposed to say a positive statement like: *My jaw is calm and unclenched.* So, I would fall asleep repeating: *My jaw is calm my jaw is calm* over and over. And because I was not awake while I was sleeping, I do not know if it worked. But I convinced myself it did. Then over the winter break of my freshman year I actually got my final porcelain teeth. (Porcelain teeth are a lot stronger than the temporary teeth. But I've *still* chipped them twice. Probably from teeth grinding that I didn't fix with my mantras.)

I also started noticing that I had lottts more dark body hair than other girls did. *Oh, no. It's happening.* I was either turning into a werewolf, OR this was the progression of PCOS. Or *both.* This was the excess hair growth they talked about, and my raw veganism had clearly *not fucking helped.* But it's OK! Because I was *now* going to reverse all my health problems and symptoms with positive thinking. I was going to *manifest* health. And I was going to reverse PCOS and reverse the process of turning into a werewolf *with my mind.*

One of the other things *The Secret* recommends doing is making *a vision board*. You're supposed to put things on the vision board that you want to attract, and then every day, you stare at your vision board and try to *feel what it would feel like to have those things*. But I had a roommate in a very tiny dorm room, and our closet was already full of my raw vegan bananas. I knew that adding a big vision board to the whole situation was officially one step too far. Plus, I knew my vision board would be weird. I needed my vision board to be full of models wearing Burberry. You know: that London-in-the-'60s look I had always been going for. Maybe like, also, a man and woman model duo in a Burberry ad holding hands, which would kill two birds with one stone: prettiness and love. Model love.

So, instead of having a standard corkboard vision board, I created a vision *tin*. I used a tin box that I got on my high school trip to France, from a cookie shop in Paris a few days before I burned a hole in my esophagus. I didn't buy any cookies in Paris, I just liked the tin. It was very *Amélie* to me (remember when she finds an old tin in her bathroom wall, and her adventure begins???). Tins were *cool*. Tins were dramatic. So, it was where my magic Google Image printouts would go.

I went on Google Images and searched for inspiring images, printed them out, cut them into little squares, and put them in my tin. And every day, when my roommate wasn't there, I would take the little printer paper images out, stare at them one by one, and try to feel *positive*.

In the tin I had: skinny models. A picture of smooth skin. A model couple (for love). A charming cottage with a wild and eclectic garden in the front, and an old-fashioned teal bike. A picture of a very charming mudroom. A picture of Amélie's bedroom. A picture of strawberries. A picture of an audience *from* a Broadway stage—like "I'm on stage." Also, I printed a picture of a Broadway dressing room, like "I'm in a dressing room." I can't remember the other things I had in my vision tin, but, so far, only the strawberries have come true.

I remember that staring at the little cutout pictures made me feel prickles of stress, because I didn't know if it was possible to have the things I'd printed out. But I wasn't allowed to think that, I had to think it *was* possible. If I thought it might *not* be, I was literally sabotaging the whole point. I *had to think positive thoughts.* I had to *feel positive emotions.* I kept trying, but I'd feel waves of anxiety and think, *Oh, no, oh, no. I'm manifesting more problems.*

At the end of the school year, once I'd finally decided that being a fruitarian was unsustainable, I decided I would start *slowly* eating whatever I wanted, but just *small* amounts. (That's still a diet, by the way.) I decided I'd say my health mantras and just "exercise a lot" over the summer, and come back to school free and beautiful, with manifested health. I'd be a newly positive Caroline, ready to take on my second year of musical theater conservatory classes and, eventually, my destiny: *Broadway.*

But as soon as I got home that summer, my brother double bounced me on my cousin's trampoline and sprained my ankle, maybe even broke it. I don't actually know, because I never went to the doctor, because I was *convinced* that I could heal my ankle with positive thoughts. According to *The Secret*, my reality was just an *illusion*, and my sprained ankle was something I had attracted through low vibrational thinking—so this was my chance to turn it all around, and to heal myself *with my mind*.

It didn't work, and I was bedridden for almost two months. And I lay there, eating pretty much only tortilla chips, and watching the entire *Sex and the City* show from start to finish for the first time on DVDs I rented from a *video store* (RIP). I spent my time trying to *visualize* myself as skinny as Carrie Bradshaw. *I want those skinny arms.* I was practicing my magical powers and trying to manifest that shit. But every time I tried, it just gave me more prickles of stress and overwhelm. And I was steadily gaining weight, which is what is *supposed* to happen when you've been raw vegan for a year and yo-yo dieting for the four years before that. I was also completely bedridden. But to me, it seemed like it was just a sign that I didn't have a good handle on the Law of Attraction.

At the end of this summer I was in a *semi*-professional musical (meaning: we got a stipend) of *Seussical the musical.* The musical was at the beach town where my family had a tiny little yellow beach house. I was playing one of the leads, Gertrude McFuzz, a bird, and I had gotten the role in the spring, *many* sizes thinner while I was still a raw vegan, and before I spent the entire summer lying in my bed eating chips and watching Carrie Bradshaw ruin her life by choosing BIG?! And *now* it was time for *Seussical*, and I *did not look like a bird*. Or, at least, I *felt very strongly that I didn't look like a bird*. I was playing a bird in love with an elephant, and the elephant was being played by this little skinny guy. So, this bird was definitely bigger than the elephant. And yes, I know that birds can be whatever size they want to be, especially in a wacko Dr. Seuss musical, but, at the time, it felt like just one more way to fail. My inability to control my weight was officially ruining *art*.

HOW TO THINK POSITIVE THOUGHTS, OR ELSE

I made a huge mistake by not going to the doctor or doing physical therapy, because by the time I got back to dance class in the fall of my sophomore year, important muscles had atrophied, and after just one dance class, my back seized and pinched my sciatic nerve, and I was out of commission for five more months. What kind of belief system makes you afraid to get help for your sprained ankle? A fucking weird one, that's what. In fact, lots of cults actually teach this: *Reality is merely an illusion, so sleep with your guru!* It's also a way to promise great things, and then blame the individual if those great things don't happen.

That year, my diet was the Law of Attraction. After the raw vegan diet, I *thought* I became anti-diet. But I did not. I just replaced diets with more magical thinking. I was still counting on getting all the things that dieting promised, but now I was going to get those things with mantras. It was all about mantras. *All* about mind over matter. *All* about thinking yourself healed and beautiful and happy and rich. I am going to heal, and become thin, by using the power of my mind. *If I focus on how unhealthy I am and how bad food is for me, that is going to make everything worse!* So, I *thought* I was eating "intuitively." But I was actually trying to use the Law of Attraction to help me to eat the smallest amount possible. I was still mostly vegetarian, and I tried to just eat *very* slowly and "not too much."

The Law of Attraction led me to believe that all my health problems were happening because of energetic and spiritual issues. According to a few different Law of Attraction writers and websites, PCOS and "womb problems" are caused by: repressed emotions *and/or* anger with your mother, *and/or* not embracing your creative flow, *and/or* not embracing your femininity. *Huh! Shit.* So, my *new* quest was to figure out *those* things, so I could heal from the inside out.

According to *The Secret* and the Law of Attraction, we create our reality. *Everything* we experience is within our control. It's *our fault*, good and bad. They lure you in with the promise that you can attract or create *anything you want*. It's *all* within your power. Not only *that*, but everything is merely an illusion. You literally think a thought, and it ripples out into the universe, and *comes back to you.* Our thoughts become reality. I mean, illusion. Our thoughts become the illusion that is our reality. We're in a video game of our own creation! Hey, just like psychopathy! Nothing is real. Sadness is unnecessary, because everything is in our control! If you don't like your reality/illusion, you can *change it*! Change your thoughts, change your life! *Aghhhhhh.*

In fact, right now, the bio for the official Twitter account of *The Secret* says: "You can be, do or have anything you want!" Well, I wanted to be, do, and have anything I wanted, but I kept getting *stressed* every time I had a less-than-ecstatic thought. In fact, I would get stress prickles and anxiety *because* of my thoughts. *Oh, no, I just thought about how I'm ugly. I can't think that! It's going to ripple out into the universe and become even more true.*

So, that was the first big problem with *The Secret*. I became stressed *just through its premise*, and then I got stressed about the stress, because according to the Law of Attraction, stress is *a problem* because it will just continue to "attract" more stress. And while I *agree* that stress can affect our bodies negatively, I don't think there was *anything* helpful about this odd, fear-mongering approach to micromanaging our thoughts.

The other problem with the Law of Attraction is that everything bad that happens to you is your fault, so you spend a lot of time blaming yourself for the bad stuff that's happening to you, and you spend a lot of time trying to figure out what the energetic cause of the bad stuff *is*. For me, this was a year when I had lots and *lots* of problems. I could barely walk because of my sciatic nerve pain, but let's not forget that that had actually happened in the first place *because* I thought I could think my ankle healed. So, I felt like I was double failing.

I was still determined to get to the root problem of my pain, and according to some Law of Attraction online charts, sciatic nerve pain is caused by:

BEING HYPOCRITICAL. FEAR OF
MONEY AND THE FUTURE.

Oh, dear. Where would I even start? *How* do I stop being afraid of money? How do I stop being afraid of the future?

Where am I being hypocritical? I don't know, but I'm going to FIGURE IT OUT. And I'm gonna heal *from the inside out and finally walk again and become very pretty.*

None of this *actually* encouraged me to be *inquisitive* about my thoughts, and where they were coming from. Instead, it made me afraid that my thoughts were happening at all. It made me think I was supposed to be stopping them before they happened. Shutting them down. Avoiding them. In some ways it encouraged me to adopt denial as a coping mechanism, and to start *avoiding* the parts of my life that needed attention and healing the most.

For instance, to me the question wasn't: *Why* do I hate my body so much? The question was: How can I never have a bad thought again so I can attract only good things and become the healthy and beautiful person the universe wants me to be, and *then* love my body. It didn't allow for any sort of real healing for me. This is probably something a therapist would have been really helpful for, to point out that what I was doing with this method was extremist and unhelpful, but therapy was not on my radar. I mean, *who needs therapy when you have the power to heal yourself with your mind?!*

What I eventually realized, way too late, is that the Law of Attraction encourages "toxic positivity." Being told that we have to be positive and happy *no matter what*, and to *only think positive thoughts, no matter what*, is terrible advice, because it leads to avoidance and denial. It also doesn't acknowledge the important fact that . . . in general, we *must* feel our pain in order to process it and heal from it. Struggle is a part of the human condition, and perfection is just an illusion. Toxic positivity makes you feel guilty for having struggles, or pain, or sadness, which doesn't allow you to heal.

I am *not* against positive thinking. At all. There is a difference between positivity and *toxic* positivity. *True*, genuine positivity can definitely breed more positivity, both in yourself and in the people around you. And negativity can breed negativity. And reframing the way you look at things, and getting into the habit of finding optimism and gratitude, can be life-changing. It can offer us resilience and calm when things get really hard, which they do. They always do. But it's *not* helpful if it's about "being happy at all costs." *Pretending* to be happy and positive is just a band-aid on top of all our pain, and unprocessed trauma, and emotions, and it *will backfire*. Avoiding your buried emotions and unprocessed trauma leads to a lot of terrible physical and mental symptoms, and it can exacerbate chronic health problems. In fact, it is probably *the last thing you want to do* if what you want is peace or healing.

Positivity isn't the problem. Believing in manifestation or the Law of Attraction isn't even the problem. The *problem* is extremism. The problem is denial and avoidance. The problem is that it's so easy to exploit people who are desperately seeking something to help them. *Those* people (and I was one of them) are desperate enough to trust anything that convinces them there's a cure-all, and they will put all their eggs in one culty basket.

There are plenty of people who would say that *The Secret* is all bullshit and all wishful thinking, but . . . I think there is *something* to *The Secret*. Our minds *do* have mysterious powers over our bodies. Just the placebo effect alone is an example of how our minds can affect our bodies, and the way we operate in the world. In fact, I believe a lot of great things happened to me, years later, once I eventually started trying to manifest better mental health and *genuine* happiness, instead of trying to manifest "being hot."

The world is mysterious. Our bodies are mysterious. And things happen all the time that can't fully be explained with our limited human means. And sometimes claiming it's because of a higher power, or the connectedness of the universe, or sub-atomic particles, makes way more sense than any other explanation, even though nothing really makes any sense at all. But we always have to look for that fuzzy line between something that helps and something that's promising to cure everything and takes advantage of our desperation.

I'm sure some people do use *The Secret* in a casual, helpful, nondogmatic way. Like my friend Sandy and her casual, pasta-inclusive raw veganism. But that was never my style. My style was going all in. *This is the thing that's going to save me.* I was looking for *anything* to be my cure-all. I was looking to buy into anything that promised to help me. I was applying an extremist mentality to *everything*. Diets. Health. Positive thinking. I was *also* twisting *Intuitive Eating* into something it wasn't meant to be.

My advice *these days* on any sort of "manifestation" is understanding that what we *actually* want from every goal we have is *feeling a certain way*. I first heard this concept from author and blogger Danielle LaPorte. We think that reaching our goal will make us feel calm, or loved, or excited, or safe, or inspired, or content, or *whatever*. And we are in fact wrong. Reaching those goals will *not* inherently make us feel the way we want to feel. In reality, we *usually* end up getting the goal and still feeling insecure and panicky and shitty, and assume that our *next* goal will essentially bring the feeling we thought the first one would bring. So, a better use of energy is identifying what we want to *feel* from our goals and understanding that *that is what we actually want*. We want to feel *safe* and rested and inspired and loved. And next, we can figure out tangible ways that we can help ourselves feel that way as soon as possible.

The other two important parts of "manifestation" are working on unlearning your negative learned *beliefs* and feeling your old, buried emotions and unprocessed trauma.

The Secret didn't address any of those things. *The Secret* was about getting anything you wanted. And it was also a very similarly dogmatic replacement for raw veganism. It promised *a lot*. And without healing the underlying dynamic, I was just going to keep searching for miracle cures over and over and over again.

Don't get me wrong—at the time, it inspired the *shit* out of me. And I needed to learn optimism, because my go-to was doom and gloom. Learning optimism and gratitude and focusing on the good things that are happening *was* really good for me. And I think, without the ulterior motive of *using* gratitude to try to trick the universe into giving me more good things, it would have been even better for me. True gratitude would have invited a *pause* and an opportunity to slow the fuck down. It would have encouraged me to stop seeking, just for a bit, and appreciate what I *did* have.

I still think taking moments to focus on gratitude and optimism is generally *good* advice. But this particular advice was coated with some strange and toxic outlooks. It made me afraid of my own brain.

HOW TO LOSE YOUR EGO FOR A MONTH

I had sciatic nerve pain for almost the whole year because I refused to go to the doctor for my ankle. I kept trying to figure out how to heal myself energetically, to heal my damn nerve pain, but I couldn't figure out *where* I was being hypocritical. I couldn't figure out *how* to stop being afraid of money. And I couldn't figure out how to stop being afraid of the future. I tried. I wrote out my mantras all the time. I wrote: *I trust the future. I trust that I will have money. I love my body.* The problem is, I didn't trust, and I didn't love, so, writing out those positive mantras just made me more stressed. My sciatica finally got better and I eventually got the use of my legs back (after *months* of going to a myofascial release massage practitioner and other physical therapy).

I *also* decided, after watching the romantic comedy *P.S. I Love You*, that I was going to Dublin for a summer semester abroad, and let *my own* life's romantic comedy begin. And I was able to choose between the Dublin acting program and the regular Irish studies program. I chose the regular, "*not* acting" program, because I was sick of my own kind.

At the beginning of that summer, a month before I left for Dublin, I read a new self-help book called *A New Earth* by Eckhart Tolle. The book is focused on teaching us to separate from our thoughts. Eckhart Tolle's teachings are a needed counterbalance for the more narcissistic bent of *The Secret*. He is very good at explaining a very simple and important truth: we are not our thoughts. And our thoughts make us miserable. Our thoughts happen, but they are not *us*, and they are not necessarily true. And we experience a *lot* of misery by identifying with our thoughts (what he calls our egos). So, being able to just *notice* that our thoughts are happening, and that they are *not* us, is a powerful habit to get into. And I've been casually aware of my thoughts in a different way ever since reading his book. So: *thank you*, Eckhart Tolle.

This was an important distinction from the Law of Attraction, which is focused on getting whatever you want by . . . controlling your thoughts. The Law of Attraction, or at least the way I was interpreting it, gives your thoughts *wayyyyyyyy* too much power. This was going a few steps further. It reminded me that even if you *do* become as rich and skinny and powerful as you want, if you still identify with your thoughts and can't tell that you are separate from them, you'll probably still be miserable.

Even though this seemed more noble, I still *always* had ulterior motives with my self-help. Yes, this was about *hopefully* becoming a better person, I *guess*. But for me, I was trying to become a better person *so I could become thin*, and healthy, and beautiful. I figured . . . if I healed on a spiritual level, then everything would work itself out, just like *The Secret* said. Once I heal my spiritual issues, not only will I be too spiritual to be upset about things, but I'll also be *hot*.

But, according to what I was reading, *before* I became hot, I had to become nice. And good. And separated from my ego. His use of the word "ego" is a little confusing, because we tend to think of someone "with a big ego" as being someone who . . . is really self-involved and thinks they are great (or *acts* like they think they're great). I was self-involved, sure, but I didn't think I was that great, at least not in the state I was in. And I wasn't particularly mean-spirited. But I was *definitely* identified with my thoughts. Eckhart Tolle's way of defining ego is: *the mind.* The more identified with your thoughts and *mind* you are, the more identified with your ego you are (according to him).

So, I implemented everything from the book. Because, beyond my ulterior motives of beauty, I *also* didn't want to be *identified with my ego!?* I don't want to suffer like that! And make other people suffer! I became *very committed* to fully separating from my ego. And it made me really, *really* nice. For a month. I was one of those people who wouldn't say a snarky word about anybody or anything. (For a month.) I purposely saw every situation as a blessing. I saw the potential good in all things. But what that also meant is that when I went to Ireland, and moved into a dorm at Trinity College with all the other new (American) people in the program, I didn't connect with anyone. I was literally too nice. I was too disconnected. I'd been trying to be egoless for a month, but now I was boring. I was a boring, nice little spirit, sitting there, smiling about the beauty of the world. You know those people who are so nice that you can't get anything interesting out of them? In that state I might have been a good spiritual teacher, but that's about it.

I was nice. I was peaceful. But I was boring. And bored. And I wasn't doing it for the right reasons anyway. A few weeks in, I was with my roommate, and I slipped up from being an egoless spirit and did an impression of one of the guys in our program while I was telling her a story about something that happened earlier. She laughed, and the floodgates opened. I felt . . . human again. I felt like myself. Turns out that my true nature is accidentally doing impressions of people.

There is a difference between being chronically mean-spirited or miserably attached to your thoughts and being a human who notices things and has human opinions about the things people do and say. If you're just a raging judgmental person doing nasty impressions of everyone, I'd say there's something deeper going on. *But* to be able to just comment and have opinions on . . . people . . . and things . . . I mean . . . what's more human than that?

Here is the thing I've realized: Eckhart Tolle's story and experience was *extreme*. He was extremely depressed and suicidal, and he had been his whole life. And one day as he lay in his bed, contemplating suicide, he had a complete and radical spiritual epiphany, so much so that he was unable to *talk or fully function* as a human for a few *years*. Unable *to talk*. He just sat on a park bench, moved to tears about how beautiful the world was. He basically was violently ripped from his identity and had to relearn who he was. And ever since, he has been explaining his epiphany to people in books and talks with Oprah and stuff.

Eckhart Tolle is *so* spiritual now that his brain isn't very human anymore. He is kind of like an alien now. An alien of peace. There are very important takeaways from his books that I will be forever grateful for, but I don't really want to be an alien. I want to be a human who learns a little from peaceful aliens, and occasionally does impressions of people while I'm telling a story, in a mostly non-mean-spirited way.

That summer studying in Dublin, I was twenty, which was underage to legally drink in the United States, but very legal in bars and clubs in Ireland. And once I stopped trying to be an alien of peace, I made friends, and we went out *a lot*. I drank a lot.

This was when I really went for it. And for the first *short* period of my life, I let myself . . . relax. And drink. And *not* sing. And not perform. And *not* have to protect my voice or get on stage and be stared at. Yes, I was always overthinking food and weight in the background—but nobody was looking at me. Nobody was going to notice if I gained or lost weight, because I wasn't doing a scene study from a Rodgers and Hammerstein musical in class. Instead, I was learning about how Ireland suffered at the hands of the Crown and the Catholic Church. There was no performance to prep for on Saturday. I just had to do my homework and write about the Magdalene Laundries and watch movies about the Irish War of Independence starring Cillian Murphy. I could just *eat* (well, half a piece of pie), drink until 4 a.m., go for a slow and unimpressive jog around St. Stephen's Green now that I had some blood and the use of my legs, and laugh with my new wholesome friends while we planned when to go to the Queen of Tarts the next day.

By the end of my summer, I was able to drink seven drinks and still be the one taking care of the other people who were too drunk. I drank a lot, but I still drank the *least* of everyone I knew. Almost half the nights out of the week I was in a club-ish bar. Compared to the anxious little control freak that I had been up until this point, this was . . . kind of . . . great? And healing? This was also my first solid co-ed experience that *wasn't* with theater people, so I *actually* dated *multiple* Irish boys. No rom-com, sadly. But it was fun and nice, if *only* for me to realize that there isn't actually anything wrong or closed off about me with dating at all. I was just usually surrounded by women and gay men.

But this summer of being normal did not come without consequence, because I ruined my voice in Dublin. I didn't *realize* I'd hurt my voice because I wasn't singing, and I was living in a dorm. Sometimes I'd try to sing in the shower, and I'd think: *Wow, this cold still hasn't gone away?* I thought it was laryngitis, but it was actually vocal nodes.

The other thing that my dedicated Irish Studies did for me was successfully make me not identify as Catholic anymore. All my new-age, woo-woo, Law of Attraction stuff already started loosening the grip, but *now* I was essentially taking classes where the teacher spent hours and hours teaching me why Catholicism is corrupt and abusive and misogynistic and empowers and protects sadistic and masochistic people and practices. I mean, as if the priest molestation scandal wasn't enough, there was *more*. And in Ireland, the Magdalene Laundries— places for "wayward" girls to be abused—were active until

1993, when *mass graves* were found, and they were finally shut down.

And I thought: *OK, well, thankfully I now have the Law of Attraction to replace this with, so I can still pray for whatever I want. I just have an excuse now not to go to mass when I'm home for Easter.*

HOW TO LOSE YOUR VOICE

Drinking and yelling in bars in Dublin had really long-lasting consequences. Years of consequences. *Lots* of existential crises. My one summer of fun and normalcy ruined my voice and affected my ability to do the thing I was going to school for and trying to make into a career. Before I'd realized the damage I'd done, I figured, *It's OK, I'll just rest up and get my normal voice back*. After a couple weeks back at school, it *almost* went back to normal. But over the holiday it seriously backslid. I don't know if it was the dry air, or the Christmas parties and alcohol, or both, but my voice got extremely raspy again, and I couldn't sing anymore.

This was also the holiday when the first *Twilight* movie came out, which is only notable because when I saw the movie, I went temporarily insane and let it hijack my brain for a good ten months—and now *Twilight* is forever inextricably linked with my memory of losing my voice.

My school holiday break ended early, because I had to go back to start rehearsals for my school program's production of *Bye Bye Birdie* a few days after Christmas. We'd already had the auditions and casting before the break, but now we had to go back early to start rehearsing. This wasn't a fun extracurricular where we had the luxury of doing a bad job, this was my musical theater conservatory at NYU putting on a musical. The director went on to direct on Broadway. And for the first time in my life, *I couldn't sing.* And it had been weeks of laryngitis at this point.

By the grace of the musical theater gods, for the first time in my entire life, I'd also been cast in this musical in a *nonsinging* role. I usually was cast as the sweetly singing princessy person (if they were brave enough to cast someone with very big boobs and an undefined jawline). But this time: I was cast as Gloria. She walks onstage for four minutes. She has a strong New York accent. She does a little tap dance. She thinks she is a talented tap dancer. She is not. *That's it.*

But on the first day of rehearsals, we had to go into the rehearsal room alone and sing for the music director so he could figure out how to place us in the group numbers, and I walked in and started trying to sing, but stopped and said, "I . . . don't know what's wrong with my voice. I lost it over the holiday break and it hasn't come back yet."

The director took me aside and said, "You should see an ENT for your voice, because you might have nodes. But, don't worry, your voice won't be ruined forever. My wife had this and she healed and is fine now." *What.*

I made an appointment with an ENT doctor for the day after my twenty-first birthday on January 5. But first, I had to have my twenty-first birthday party, where I exclusively provided bottles of chardonnay for the party. *Chardonnay, the nearly objectively grossest wine.* For some reason, in college I thought I liked chardonnay. I thought it was sophisticated. I live in New York. I'm in my *twenties*. I drink *dry wine*. I was convinced chardonnay was "dry" and "not sweet." Today, if someone gives me a wine that tastes *anything* like chardonnay, I will literally spit it back into the glass. (Try me. *Try me.*)

So, the day after I partied with some magnum bottles of Barefoot Chardonnay, I went to the ENT. He did a vocal scope, and voilà! Nodules on my vocal cords. They probably didn't need surgery, just a change in lifestyle.

I was told I had to: go on vocal rest for five days. (No speaking *at all*). No drinking *for a while*. And I needed to see a speech therapist. I think he also gave me a prescription for an acid reflux medicine "just in case I had it," but I was still in my Law of Attraction, *no pharmaceuticals for me especially if you're just guessing* phase, so I never filled the prescription.

But I took all his other advice. The *day after I turned twenty-one*, I had to stop drinking for a while. *Great.* Goodbye liquid drug for my undiagnosed anxiety. I had to carry around a huge pad of paper so I could communicate with people. I walked into my apartment after that ENT appointment and grabbed a pad of paper and wrote to my roommates: I HAVE VOCAL NODES. I HAVE TO REST MY VOICE FOR A WEEK. My roommate's boyfriend offered me a glass of (my own bottle of) red wine. I frowned and wrote in big letters on the pad: CHRIS, I CAN'T DRINK. I CAN'T DO ANYTHING. I figured that they may as well drink the bottle if I couldn't, so I went to go sit in my room and be sad and think about *Twilight*.

What was I *going to do??* I had to email my director and tell him, "Yes, I *do* have nodes, and now I have to be on vocal rest for a week. I'll be attending rehearsals, and just sitting there watching everyone sing."

I went into rehearsals carrying a few important messages written on different pages of my notebook so I could flip to them over and over again depending on what I needed people to know:

- I have nodes and I'm on vocal rest
- I can't talk for five more days
- Yes it SUCKS
- We should go see the *Twilight* movie this weekend, though. I know you've heard it's stupid, but it's actually *amazing*

At the time, to dull my misery, I became a small-time, in-person, silent *Twilight* influencer. I became a *Twilight* cult recruiter. What can I say, my life was sad. I couldn't talk. I couldn't drink my dry chardonnay. But I had *Twilight* to dull the pain. It was just another bout of extreme escapism to numb my misery.

After my vocal rest was over, I had to start seeing a German speech therapist named Fritzy. And I remember being amazed by her name, because that's what I used to say to my friends when I was starting to lose my voice and had to stop talking for the night: "Agh, *my voice is on the fritz!*" And *now* my speech therapist's name is Fritzy?!?!?!

In one of our sessions, Fritzy told me I had a "special" voice. *Huh?* "It's a really pretty, special voice. I hear a lot of voices of professional singers, and I work with a lot of opera singers, and yours is special." "Wow . . . thank you." This was the kind of vocal validation I had grown emotionally dependent on, but it was also the kind of praise that stressed me out. *My voice was special. See!?!?!? This was why I had to get my shit together. And why I have to make sure I can be skinny and beautiful and darling to match my pretty little voice!* But now I'd ruined my voice too.

For the next few years, I became absolutely obsessed with vocal health. I had to start speaking in a way that didn't put strain on my vocal cords. I had to *stop* speaking as soon as I noticed my voice was tired. Nodes are sort of like a callus on your vocal cords. And every time you use your voice, it re-irritates the callus, which just becomes a vicious cycle. Which is why you have to start off with vocal rest. Your vocal cords need a chance for the nodes to become less inflamed. I had to start speaking softly, but *not* whispering. Whispering is really hard on your voice. And I had to start speaking in a *higher* register, which is easier on the voice. So, I walked around speaking in a soft, sweet little voice. It was annoying. But I had to do what I had to do.

For me, alcohol or no alcohol, *any* socializing, going out, speaking a lot, or speaking loud *at all* would re-irritate my voice. Even just going to eat with a friend in a loud restaurant. And it would make it so that I couldn't sing normally for a few days. I'd quickly start to feel vocally tired and raspy, and I'd panic and stop speaking. My friends would say, "What?" And I'd softly say, "My voice. *My voice.*" Then I'd go home and lie in bed miserable that I ever tried to have fun.

In case you're wondering, vocal rest is . . . not rest. It makes everything harder. And any sort of socializing I tried to do just kept fucking with my voice, and therefore my career, and therefore my destiny. And so, I was never calm. I was never able to relax. But what else was new?

HOW TO HAVE A
NERVOUS BREAKDOWN

My voice had been off-and-on inflamed and raspy for months since the holidays, and now it was April of my junior year. Healing my voice was going to take time. And austerity. No socializing. No *anything*. And as stressful as it was, it also became an excuse to never go to an audition. *My voice isn't healed enough! Sorry!*

I hated auditioning. I looked for any excuse not to audition. I dreaded each and every one. It always put my body in a high-alert, shaky state that usually left me exhausted for the rest of the day—and sometimes for the rest of the week. *Never mind the fact* that I was going to school to study acting, and it was fully illogical that I was ignoring what it actually *meant* that I detested and avoided auditions. It would be like someone going to school to become a chemist but going into full-blown panic every time they had to step into a chemistry lab. *Uh . . . what do you think you are signing up for here? What do you think you're going to be doing every day of your life?* Most people I went to school with were eager for the opportunity to flex their little auditioning muscles. Not me.

I couldn't admit to myself that this was a huge issue, and that it wasn't just going to magically disappear at some point along the way. For so long, I thought that I could heal my nervousness by losing weight. I thought I wasn't confident acting in auditions because I *shouldn't be. I didn't look right—yet.* I assumed that losing weight and being prettier was going to cure my audition nerves. I knew I was talented, but I had a puffy face and a double chin, and I believed that I just didn't *deserve* to feel confident, especially auditioning for the pretty lead lady.

Some actors love auditions. Some actors just tolerate them. Some actors, I've since learned, do cocaine, which apparently helps you feel invincible. I never felt invincible. I *was*, however, calmer and more confident once I was already cast in a show and had the director's vote of confidence. But the subtext of showing up to an audition was: *HI, I think I'm good enough and pretty enough to be in your show!* And I didn't believe that. So, I shook. I literally *shook.* My hands shook. My body shook. My voice shook. And I did a bad, shitty, shaky job.

I hoped that once I was pretty and thin, I would finally arrive at a point where auditioning was fun, or at least tolerable. Then I'd magically revel in everything about the path I'd chosen. But the one thing I could not do was admit to myself that my aversion to auditioning was a bigger problem.

In the middle of my voice crisis, I went home for the weekend to be the Catholic confirmation sponsor for my sister, Margaret, and my cousin, Fiona. They were both twelve, and going through the final Catholic sacrament before, I guess . . . MARRIAGE? (Or THE NUNNERY!) During this sacrament, they became official members of the Catholic Church. At twelve. Margaret's confirmation was Saturday, and Fiona's was Sunday at a different church an hour away from my parents' house.

When they first asked me to be their sponsor a few weeks before, I told my mom: *UGH NOOOO. No. I already told you: I am not even Catholic anymore.* She told me that was ridiculous, and that it meant a lot to these little twelve-year-old girls that I be their older sister/cousin, Catholic sponsor.

I wanted to sit them down and say: *Don't become Catholic, children! Just—just fifteen years ago in Ireland you could have been sent to the Laundries to be abused and maybe even thrown in an unmarked grave just for being flirtatious! Don't do it! It's a broken system! God is everywhere and he isn't even a man with a beard! Run!*

But, I dunno, maybe I was too broken to stick to my guns. Or maybe I imagined that if the situation were reversed, and *I* asked my older cousin to be my sponsor and she said, "NO," that I'd be really crushed by that. So, I didn't do it for Catholicism, I did it for my sister's and my cousin's fragile little hearts.

I took my broken voice on the new BoltBus back to Philadelphia to be their sponsor. *Not* graciously, at all. I was in a pissy mood. I was miserable. And I didn't know why. I was miserable because of—*everything*. And I didn't even know how to begin to unravel what was at the root of it.

I hated every day. Every single day I felt guilty that I was avoiding auditions. Auditions caused me a lot of dread. But

I also felt dread *avoiding* the things that caused dread. Acting class? Easy peasy. Vocal performance class? I could do it in my sleep. But auditioning for a *real* acting job in front of real directors? Trying to find a dress that made my boobs and arms look smaller? NO no no no. I'd rather go for a run and then stop to hyperventilate on a bench in Washington Square Park after twenty-two minutes.

And now here I was, back home for the weekend, with a damaged, temperamental voice, and I needed to fit into two different outfits I could go to church in. And *great.* Everyone will see that I've gained weight *again. Isn't she studying acting? Wasn't she raw vegan two years ago? Is it responsible for her to not have her eating under control when she is going into such a weight-centric business?* Great. Great great great. I. Can't. Wait.

I was in a bad mood the whole weekend. I didn't want to be there. I didn't want to be Catholic. I didn't want to have to go to church *twice in one weekend.* I didn't want to have to wear church clothes. I didn't want to have to be their Catholic spiritual guide. And I didn't want to be home, where my mom was asking me all sorts of questions about *what I was doing.* And *how it was going.* And *how my voice was.* And *what I was going to do this summer.* And, despite my misery, I had to speak the whole weekend in a soft, high-registered voice, because it was raspy again. At this point, I didn't even know why my voice was acting up. It would just randomly *decide* to be raspy, for no reason, even if I was being a little nun and not socializing and not drinking and diligently doing my vocal stamina exercises that Fritzy gave me.

The morning of my cousin Fiona's confirmation, my mom

called me into the other room and said, "Caroline, I was thinking, what if you switched majors for your senior year and
majored in something else? You could stay in school a little
longer to finish the new major. And if you do it now, there's
still time."

Wait. What? WHAT?

"What do you mean? No. Mom—No no. This is just a bad
year. A bad semester. I . . ." *What was she doing?!?*

"But . . . you aren't auditioning for anything. And you aren't
doing anything this summer. You don't really seem to *want* to—"

"YES I DO!" Ugh. I had to speak softly so I didn't do more
damage. "I do. I do. I *just* damaged my voice! But it's going to
get better. Mom—I can't . . . talk right now. This is going to hurt
my voice." I wanted to scream.

"OK, we don't have to talk about this now. But, Caroline,
this career seems to really . . . stress you out. I don't think it's
making you happy. And I don't think you're willing to really do
what it takes. To *go* on all of the auditions."

(Softly): "MOM. I . . . No."

"You could go back to school for nursing! Then you'd always
have a good job, *and* you can always still act if you want, with
or without a degree." Why *nursing*? Nursing was always her
go-to backup career for me, never mind the fact that I never
showed *any* inkling of nursing being the right career for me.
I hated blood. Hated needles. I mean, at this point I basically
refused to take medicine and said I hated hospitals "because of
the fluorescent lighting."

Softly, I said, "Mom. I am going into my senior year. . . .

They are already asking us to choose which semester to do our agent showcase. . . . Also, really—*everyone* . . . says I'm so good. My teachers . . . *FRITZY!* Mom—"

"I know you're *talented*, Caroline. I just don't know that you actually want to—"

And I started sobbing. And, as you might guess, sobbing is really bad for your voice.

I cried—violently—for two hours straight. I couldn't stop. And I didn't even really know why. It's not even like my mom told me I *had* to switch majors, she just . . . brought up the possibility. I could have just said: *No, Mom, that's ridiculous. I do really love it, I just have to let my voice heal.*

But the problem was—I knew she was right. I knew something was wrong. I knew my audition avoidance was a really bad sign. But, at the time, I couldn't fully identify that. All I knew was that something snapped, and I was broken open. And I was sobbing. And the crying was just hurting my vocal cords more and more.

I hated everything. I hated this weekend. I hated whatever feeling I was feeling that I didn't understand. And I had to go upstairs to get dressed to go be a Catholic confirmation sponsor in a slightly stretchy gray pencil skirt from Express. Because that's all I brought home and all that fit.

I hated my life. And I didn't even fully know why.

I was sobbing while I put on my stupid tight clothes. I was sobbing while I did my makeup. I cried all my makeup off. I had to put it back on. My face was splotchy and red, and I'd stare in the mirror and just burst out crying again. Sometimes I'd stop crying for forty-five seconds, enough to pull on my *stupid* pantyhose and realize there was a run in them, and then I'd start sobbing again.

I was crying while I was doing my hair. *Doing my hair for WHAT? For CHURCH!?* It felt like a dam had broken. It felt like something that I had been trying to squash for my whole life was finally bursting out. *I am miserable. I don't know what to do about it, and I feel trapped.*

I kept *trying* to stop crying, because I couldn't put makeup on again for a fourth time, but I kept crying. I mean . . . it *had* to stop eventually, because in an hour I had to be standing by my cousin's side, while she joined a CULT. *Oh mY GoD.* At this rate, I was going to be sobbing while I stood next to her in church. I'd never cried for this long and not been able to stop.

My dad stopped by my room while I was blow-drying my hair with a stupid round brush, and he said ". . . Are you OK?" And I just looked at him and kept crying.

"I don't know what's—wrong with me." I was gasping. I also tried to say it in a sweet, high voice to protect my broken voice, but it was futile.

"OK . . . well, we are going to leave in twenty minutes . . ." I nodded. He walked away and I kept blow-drying my hair. And I kept crying.

In the next ten minutes, the crying stopped, temporarily. I went downstairs five minutes before we had to leave. My face was red and puffy. My mom usually tweaked my outfit before we left for any sort of event, but I think she could sense that now was . . . not the time.

Later that night once we were back home, she said, "Clearly

this is upsetting you, but I do think this is something that needs to be talked about. You don't *have to* be an actor, or you can major in something else so you have options, *and then still be an actor!*"

I started sobbing again. My voice was raspy. "Mom, *everything* I have ever done was for this." I was panicked and angry with myself. This was only happening because I had *failed*. I had failed at dieting. I had failed at getting my audition nerves under control. This was happening because I had *ruined* my voice in Ireland, stupidly trying to be normal and free for a summer.

I was standing there, crying again, and all I could think was: *I can't fail.* No. No. I can't give up. I can't be one of those people who *quits and can't make it. EVERYBODY EXPECTS ME TO BE ABLE TO FIGURE THIS OUT.*

"My God, Caroline, you would probably be happier just stopping all of this and being a waitress for the rest of your life. What is the point of—"

"But, my *LIFE*. What about my LIFE?"

"Caroline, *who cares about your life!?*"

This was honestly something I'd never considered before, that nobody cared what I did. That nobody, but me, cared about my life. That the people in high school who said, "Doons, you're going to be on Broadway" did not, in fact, care whether I actually succeeded or not. *Nobody cared.* And not in a cruel way—in a *freeing* way. I had a moment of relief, at the idea of dropping off the face of the planet and not caring what anyone thought.

"You're miserable! I wanted you to be able to do this if you enjoyed it. But who cares about any of this if you are going to cry for hours over it."

I know that this is a specific kind of privileged misery. There are lots of people who grew up *wishing* they had people to *care too much* about what they did. Neglect was not my childhood trauma. Mine was feeling like I was under a microscope.

But in *this* moment, my mom was giving me an out. And if I had actually been able to hear what she was saying to me, maybe I'd have gotten some relief, then and there. I could have started again and chosen a new path with less pressure and fewer eyes on me. But I couldn't hear her. Crying for two hours straight and absolutely hating my life was, apparently, not rock bottom for me. The tough pill I was refusing to swallow was that no matter how talented everybody told me I was, and no matter how much I actually loved performing, my nerves weren't built to go from audition to audition for the rest of my life. My nerves weren't built for the reality of being an actress.

But I wasn't ready to admit it. Because even though the idea of leaving it all behind *was* relieving, 15 percent of me knew I would miss it and be heartbroken. And 85 percent of me felt like giving up was too much of a failure. My mom was giving me an opportunity to change my trajectory, but it almost didn't make sense to me. *How* could I choose that? The opportunity to start over again didn't line up with the version of reality I'd known my whole life. Changing your trajectory was . . . weak. It was admitting failure. You couldn't be good at something and get into a top college program and go through 75 percent of your major and then . . . *not do it?!?* (Thanks, *culture that makes us believe that college is the be-all-end-all and will make or break your entire life.*) I was still so concerned about what giving up would *look like* from the outside. So, I didn't let myself.

No, no. I couldn't give up. I couldn't drop out. My solution? *I was going to get more plastic surgery instead.*

HOW TO GET
ANOTHER NEW FACE

After my breakdown, I convinced my mom, and myself, that things were going to change. I was going to snap out of it. I wasn't miserable. (I was.) I didn't hate auditioning. (I did.) I was just having a bad weekend! I *was* going to *start enjoying it more.* I was going to *appreciate* my talent, and not squander it away, worrying in my room. And I was going to start *auditioning.* (Well, I would once my voice healed . . .)

My summer plan was to stay in NYC, get a waitressing job, eat a diet of primarily Luna Bars, and heal my voice. And then in the fall, I was going to start the final semester of my conservatory and acting major. This last semester was when we were *coached* on how to market ourselves. We would have master classes with agents and directors and casting directors. And at the end of the semester, we would have our "industry showcase," all curated to show off our unique talent and "type," so you could show agents: *This is who I am. This is what I do. I am versatile! I am beautiful. Sign me to your agency. I will make you money.*

My conundrum became even more overt and crystalized:

my voice was sweet and pretty, so I had to be too. So . . . I also convinced my mom to convince my *dad* to pay for me to get liposuction under my chin over the summer. *Then* I'd look thinner even if I couldn't lose weight in my boobs or arms or stomach or legs permanently. At *least* my face would look thin. Then I'd look more like the stupid princesses I always had to audition for. Then I could become confident in auditions. Then I would be unstoppable. Then then then.

I got a job at the Chat 'N Chew, right next to Union Square, and I was *not* a good waitress. I mean, I tried. I *really* tried. But my problem was that I was extremely anxious, which inherently messed up my ability to just calm down and trust that *if I didn't get them their Coke refill in one minute, the world would not fall apart.* So, maybe I *was* a good waitress, because I cared *too* much about their Chat 'N Chew dining experience. I just wasn't good at taking care of my own nerves.

(Have I mentioned yet that I'd never been diagnosed with anxiety? Because at this point I'd never been to a therapist? And I thought I was going to heal my misery through dieting and positive thinking? Actually, I went to a therapist *one* time, two years before, who I found from a flyer at a health food store. And she recommended I see a spiritual healer she knew. And I did, while I had sciatica. And he could psychically tell that I had just had a Perrier a half hour before our session and told me to limit them because it does something to your blood. He did not heal me of my health problems OR my mental problems, but he did psychically know that I had just drunk carbonated water.)

This is the summer I also started essentially drinking an

infinite amount of coffee every day. I don't know how much, because I just poured myself coffee after coffee at work. It could have been four cups. It could have been twenty. It's hard to say, but it was definitely too much coffee, and not enough food.

Remember: stress and stress hormones are, arguably, a big root cause of PCOS and all my health issues, and *a lot of people's health issues*. I thought the answer was dieting and living off caffeine, when the answer was probably to lie down for two years straight.

Even though I felt horrible and was starving and anxious and overcaffeinated all the time, this is what I *thought* intuitive eating was. I thought: *OK, maybe this is a solid, casual weight-loss lifestyle*. Intuitive eating! Look! I can eat whatever I want! I just won't eat *much* at all, and I'll walk TO and FROM the restaurant, and *then* I'm on my feet for another six to eight hours, and I'll *also* go for runs every other day. Health! Beauty! Success! Confidence! Happiness! Money!

My feet had never hurt so much in my life. I remember asking the other waitresses *how do you get around your feet killing? Every night they throb while I'm trying to fall asleep.* And they didn't really know what I was talking about. So . . . OK, great. I am the only person whose feet hurt when they stood for ten hours. Let's just add it to the list of problems.

Then halfway through the summer, I took off from work for a week to go home to Pennsylvania to get double-chin liposuction. And there are many things I want to say about this:

1. Obviously this is messed up. I mean, I had a nervous breakdown over the absurd pressures of my chosen career path.

And, instead of the breakdown helping me to realize that acting maybe *wasn't* the right path for me, and was making me pick myself apart in ways that weren't mentally or physically healthy, I decided to see if more plastic surgery would help.

2. This procedure didn't even work. I looked exactly the same before and after, maybe worse, actually. It did *not* give me the tight jawline it was supposed to. This might be *partially* because I got it when I was at one of my *thinnest points*, thanks to being on my feet for ten hours a day on a diet that consisted primarily of Luna Bars. So, when they did the procedure, there wasn't much to liposuction anyway. And then when I inevitably gained some weight again over the course of the next year, the fat just came back. But I also probably needed an even more invasive procedure to get the results I wanted. *Ugh.*

3. At first, I couldn't tell whether it had worked or not, because I was supposed to be swollen for a bit. But it became clear pretty soon that it hadn't done anything, and I couldn't emotionally handle that fact. So, I ignored and repressed it. I repressed it so much that I usually forget that it even happened at all. I couldn't deal with the fact that not only had I been desperate enough to go through with it, but it literally didn't do *anything*.

4. It might have made it actually look *worse,* because all of a sudden, there was loose skin, and I didn't wear the post-op face compression thing for the full week, because I had to *go back to work at the fucking Chat 'N Chew.* I also never got the follow-up "skin tightening" procedure because I was

traumatized and horrified and couldn't force myself to go back.

5. This is clearly the way my face and jaw wants to be: undefined.

After a week, I went back to abusing my feet at my waitressing job again. And then, at the end of the summer, I sprained my ankle while I was running, probably because my feet and ankles were protesting. STOP IT, STOP IT, CAROLINE, YOU ARE TORTURING US. I had to take a few days off work to let my ankle heal. But *then* I realized that this was my out. I just pretended my ankle never got better. "Sorry, my ankle isn't healing. I guess I'm going to have to change careers."

I went into my final semester with the same undefined jaw. And, thanks to my unsustainable summer "lifestyle" of overexercising, overcaffeinating, and living on 50 percent Luna Bars, I slowly gained weight over the course of the fall semester, no matter what I did. As is the way.

As part of our curriculum, we did lots of mock auditions for casting directors who were paid to come to our school, give us a fake audition, then give us all notes afterward. This was . . . *slightly* helpful exposure therapy for my audition anxiety, but I still hated it.

The showcase was in mid-January, after our holiday break. And over my holiday break, I lost my mind and cut my bangs *extremely short*. I blame my mom. I'd had normal length bangs for the past year and a half in an effort to look like Zooey Deschanel, and my mom was constantly telling me that if I was *going* to have bangs, the *most* flattering bangs for my face were tiny little Audrey Hepburn bangs. She said it constantly: "Caroline, your bangs are so long, I think you should have short little Audrey Hepburn bangs."

So, after hearing that for over a year, in a fit of madness, three weeks before my industry showcase, I went upstairs and cut my good, normal, eyebrow-length bangs into tiny little bangs.

I went downstairs and said, "OK! Look mom, I—"

"OH, WHAT? Whoa! Caroline. Why did you do that?"

You've got to be kidding me. "Um, because for the last year you've been telling me that they'd look better if they were SHORT LITTLE AUDREY HEPBURN BANGS?!?!"

"No, I—didn't mean . . ."

"YES! YES, YOU DID?! ARE YOU SERIOUSLY TELLING ME THAT YOU DIDN'T??! . . . DO THEY LOOK BAD?"

"They. . . . They don't look bad, but . . . I . . . I never told you to actually CUT them."

I stormed off.

Great! Great. Now I was stuck. I mean I was really stuck. Unless I literally wore a wig, I was stuck like this for the showcase.

I *willed my bangs to grow* in time for the showcase, and they didn't. I mean, they did a *little*. Y'know . . . millimeters. But they were still extremely short and weird little bangs. It would have at least been *a deliberately quirky look* if the rest of my hair wasn't really, really long.

A few days before my showcase, my voice got raspy again, and panic set in. My voice was *still* temperamental, and I had to spend the few days before my showcase not speaking at all. Even during our dress rehearsal the day before, I didn't speak and I didn't sing. I spent the days before just sitting around, while all my classmates talked, silently thinking about how horrible everything was, and staring into the mirror at my stupid bangs.

The day of our showcase, I got my period for the first time in four years. Out of the blue. *Are you kidding me, period? You leave for four years? You leave me searching for ways to get you back—dieting and saying mantras and praying to heal myself on a cellular level. And I don't hear a WORD from you? NOT A WORD? And now you come back on a day that I do NOT HAVE THE PHYSICAL, EMOTIONAL, OR MENTAL CAPACITY TO DEAL WITH YOU. I DON'T!*

After my showcase, I had two really good agents who wanted to meet with me. *Phew. So, my bangs didn't disqualify me.* A lot of people in my class got no agent interest at all, so I was lucky. And my temperamental voice and undefined jawline hadn't sabotaged me *yet.* I met with the first agent who was interested in signing me at their midtown office, and I fully bombed the interview. Bombed. He asked me questions about my career dreams and the roles I wanted to play, and I could barely answer his questions.

"Do you see yourself as more of a Glinda or Elphaba?"

". . . Ummmm, a Nessa?"

Nessa is Elphaba's sister. I am probably RIGHT that I was a Nessa, but I was not confident, and it showed. He had been interested based on my performance in the showcase, but once he sat down with me and saw how unsure of myself I was, it was a hard no. He was smart. I was not a good bet.

The *other* agent who was interested in me first reached out to my teacher, Kate, and asked her what she thought of me as a performer. He used to be *her* agent, and they still had a good relationship, and she had been my acting teacher the year before. She told me that she told *him* that I was "one of the best actresses she knew."

See, it was little things like this that killed me. On one level, it was all I ever wanted to hear. This acting teacher who I loved and respected so much said I was *one of the best actors she knew*? This woman who had been on Broadway with Jennifer Garner the year before? Who taught and worked with *so* many actors over the years??? She told me about their exchange on purpose. Maybe she knew I needed a little boost.

But on another, deeper level, hearing things like this from Kate, and from Fritzy, was the reason that I couldn't admit that I was miserable. Because it was *those* little comments and compliments that made me feel like I could never quit. *How could I give up if I'm really that good? Wouldn't I be so angry with myself? Wasn't I letting people down? Wouldn't I be letting her down? Wasn't it worth pushing through and figuring it out?* I was stuck, *because* I was, apparently, good. So, I had to keep trying, even if I was miserable all the time. As if it was worth it.

HOW TO BECOME
A FRENCH WOMAN

The first summer after college I was *very thin* because of my new cult life-view: everyone should be *more French*. I'd tried to start this French life six years before. But now I was back. I read the book *French Women Don't Get Fat* and I converted. I converted to full Francophile. I wanted everything to be artisanal. I drank a lot of wine. I ate like a person afraid of eating a whole banana. I drank a lot of coffee, wore scarves, ate lots of yogurt—I thought I had everything figured out. It was like a sneaky eating disorder, but in *French*.

I was cast in *Sunday in the Park with George* in Philadelphia, which is a musical about the painter Georges Seurat and how he was bad at relationships and good at painting. A musical set in *Paris*. (*And* I was also *going* to France later in July. We were going to do a "bike tour" where we had to bike through Provence from town to town, and separately, a van would take our suitcases from hotel to hotel. And I want to tell you: *never again*. According to the tour website, this was supposed to be one of their "easy" bike tours. But we learned halfway up a mountain that what that meant was "easy for *mountain bikers*," which we were not.)

In August, I moved back to New York City, which is one of the most ridiculously expensive cities in the world. So, being as supportive as they always were, my parents were going to help me pay for my apartment for *two years* to make it easier to jump-start my career. "You're so close! You have an agent now! We are proud of you! We want to help you." The fact that my parents *could* help me financially, and that they *wanted* to help me financially, I do not take for granted. And . . . spoiler alert: I *still couldn't get my act together*. My day job was babysitting for a family I'd started working for the previous winter. Even though I had parent-subsidized rent, I had to be able to afford, y'know, everything else, like yogurt and little French sneakers.

The apartment was a studio on the Upper West Side of Manhattan in an old converted brownstone. It was adorable, but the walls were crumbling. There was no kitchen, just a tiny sink, a tiny stove, and three cabinets. So, my mom bought a small fridge and we put it in the closet (almost definitely not up to code). There *probably* was black mold in the bathroom that I only noticed a year in. The building was infested with cock-roaches. The windows were infested with carpenter bees. *But* the bee-infested windows were big bay windows that looked out onto a beautiful tree-lined street.

Two days before I moved into my new apartment, I got really sick *and* my great-aunt Bernie died, so I had to take the bus to Philadelphia to sing at her funeral, with a fever, swollen tonsils, and lumps sticking out of my throat.

I went to the doctor to see if I had strep. And I didn't, I

had . . . mono. According to the mono incubation period, this meant that I contracted mono while I was in . . . France? *France! Why do you keep forsaking me?! I didn't even make out with anyone there! All we did was bike over mountains and sleep.*

The day after the funeral, still very sick, I moved into my uptown sick ward. I was very ill and incapacitated, and then deeply exhausted for *months*. (Years? Seven years later, I finally had a doctor diagnose my chronic exhaustion as stemming from chronic *Epstein-Barr*, which is the mono virus. So, not only did this sideswipe me right as I was graduating from college, but it affected me *long* after that.)

A few weeks after being bedridden, I went back to work babysitting once I wasn't contagious anymore. I loved that family I babysat for, so at least there was that—a little light in my confusing, tired life. And the little three-year-old I babysat was *also* named Caroline. But other than babysitting, I lay in bed. I panicked. I cried. I complained to the sky. I worried I was manifesting more problems. I worried about my weight because I wasn't working out. I listened to dramatic songs and cried some more. I went for very slow walks in Central Park once I had a little bit of energy. I barely had energy to go get groceries, let alone become a Broadway star.

Though I was doing very little, I would never call this "rest." Even if I was physically stuck in bed and acutely ill for weeks, there was nothing peaceful or restful about it. Not only that, but mono causes extreme fatigue that can linger for a very long time.

During that first month of mono, after my throat didn't hurt as much, my new agents got me my first Broadway audition. It was for the understudy of Hope (the ingenue) in the Broadway production of *Anything Goes*. I got the email about the audition while I was lying in bed at 11 a.m. and replied, *Yes, I can make it!* And, strangely, I was so tired at the audition that I didn't even have the energy to be nervous. So, for one of the very *few times in my life*, I did a good job, and they called me back.

I had a callback for *Broadway*, and I had mono, and now I finally had time to process what was happening—and panic. *Am I actually thin enough to understudy Laura Osnes? She doesn't have any BOOBS? I won't even fit into her dresses.* (This might seem absurd, *but* when you understudy, you're expected to fit into their costume, and my boobs would not have.) I walked into the callback a shaky mess, like usual, and totally bombed.

I always thought I was going to eventually wake up and "snap out of" my anxiety, because I would *finally* be thin or beautiful or confident . . . and that just never happened. I was still me, living in an extremely expensive mold, cockroach, and bee infested apartment, now with another chronic illness. And every day I woke up and panicked.

Though France had forsaken me by giving me mono, I was still dedicated to becoming as French as I possibly could. This was the diet that I (again) thought was finally working for me. This was the *definition* of "it's *not* a diet, it's a lifestyle." *Being French* was my *lifestyle*. My French diet had been very wine-dependent. I used to say that I drank "often and lightly." It was my self-medication for my undiagnosed anxiety, and I never thought I had a problem, because compared to everyone else I knew, I didn't really drink that much. I *couldn't* physically drink as much as other people. It messed up my sleep and gave me horrible headaches. My body just couldn't handle it like other twenty-two-year-olds, and now that I had mono, my body *really* couldn't handle it.

When I got mono, I stayed away from wine for . . . a month or two. But my French lifestyle was calling to me, so I started drinking wine again, and probably way too soon. Wine and mono aren't a good mix. Poor liver.

The other thing I tried to do during this period was try to *feel all my emotions*, in an attempt to stop "eating emotionally." This was partially inspired by Geneen Roth, and partially inspired by those charts that told you the energetic causes of different health problems. PCOS was apparently caused by "repressed emotions." So, by feeling all my emotions, I was going to be killing two birds with one stone. Healing my health *and* healing my eating problems.

I assumed that because of my lifelong "food addiction" and inability to stick to a diet, I was an *emotional* eater. I also assumed that my binge eating *was* emotional eating. I mean, why else would I be doing it? If not because of my weakness and inability to get a handle on my unruly emotions? I read enough self-help books that made it clear that people ate because they couldn't handle their emotions, so I decided I was going to handle them.

My goal became to *feel everything* so I didn't use food to numb myself out. And while I do think that, in general, feeling what we have been afraid to feel is a *good thing*, and something I even talk about now in conjunction with The F*ck It Diet, I was still trying to use the premise as another diet strategy. This was *mindful* eating, I thought. You eat artisanal, snobby foods.

You pretend you are French. You drink wine. You drink coffee. You wear scarves. And you process your emotions *in order to eat less*. And while you are eating, you eat *extremely* slowly, leaving lots of food on your plate, because you are mindful, French, and becoming more beautiful by the day.

It wasn't healthy. It was obsessive. I didn't think it was obsessive because, relatively speaking, it was *less* obsessive than *other* diets I'd been on, because I didn't need to worry as much about avoiding certain foods. "All foods fit" on my mindful French diet. Kind of. I mean not like, sugary American food. (*Stupid Americans.*) But *most* foods fit. All snobby foods fit! So, I thought I had finally made intuitive eating work for me, *French*-style.

That following summer I followed my French lifestyle plan extremely closely on a family trip we took to the Canadian Rocky Mountains. I was skinny, but I was eating so little that I eventually burst into tears at a restaurant while we waited for our dinner because my blood sugar had gotten so low. And the rest of my family stared at each other: *Well! There she goes again! Crying because she is hungry and obsessed with food!*

Oh, no no no. This is not *good!* I'm not supposed to be crying over food anymore. I'm supposed to be smoking a cigarette and humming "La Vie en Rose" while all my silly American family members complain about how they ate too much. Then I can sit there sipping my after-dinner espresso while they kicked themselves for eating the entire piece of cake they ordered for dessert. Also, I was supposed to be *feeling my emotions in private* so I didn't burst into hungry tears at the dinner table in this expensive Canadian restaurant!

Help. Why isn't anything working?

HOW TO BECOME
RICH ON THE INTERNET

I was supposed to be doing a lot of things that I was *not* doing. I was supposed to be going to auditions on my own, *not* just when my agents got me a Broadway audition. I was supposed to be *out there* schmoozing and making connections and impressing casting directors at open calls. I was supposed to be spending my days looking up auditions, self-submitting, asking my agent to submit me for specific things, doing research on what *kinds of shows were coming to Broadway*, reading plays, getting cheap rush tickets to shows so I could see everything that was currently running, finding new monologues, finding new songs, going to voice lessons now that college voice lessons were over, going to *classes* with directors and casting directors to let them know who I was. I was also supposed to be working on *original content* for the internet! A web series maybe? And hiring an accompanist and recording songs to put on my website! There was a list a mile long, and I wasn't doing any of it.

I was lying in bed, exhausted, going to the bodega a block over and buying kombucha, and writing absurdist essays on my blog that no one read about how anxious I was. The only thing I started doing when I finally had energy, besides babysit, was start going to improv classes at the Upright Citizens Brigade, which was a nice and terrifying change of pace. But if what I wanted was to be in musical theater, I was *supposed* to be waking up every morning at the crack of dawn, warming up my voice, washing and blow-drying my hair, putting on a dress that made me look in the *essence* of the show style I was auditioning for, and lugging a big bag that carried my huge binder of sheet music plus a few different kinds of dance shoes *just in case* they wanted me to stay and tap dance on the subway down to midtown. And once I got there, I had to wait in line to see if they had room to see people who weren't in the actors' union.

I did the whole "open call" thing a few times: getting up at the crack of dawn and waiting around all day only to be told at 3 p.m. that they wouldn't have time to see me. Or to be given an audition slot at 3:40 p.m. and do a terrible job, of course. *No. This is a waste of time and energy!* I had agents now! I was going to wait for my agents to get me Broadway auditions. And every few months, they *would* get me a Broadway audition, and then, because I rarely auditioned, I'd absolutely bomb out of sheer terror.

At some point, another actor friend told me that "all musical theater actors use beta-blockers for auditions." Apparently, it's just standard. I don't know that that's actually true, but there is probably some truth to it. So, *what did I do*? I borrowed a few of my brother's beta-blockers, and I've since been prescribed some for performance anxiety. Beta-blockers block adrenaline, so it helps with the shakiness of your hands and voice in auditions.

I tried them a few times in auditions, and honestly . . . they helped a little, but they didn't really help *that* much. So, I decided to move on to another drug: a shot of vodka, out of a water bottle, twenty minutes before my audition slot. I only did this *one time*, thank God, and it was for my audition for the national tour of *Mary Poppins* the musical, for Mary Poppins. *Hello, I'm here to audition for drunk Mary Poppins.* This method didn't work very well either. I probably needed more shots. But thankfully, I didn't try it again.

Then, just six months into my new life with mono, my agent quit the business. He was leaving the entertainment industry to go back to *medical school.* This felt especially ominous to me. *No! God! Mom! I don't want to be a nurse!!* His partner took over and formed her own management company that I was half-assedly a part of for the next three years. They would *sometimes* send me out for Broadway auditions, and, of course, I would bomb them.

I didn't have a meteoric rise to Broadway like I had hoped for, being "one of the best actresses" my teacher Kate had known. And *she* had just left the business to get married and move back down to Georgia the year after I graduated. So, I had to figure out some other jobs in the meantime, because I wanted to become independently wealthy, so when my parents informed me I was being cut off from their rent support because I had squandered my time being ill and anxious, I was going to be able to say, "Thank you so much for your support, parents, I've been saving money and I can afford a studio apartment all on my own. I've become independently wealthy from all of my babysitting and my side gig as a birthday clown."

I'd been babysitting for little Caroline three days a week. And I had another family, with twin boys who I babysat the other two days. And I would fill in other times with other families, like mornings and nighttime. Which, if you're doing the math, left me with no free time to audition, which was, maybe, my subconscious goal.

I *also* joined a small company that employed actresses to be birthday princesses *and* birthday clowns. Not like a John Wayne Gacy clown with a painted face, but think more "quirky woman from *The Big Comfy Couch*" doing silly games with largely uninterested two-year-olds for two hours, while their parents looked on in their expensive sweaters and thought, *Wow, this is cringey?* I learned how to make balloon animals in a twenty-minute seminar with other new princess/clown hires and was booked for my first two-year-old's birthday party.

I did a few two-year-olds' birthday parties as a clown and realized that the pay was not worth the effort and existential pain of being a clown, so I went back to the more monotonous, but way easier, babysitting. Babysitting wasn't helping me become independently wealthy like I needed—but I had another plan. I became really passionate about sitting at my computer and learning how people became rich on the internet.

It's a *miracle* that I and my cult-susceptible brain didn't get sucked into any multilevel marketing scams, selling wares on the internet and being told you're becoming a "business owner," not knowing it's a rigged game that very few people can make money with, until you've already lost thousands of dollars and spammed hundreds of acquaintances on Facebook.

MLMs are like business cults. They're pyramid schemes that

get around the *technicality* of being a pyramid scheme, because they sell products. But it's still a scam, because what everyone is encouraged to do is to recruit new salespeople, *not* actually sell leggings or weight-loss shakes. You don't make enough money selling the actual products, the way you make money is by recruiting people below you and selling them the business starter kit. And then every sale THEY make, you make a cut of. But *they* are also encouraged to recruit people under *them*. (And that's the pyramid part.) Most of these businesses have monthly minimums of inventory you have to buy, so a lot of people end up thinking they are starting a side business but end up with a garage full of skin-care products they haven't been able to sell.

I really lucked out by avoiding this particular cult trap. If there had been a French Diet MLM, I probably *would* have joined. But thank God I didn't start selling French weight-loss yogurt shakes on Facebook. Either way, "sales" is NOT my thing. The *only* other thing I wanted to do besides act was write. During my senior year of college, I created a BlogSpot called *Non-Quick Oatmeal*. I started it with the intention to make a *food blog*, an ode to "slow food." It was all part of my new French lifestyle. But the blog started as just an extremely boring documentation of all the restaurants I went to with my friends. See, *this* is what happens when you have disordered eating and are always slightly underfed. You think that food is your passion. I truly thought I wanted to be a food writer because I thought about food *constantly*. In reality, I was just chronically hungry and micromanaging what I allowed myself to eat, and I misinterpreted that fixation as being a "foodie."

However, *thankfully*, I very quickly realized that I was a horrible food blogger. So, *Non-Quick Oatmeal* eventually turned into a blog filled with absurd essays. Nobody *read* the blog besides a handful of friends, but I loved writing it. It was one of my few true joys. I would spend *hours* writing. All I wanted to do was stay home from auditions and write essays.

At some point, I stumbled across Marie Forleo, an online business coach who teaches people how to turn their "multipassionate" business into an online empire. *Wait! I'm multipassionate, right!? I like acting, singing, writing weird essays, and I am passionate about farm-to-table artisanal foods, being French, and self-help books!*

According to Marie, the way to grow a following online was to *offer something*. Produce free content that teaches or offers something people *want*, put your blog on a self-hosted site so you own everything (as opposed to social media, where you own nothing), and then offer a freebie where people can "opt-into" your *email list* so you can contact them when you want to communicate or market something. And how to figure out what you should be offering? Focus on what you're *passionate about*.

But . . . what *was* I passionate about? Well, at this point in my life, I was passionate about being a French woman. And I was passionate about expensive, artisanal, "slow" foods. I was passionate about pretending my disordered eating was my passion. I wasn't sure how to turn that into a business, so I gave up trying to become rich on the internet and I just kept writing.

HOW TO EAT LIKE
A CAVEWOMAN

I wasn't feeling great. I'd been tired and unmotivated and pan-icky for a whole year. I was hungry all the time. I still rarely, if ever, got my period. I was sleeping really poorly, unable to fall asleep unless I ate something to take away some of my gnawing hunger. And I still had all these annoying skin and hair symptoms of PCOS that let me know my hormones were still out of whack.

Through the internet, I came across the Paleo diet. I wasn't looking for it. It found me. It sought me out and whispered: *Maybe you should cut out major food groups.* At this point I *thought* that I was eating intuitively. I thought I'd figured out the way to not diet but still be skinny, the French way. I *knew* what had happened to me when I'd gone on more formal diets: I got dogmatic about the rules. I panicked over little details. And eventually, I'd binged. *A lot.* But the Paleo diet was promising some pretty exciting things: healing from the inside out. Healing *hormones.* Reversing PCOS symptoms. *And* becoming low-carb was also supposed to cure my food addiction and bingeing. It would "reset" me, apparently, and I would become *so healthy* that I wouldn't crave food. It would heal my body and my *cravings*. And, as you know, spontaneous and miraculous healing had been my goal for a very long time.

But if I were to try the Paleo diet, one of the things that I'd have to do, besides give up grains, was give up dairy. Oh, *nooooo*. I'd given up dairy *many* times before, with the longest stint the raw vegan diet. But that diet was very different from this diet, so maybe I needed to give up dairy *while* giving up carbs, and *that* would heal me?

And . . . *what if this is it? What if this is the way to heal, and I'm being blinded by my French lifestyle and my love of cheese? What if I need to give up dairy, and that's what will really heal my hormones?*

So, my plan was to *casually* cut out grains and dairy for a short, *casual* month, to see if it helped. I knew that extremism would be my downfall, which is why I was trying to do this one *differently*. But, as you might guess, by the third day of my new "casual" Paleo experiment, I was sucked into a Paleo vortex. As *soon* as I'd cut out all grains, most carbs, and dairy, my stomach became seriously bloated. It was like the opposite of what you'd expect. I immediately felt *horrible*. So, like I'd done before, I assumed this was just the detox, and to speed up the detox, I became even stricter.

Pretty soon, not only was I religiously Paleo, but I was on the GAPS diet, where you only ate bone broth soup for a few weeks, in order to heal your gut, in order to heal your *brain*, in order to heal your whole being: body, mind, spirit. Y'know: *my jam!* This whole experiment was like *considering* attending a church service one Sunday, and then converting to the Amish religion three weeks later. I went from zero to sixty.

I started the Paleo diet in early fall, and by October I was only eating bone broth soups and the occasional cup of applesauce. I spent hours a day on a Paleo message board reading people's takes on whether coffee was Paleo or not (I still drank coffee, I'm not a complete masochist, just no cream). Over the holidays I was eating primarily meat and vegetables, specifically lamb and kimchee, but I was *also* nonstop baking Paleo pumpkin pie with almond flour for the crust and almond flour Paleo gingersnaps. I started binge-baking and binge-eating Paleo Christmas desserts. Almost every day, I'd make a new pie, and almost every day, I'd promise myself I would only eat a tiny piece, and almost every night I'd eat the whole thing at 11:30 p.m.

I was also following lots of Paleo bloggers and reading Paleo books and listening to Paleo podcasts. *Nonstop Paleo podcasts!* Paleo podcasts while I walked to the grocery store to buy more meat! Paleo podcasts while I cooked my Paleo dinner! And one day in December, I heard someone on the Paleo podcast say: *Well, when you eat super low-carb, you actually become* more *insulin resistant, but that's OK, because you aren't eating carbs anyway.* I stopped in my tracks. *WHAT?!* I rewound it and listened to it again. *Oh, my God.*

The whole *premise* of my lifelong fear of carbs and sugar and fucking *rice* was because I apparently had insulin resistance, which was apparently causing my PCOS, and a low-carb diet was supposed to *heal me.* Now you're telling me it's making it *worse?* I was shaken, but I wasn't ready to *leave my new religion yet*. Not after alllll of those bone broths I'd made. But I tucked away the new knowledge that dieting was *maybe* making everything worse to bring out another time.

Then on one woman's blog, she wrote that eating a Paleo diet, and becoming super low-carb, had messed up her hormones and made her temporarily *infertile*. And because of her sharing that experience, other women were reporting back the same thing in her comments. She wanted to have another baby, and so in order to "turn back on" her hormones, she was purposely eating *more* food, way more carbs, purposely gaining back the weight she had lost while eating low-carb, and focusing on sleeping as much as possible to get her body out of the sort of crisis state it went into when it was low-carb that stopped her ovulating.

WHAT—and I cannot stress this enough—*THE FUCK*?!! I've been over here, for *ten years*, petrified to eat potatoes, because I was trying to heal *my hormones*. And you're telling me . . . this . . . is maybe . . . making it *worse*? Gaining weight and eating food is going to help her *heal*?! I'd always been under the impression that losing weight was *always* the goal for health, and that gaining weight was always a *bad* sign. Now someone was doing the opposite?

How was I supposed to process this information? I was hearing whispers in the online Paleo community that Paleo had *not* helped them the way it promised to. For every person who was claiming that Paleo had healed them, just as many were saying the opposite. It had messed up their hormones. It had exhausted them. It had made their health . . . worse.

And what had it done for me? How was *I* doing? Not well.

I was bingeing every day on homemade Paleo gingersnaps and bars of 90 percent dark chocolate. And my bone broth–focused, no-dairy, no-grain lifestyle hadn't spontaneously healed *anything*. I still had acne. I still didn't have my period. And I lay in bed starving every night, unable to fall asleep.

So . . . what now?

HOW TO STOP DIETING

My twenty-fourth birthday is the day it all came crashing down. I'd been Paleo for about four months, which doesn't seem like *that* long, but I had already allowed it to chew me up and spit me out. I'd already gone through a low-carb Paleo phase, and a bone broth and applesauce *only* phase, and I still wasn't healed. And though I'd *just* learned some things about weight and health and hormones that I couldn't shake, I also hadn't felt ready to give it all up yet—though the seed had been planted.

My high school best friend Annie had moved to New York and was living with three other actresses in Queens, but she was hanging out with me and staying overnight on my couch the night before my birthday. I had my apartment stocked with meat and vegetable snack options, as usual, but I'd decided to make myself Paleo birthday treats. I found a Paleo cupcake recipe off the internet, and I cut out 85 percent of the sugar from the recipe and didn't make the coconut oil icing. So, what I'd really made were twelve extremely dry, crumbly, unsweetened almond flour "muffins."

"Annie, do you want a cupcake??"

"Uh . . . no, thanks!"

Annie didn't want any, so by the end of the day before my birthday, I'd eaten all twelve of them. They didn't taste good. At all. But I just kept putting them in my mouth thinking, "Wow, this is gross," and then putting another one in my mouth once I'd swallowed the one before. We went out the night *before* my birthday to celebrate with some other friends, some of her friends from school, and some of mine. I was "allowed" to drink lightly on the Paleo diet . . . I just couldn't drink *grain-based alcohol.*

The next morning on my actual birthday, after barely sleeping, I decided I was going to carpe this diem, continue my Paleo baking spree, and make myself Paleo squash pancakes. I pureed some butternut squash, mixed it with eggs and a dash of salt, and because it was a special day and I was losing my grip, I added a teeeeensy little bit of maple syrup.

"Annie, do you want any squash pancakes?"

"Eh . . . no, thanks!"

I made enough squash pancakes to feed six people, slathered them all in butter and another *teeny* drop of maple syrup, and ate all of them in five minutes. Just like the "cupcakes," these "pancakes" were also disgusting, but I couldn't stop. Once I'd eaten all of them, I felt nauseous and stuffed and sick and panicky. And this birthday binge, while not outwardly different from any of the previous one thousand binges in my life, was the final straw that broke me. It was the experience I needed to crystalize the whispers I'd been hearing on my ex-Paleo blogs:

This is a flawed concept. Dieting is a flawed concept. You can't heal binges by cutting out food. Weight loss isn't going to heal you, and it might make things worse.

Annie left late morning and went home to her actress compound in Queens. I kept it together until she left, but once she was gone, I walked into my bathroom, still extremely stuffed and uncomfortable, and miserable, and looked in the mirror. I thought: *This is it. This is the end of the road. This stupid diet hasn't healed me of anything. And if I don't stop this miserable cycle, this is never going to end.*

It was clear. Dieting was *definitely* messing with my eating. There was a direct correlation between my dieting and my bingeing. The more I tried to follow a specific plan, the more out of control I became.

But in *this* moment, I finally realized a way more important part of this entire miserable puzzle: weight. *Weight.* The reason this keeps happening is my obsession with weight. *That* is the core issue. *That* is the reason my intuitive eating was never actually intuitive. *That* is the reason I have been trying to eat the smallest amount of food and carbs for a decade. *That* is the reason I keep putting myself on new diets. *That* is the reason I eat so little that I start crying when my Canadian dinner doesn't come out fast enough. It's *weight.* I've been trying to become skinny or stay skinny or become *skinnier* for ten years, and it's done nothing but make me exhausted, hungry, obsessed with food, and hate myself. And it has almost certainly made me more unhealthy.

I'd told myself for years that all I really cared about was *health*, but I also thought that health and weight were the same thing. I thought it was a *fact* that carbs were my enemy, as well as the enemy of our nation's health. But now I was being faced with an alternate reality: that eating low-carb could mess up your health. And I had been *constantly* trying to eat the bare minimum to get by and to keep my weight as low as I could, and now I understood that it wasn't necessarily good for me. And once I learned that, how could I ignore it?

During all those years when I'd tried to heal my eating, I thought the *goal* was to lose weight. All the while I thought I was eating intuitively I was still always obsessed with eating the smallest amount possible. I was *still* trying to make sure that I ate in a way that kept me as small as possible. And *that* was the problem.

It was like all of a sudden I saw the cult I'd been in for a decade for what it was. So, I made a decision to leave. I was going to stop dieting. I was going to *actually* deal with my fear of foods, and carbs, and my fear of gaining weight. I was going to eat. I was *going* to gain weight. And . . . I was going to quit acting— at least temporarily, if not forever. I knew that I couldn't keep up my decision to let myself gain weight if I kept going on auditions for Cinderellas.

I had no idea what I was doing. I didn't know what it would be like. I just knew I was miserable, and I'd hit my breaking point. I didn't *know* how much of my gut instinct about weight and dieting was actually right yet. It *felt* right, but I didn't know *anything* except the few things I'd read online about carbs and weight gain helping people to heal their hormones. I'd figure out the rest as I went.

HOW TO RULE OUT
EVERY MIRACLE CURE

I often wonder if there had been a way to avoid all the diets and all the dogmatic self-help plans I tried. Could I have? I think . . . no. At least not in our current environment, where everywhere you look there is some new diet promising to cure everything. Not in this world where the mainstream conversation is pro-diet. I would have needed a culture that didn't raise up wellness diets as the answer to everything. And a world that didn't terrify me into desperately seeking beauty and thinness.

I wanted solutions. And when it became clear that my doctors *weren't* offering me spontaneous and miraculous healing, I decided to turn somewhere else. I wanted a magical cure. And it *just so happens* that extreme diets and extreme spiritual self-help ideologies were the things that were promising me what I wanted: *miraculous healing*. They promised that they had *the answer*.

Both my extreme wellness diets *and* my woo-woo self-help books all said: Don't trust most of the narrative of Western medicine. Big Pharma doesn't have the solution. They're keeping *the real secret from you. They're keeping you sick. The secret is* fill in the blank: low-carb, no-carb, no cooked food, only fruit, changing your thoughts and manifesting everything you want from an *aligned vibrational state.* This fit with my experience and worldview. I'd already tried the drugs, so after that I needed to try . . . everything else.

Don't get me wrong, Big Pharma is corrupt as *shit.* There's copious evidence to support that drugs that should *not* be on the market get passed because of money and lobbying. I do not blindly trust pharmaceutical companies *or* the organizations that are often bought off by them. But there's also nuance. Just because lots of pharmaceuticals and Western medicine may primarily offer band-aids with side effects instead of cures, that doesn't mean that the wellness industry doesn't *also* prey on us. They *definitely* prey on people's desperation and exhaustion with unregulated supplements and the newest miracle cure that promises to fix every problem in your life. *Tired? No need to rest! Just take this supplement and cut out all of your favorite foods!*

The other thing that's worth saying is that for some people, pharmaceutical "band-aids" instead of cures are better than nothing. That is our personal prerogative. For me? It wasn't good enough. I wanted to get to the *root of it.* If possible. But it's not always possible.

What I've realized is that I *had* to try all the things I tried. I had to try *everything.* Because what if it really *was* carbs or gluten or dairy keeping me sick? Wouldn't I have wanted to know? Wouldn't that be so *simple?* I have a friend who had really bad digestive issues, and she was eventually diagnosed celiac and *now* that she knows what to avoid, she is fine. I wanted a simple answer like that. So, I *had* to try everything, just in case. I had to see. And now that I've tried fucking *everything*, I know first-hand that most things that claim to be miracle cures are just . . . not. *Now* I know. Now I can look at a new miracle cure and see it for what it (most likely) is: fearmongering. I believe some of those miracle cures *do* work for some people, sure. Or maybe it's the placebo effect, which is one hell of a drug. What I do know is that they do *not* work for everyone.

So, what's the actual solution? Is there a way to create a world where people *don't* go on a wild rabbit chase looking for miracle cures, and only stop once they have spent years or decades and end up exactly where they started, only now they're poorer and older and their nerves are shot? And maybe they've spent decades hating themselves instead of befriending their bodies? Is there a way to avoid this?

Probably not. This *is the way*. Humans just . . . *do this*. We are so adorable and stupid! We do this desperate seeking, and we have done this through the ages, like making pilgrimages to distant spiritual healers and wearing corsets and makeup made of mercury and lead. We want to be *beautiful*. We want to be *loved*. We want to be *healed*. And sometimes we *are* healed. And sometimes we are not. But I guess what we *really* need is informed consent. We need people talking about the dark side of drugs, diets, and so-called miracle cures. We deserve to hear the dark side of desperately seeking beauty.

All I know is that if we had a less diet-happy culture, and a less beauty-obsessed culture, and more people talking about their horrible experiences, I may have avoided at least some of my madness.

HOW TO HEAL YOUR CREATIVE SOUL

The problem with my plan to quit acting was that, in a rare turn of events, I actually had an acting job lined up for the spring in Philadelphia. And it was a role I was excited about. I could have pulled out of the play, but I really didn't want to. I loved acting, I just hated auditioning. *So,* I decided I'd do this *one last show,* and then figure out how to get a real job.

Those three months between my birthday epiphany and the start of this show in early April were not easy and they were *not* fun. The bulk of my misery came from not knowing what I was doing with my life. I'd spent the past ten years with a laser focus on dieting and planning on being a skinny actress, and now I'd lost both of those things. I lost my focus. I lost my community. I lost my goal.

I knew it was for the best, but I felt unmotivated, directionless, and depressed. And because of this show in the spring, I *couldn't* jump into looking for a new job, I had to wait. So, while I started eating more food and beginning this healing process, I kept babysitting. And I spent a lot of time sitting around my apartment watching *Friday Night Lights* and worrying about my life. When you start watching *Friday Night Lights* in the morning *before* babysitting, you know you're not doing well. *What was I going to do? What* career *was I supposed to go into if I wasn't acting?*

This would have been a great time to go to therapy, but that wasn't even a thought that crossed my mind. There are a couple reasons for that. One . . . I had no context for what I was about to do. I actually did not realize that it was, essentially, mild eating disorder recovery. Because I didn't realize yet that what I'd been experiencing for the past ten years was somewhere on the spectrum between disordered eating and an eating disorder. All I knew was that what I'd been doing was dysfunctional, and it wasn't working. I think I also had a vague sense that nobody in the entire world would understand what I was trying to do with food. I didn't know there were weight-neutral, intuitive eating practitioners out there. I didn't know there were fat-positive eating disorder therapists out there. I had no clue. As far as I knew at this point, intuitive eating was just another diet where you rated your hunger and tried to not overeat, because that's how I'd interpreted it years before. And I now needed to let myself eat a lot. *Fuck the hunger scale.* That was the only thing I was sure of.

But even if therapy *had* crossed my mind, I wouldn't have felt like I could afford it. Yes, I lived in a semi-expensive apartment that my parents were primarily paying for, but I had very little extra money myself. The money I *did* have had to be spent on lots of food, new clothes from Old Navy in the next few sizes up, and new, bigger bras. And good, big bras are expensive.

However, I *did* finally go to a new doctor, who ran blood tests and said my glucose was totally normal, but that I just had extremely low estrogen and progesterone for my age. It's hard to know if that was because of *years* of dieting, or PCOS, or both—he certainly didn't know, or have any real understanding of how disordered eating can mess you up. But either way, he prescribed me bioidentical hormones to try to jump-start my cycle again. A few months of bio-identical hormones, plus *actually* consistently eating calories and carbs, *did* jump-start my cycle. It's not always a regular cycle, but I've had it ever since.

So, *how did I start healing my relationship to food?* First, I just want to say that *The F*ck It Diet* is essentially a self-help book *all about this*, and it is specifically geared toward people who want to heal their relationship to food. But, for the purposes of this book, *this* is what I did (besides babysit and watch *Friday Night Lights* and panic):

First, I added in foods I was afraid of. I'd been eating Paleo (no dairy, no grains, low-carb . . .), so I *immediately* started eating dairy and more carbs. In the beginning, I was still very afraid of gluten thanks to my fun Paleo dogma, though I did have the *general* plan to eventually stop being afraid of gluten. But for now, I was just going to take it one scary thing at a time. I was going to wayyy up my calories and carbs and just try to feed myself an abundant, gluten-free diet. I would eventually add gluten, when I mustered the emotional strength.

Second, I expected to gain weight. And I prepared for it. I didn't know how much, but I guessed it would be based on the way I'd yo-yod up and down in the past. I assumed I'd go up to the weight where my body had always tried to go every time I went off a diet and on a food bender. Again, I knew I might be wrong. I knew I couldn't fully prepare, or fully know, or control it, but that was my *general* sense. And I prepared by buying roomier pants and inexpensive flowy shirts. I bought bigger underwear, and immediately thought why the HELL have I been forcing myself to wear size small underwear? And I planned on ordering myself lots of big bras that had a little bit of wiggle room to get bigger.

These were the steps I took to show myself: look, I really mean this. I'm *really* doing this. I'm really going to allow this process to happen, and these clothes I'm buying are proof.

Third, I'd realized that being afraid of weight gain was keeping me stuck and miserable. And I knew that the only way to heal was to radically accept wherever my body ended up. The days of obsessing over my weight were over. I'd devoted my life to weight control, and at this point, since it basically fucked me over, I was *done*. I looked up books on accepting your weight, and I found two books on radical fat acceptance. Now, as "fat" as I always *thought I was* for a musical theater ingenue, I was never fat. And never ever *ever* had I looked at dieting and our cultural fear of fatness from a fat perspective. Most of us assume that all fat people have eaten themselves fat, and that's just . . . incorrect and extremely stigmatizing.

Reading up on fat acceptance gave me the research and the perspective shift that changed everything. Not only did dieting backfire, but our cultural fear of fatness was toxic, and at the root of all of it. And if you want to go even deeper into learning about this, it actually stems from white supremacist beginnings and an association of fatness with blackness. A really good book on the history of fatphobia and white supremacy is *Fearing the Black Body* by Sabrina Strings.

To this day I am 100 percent sure that the most healing thing you can do, if you are trying to heal your relationship to food, is to learn about radical fat acceptance and let it wash over you like a healing light. Becoming fat was always the looming threat of PCOS. (Which isn't even true, but when you have insulin resistance it *can* often lead to weight gain.) I had always tried to become skinny at all costs, especially because of acting, but now I knew that I had to just surrender. If my biggest fear was becoming fat, wouldn't I feel more peaceful if I could accept it? The books that shifted things for me back in 2012 were: *Lessons from the Fat-o-sphere* by Kate Harding and Marianne Kirby and *Fat!So?* by Marilyn Wann. *Those* books led me to the book *Health at Every Size* by Lindo Bacon, a weight science researcher, which really blew my mind. It gave me *evidence-based reasons* that the best thing I could do for my overall health was to *stop* trying to lose weight and *stop* trying to micromanage my food, and to learn to take care of myself and engage in health habits *wherever* my body wanted to be. *This* was the science that corroborated my hunch that stopping the diet madness was the best thing I could be doing for my mental *and* physical health.

I had been pretty depressed for the past few months, waiting in limbo, eating lots of potatoes, gaining weight, reading about fat acceptance and Health at Every Size, and getting scared about what the hell I was actually going to do with my life. And then . . . in the middle of all of this, I had to uproot my life for two months to be in this *play* in Philadelphia, and I was going to be living at home with my parents in the suburbs and driving their car down to the city every day for rehearsals. I was almost burning more money on gas and parking than I was making each week, and it made me *extremely anxious*. I appreciated my parents for being so generous, and so excited about this play, but going back to live at home, especially when I was so disenchanted with acting, and making no money for this to even be a sustainable life choice, made me very antsy.

When I moved home, I sat down with my mom and I told her I was going to quit acting. I told her I wasn't happy, and that I had to heal my relationship to food and weight.

"I have a problem. I have . . . well, basically, an eating disorder, or disordered eating, or something. And I need time and space to heal. So, I'm going to eat everything, and let myself gain as much weight as I need to, and just see what happens."

She understood that I wasn't happy. She could see it. And she knew I was stressed over food, but she had never understood *how* stressed. She didn't understand how much space it took up in my mind. She was always going on her own diets, like most women who grew up in our culture. You know, she *loved* her health food. But for her, it never affected her quality of life like it did for me. It was an ever-present interest for her, but it ended up being debilitating for me. So, in some ways, she didn't understand how I could have had an eating disorder if I'd never *looked* like I did. It never *seemed* like my problem was restricting, it seemed like my problem was bingeing. She didn't understand why I had to go "so extreme in the opposite direction" from diets to eating everything. And she also was worried about my health, because everything we *both* had read about PCOS for ten years made us both afraid of food and of my apparent food addiction. *But* she listened to me. She didn't understand it, but she supported whatever I felt I needed to do to heal and to be happy. And that was what I needed.

While I was living at home and doing this play, there was another woman in the play who was *clearly* insecure and miserable, and she took it out on me. She had been the beautiful, successful leading lady for years, and now she was in her forties, and she was annoyed. She had just become vegan. She talked about her weight all the time. She talked about looks all the time. She talked about aging all the time. And she was . . . kind of an asshole. She would say passive aggressive things to me constantly about being young and having a role with more laugh lines than her, which she also wasn't happy about.

Little did the snarky woman know that *I too* was miserable and insecure. But because I'd had my epiphany a few months before, and deciding to quit this cruel business, I saw this all with fresh eyes. *Hah. She thinks I'm confident. And! She gets nothing but roles, and praise, and awards, and she is* still *miserable and insecure and taking it out on me. . . . I never, ever, ever want to be like this. This stupid career makes you miserable, and it is not worth it.* If I hadn't already decided to quit, she might have put me over the edge. I could see clearly that this was the mentality that could *easily* happen to me if I stayed in this business. And I never ever want that to happen.

Her misery helped me stick to my guns, actually. Because I *loved* this role I was playing. It was a dream. It was right up my alley, comedy-wise. And it made me really sad to be quitting when I was finally getting to do a role that was fun. And the other amazing thing is that this role could have been done in any body and at any weight. So, having this woman be such a passive aggressive monster to me helped me remember why I was quitting: *I don't want to scrutinize myself the way she does. I want to be free.*

I didn't feel free, though. I felt lost. I was isolated. I lived at home with my parents. And I was sad. And I was trying to eat a lot. One day a few weeks into my time living with my parents and driving into the city for the play, my mom said, "Oh, SHOOT, Caroline, I forgot to buy the book for this book club I'm in, and we are having the first meeting tomorrow. Can you download it on your Kindle and I'll pay you back? And can I borrow the Kindle until I get a copy of the book? I have to read the first part tonight."

"Sure."

The book was *The Artist's Way*. I downloaded the book and showed her how to use the Kindle, and went to go eat something and lie down and think about my life.

The next day, as I lay on the floor complaining about my abuse at the hands of a jaded middle-aged actress, my mom said, "OK, Caroline . . . I read the first part of this book, and I've realized why I joined this book club in the first place. . . . This book is for *you*. You need to read this book. It's about creativity, and being an artist, and perfectionism . . . I think you'll love it. Please please please read it. Or just read the beginning."

"Ugh, Mommmmmmm. I'm so tired. And I don't even want to be an artist right now."

"I know I know, but I still think you'll like it. I think it'll be helpful."

The last time she made me read a book, I became a raw

vegan. So, I put it off for a couple days, but eventually I opened my Kindle and read the first part. *Oh. I see.* It was about creativity *as* spirituality. It was about creativity as a healing force. It wasn't just for "artists," which was important because I didn't know if I even considered myself an artist. I didn't know if I *wanted* to be an artist anymore. The book was about how perfectionism, and self-judgment, and cruelty to ourselves dull our creativity and joy. It's about how creativity can be healing all by itself, even without an outcome. It's about how important joy and fun inherently are, all by themselves.

Joy and . . . *fun*? What!?

OK. Maybe I do need this. (Also remember, "blocked creative flow" was apparently one of the *energetic* reasons for "womb problems." That was probably in the back of my head too . . . some things are hard to shake.)

I started reading and doing all the writing exercises and following all the prompts. I would get up early before rehearsal and write my three Morning Pages where I would dump all my brain noise out onto these pages. The morning writing exercise didn't feel profound or life-changing, but I still had a sense that on some level, no matter what the outcome was, this book was going to help me. And the thing that made this one different from other books and self-help "methods" was that it constantly nudged you back to *yourself* in a way that felt very doable. And it was allowed to be small. Subtle joys were enough. Writing three sentences was enough. All of that was *enough*.

Weirdly, I'd never thought of myself as particularly creative. I used to actually say: "I'm not very creative. I'm just good at taking direction from a director!" Or "I'm just a good mimic!"

I never saw singing or acting as creative. I thought it was just a skill. I was wrong, though.

Humans are creative all the time. I mean . . . even decorating your home is creative. Cooking and baking are creative, *even* when you take out all the sugar from the recipe. And I felt that somehow, this shift would heal a part of me. I didn't know what, and I didn't know how, and I didn't know why, but I was going to do what the book said to do, and see what happened.

HOW TO BE A RECEPTIONIST WHO'S AFRAID OF THE PHONE

One of the things that was so profound for me about *The Artist's Way* was that it was addressing perfectionism and joy in a way that ended up running parallel to what I had just started addressing with my eating and body image. And so, very accidentally, it gave me some tools for introspection, and it also gave me a new life view that was a lot more forgiving and joyful and sustainable than the way I'd been living before. I had been pretty depressed before that play, but *now* I was back in New York City, and I had *The Artist's Way* to use as my anchor as I tried to figure out how to learn to be happy. Or, *happier* at least.

I now ate gluten. Which meant that I *officially* ate everything. I ate a lot of toast and cheese. I ate a lot of granola and cream. I ate a *lot* at night, because that's always when I was the hungriest. And I ate a lot of Häagen-Dazs ice cream. I also ate a *lot* of nachos. I was very committed, but I found it terrifying for a while.

Every morning when I wrote my Morning Pages, I would notice that I was going over the things I was eating and my fears about what the foods would do to me, and my health, and my life. And I started to be able to really *see* the way my brain worked, day after day, worry after worry. I was able to begin to unpack *why* I was so afraid about eating imperfect things, like "bad industrial seed oils." And one day I wrote "Oh, my God. *Fuck it*. I need to just go on the FUCK IT diet. I am *so so sick of my own brain*. Fuck it and fuck all the noise."

As soon as I wrote "The Fuck It Diet," something clicked for me. *That's a great name*. I immediately opened up my computer and typed in "thefuckitdiet.com" to see if it already existed. *It had to. This had to already be a thing*. It didn't exist, and before anything else I immediately bought the domain name. Then I googled some more, totally unconvinced that it wasn't already a thing. It had to be a big movement. A book. *Anything*. It *had* to already exist. The sentiment spoke to me. It spoke to the *exasperation* I felt after caring too much about my diet for way too long. It *had* to be a sentiment that other people felt too? There were little blogs called *Fuck the Diets* and *Fuck Diets*, but for the phrase *I* wanted, "the fuck *it* diet," I found a joke by Margaret Cho from 2003, which *was* along the lines of my sentiment. But that was it? Just her joke? There was no big movement . . . no website, no book, no nothing. I couldn't believe it. *OK, I'm going to start writing about what I'm learning and what I'm doing. And this will be my healing creative project.*

This was just a little creative writing side project. I didn't think it was going to turn into anything. I wasn't even going to use my full name. I was *just* going to use this domain as a blog to write about what I was learning. Maybe it would help me process what I was learning? Maybe it would keep me accountable? Maybe a few people would read it, and the creativity alone would be helpful? I didn't have any reason to believe that anyone would read it, because I'd had blogs before that only about seven to ten people read. But, thanks to *The Artist's Way*, I was learning that creativity *just for the sake of it* is healing in its own right. It didn't *need* to go anywhere. Nobody *needed* to read it. It was allowed to just *be*.

I was learning things about weight and health and food that were blowing my mind, and I *needed to write about them*. Like: *Did you know that being fat is not inherently unhealthy?! Did you know that we have weight set ranges where our body will force us to stay? Did you know that going low-carb can fuck you up??? Did you know that we actually need way more food than most diets say? Did you know that undereating can mess up your metabolism? Did you know that too much cardio can mess up your metabolism? Did you know that dieting directly leads to bingeing? Did you know that bingeing is just repairing your body from years of dieting or yo-yo dieting? Did you FUCKING KNOW ANY OF THIS, WORLD?!*

Also . . . it was almost the end of the two years when my parents were helping me pay for my apartment. So, I told my parents that I was cutting *myself* off before they even had a chance to officially do it in three months. The two-year pressure cooker had backfired. I *BURST* like a potato that hadn't been pierced. I burst from the pressure and the heat, and now I was quitting my life and writing stream of consciousness Morning Pages every morning to try to save my raggedy little soul. And

I had just bought a website domain called The Fuck It Diet. *AGHHHHHH.*

Annie and I decided that we should become roommates and move to Washington Heights, where we could actually afford rent. I was moving to Washington Heights so I could afford my own life. And I was going to find a real job. When I told the families I babysat for that I was switching life paths, I luckily had Annie for them to take over once I was gone.

I bumped into someone I'd known from high school, and she told me that she just started working at an arts PR firm and they were looking for a new administrative assistant. Entry level. *Check.* Arts! PR?! I don't know what that is, but *check*. It sounded cool, like a job someone has in a movie. *ARTS PR. Yes. Perfect.* Even more than just a temporary 9 to 5, I was looking for a *career* change. I was looking for *another life option.* And, no, I didn't know if arts PR would be right for me, but in *theory* it sounded like I could enjoy it. Maybe I'd be doing a cool NYC street walk and talk using the words "account" and "client" and "pitch."

I got the job, and two days after Annie and I moved to Washington Heights, I started as an administrative assistant (receptionist) in an arts PR firm, in an office building right off Lincoln Center.

After two weeks, once I'd gotten the swing of things, I remember thinking, *Wow, I can't believe how boring this is. This is life, huh?* The only thing that got me through was pretending I was Pam from *The Office*. There was no Jim. Only Angelas and Merediths and Phyllises and a sort of Toby situation. I made *just* enough money to make ends meet with my rent in

Washington Heights, and pretty soon I was shocked by how mundane everything was. When all you do is wake up, feed yourself (and now you eat toast and butter), commute, get exhausted by work, live for your one-hour lunch period that *you take full advantage of because you don't actually care about rising in the PR ranks after all*, spend your days sitting at a desk and praying the phone doesn't ring, but all it *does* is ring, and it's your job to pick it up! *Dunder Mifflin this is—wait, sorry,* then take an extremely crowded subway home, be exhausted, eat dinner, watch an episode of Bravo, and wonder how anyone ever has time or energy to do anything, go to bed early so you can wake up again, and do it all over again . . . you wonder . . . *and for what?* You're doing it so you can pay for a life where all you do is answer the phone. *Man.* This is what everyone is doing, isn't it? No wonder we're all tired and miserable.

As monotonous as it was, I *needed* it. I really needed monotony. I needed a buffer. I needed to just . . . do something mundane and do *just OK* at it and survive and know that this was an acceptable life choice.

I think this extreme pressure to *be something* and *do something impressive* is more prevalent now than it used to be for previous generations. It's the dark side of individualism, that belief that we can and should do *anything* to become personally fulfilled and fully realized, and in the process: maybe even *change the world*. A full 67 percent of millennials said they felt "extreme" pressure to succeed, compared to 40 percent of Gen Xers and 23 percent of boomers. We put so much pressure on ourselves to be successful and impressive that we never stop to wonder if it's actually going to make us happy. We assume it will, but we're ignoring the fact that success *does not inherently make people happy*. In fact, it just sets up even more expectation to continue living up to. We *won't* be happy if our underlying dynamic is always to be impressive, no matter how impressive we become.

I don't think life is more stressful for younger generations than it was for our parents' or grandparents' generations. Obviously, there's always been societal pressure and hardship, in many ways wayyyy worse than the pressures and hardships our generation faces (world wars, segregation, etc.), but the pressure has shifted for us. Millennials have taken on the pressure to be successful and impressive and unique in a way that few generations before have. Social media probably has a lot to do with that, because not only have our brains adapted to constant stimulation from notifications, but we are constantly comparing ourselves to the curated feeds of old acquaintances. You don't know the pain they're facing, you just see their gorgeous wraparound porch and you think, *Ugh, what's wrong with meeeeeeee? I just have this little stoop!?* Plus, the more time you spend on social media, the more depressed you tend to be. Beyond social media, our generation thrives on the delusion of our own importance. *We can and should be doing amazing things! We should be starting a cool multimillion-dollar business! We should be doing this all by age twenty-nine!* We don't want to settle for a job that we hate, we want *more*. And in some ways, that's amazing. Why *shouldn't* we reach for the stars? But in other ways, it's setting us up for constant disappointment. The pressure to be something and be somewhere impressive by thirty—most of us have internalized that, and it's just not a fair expectation (*especially* with the economy and job market we've inherited).

I've never read the book *The Defining Decade* on purpose, because I hated the premise. *Oh, I'm supposed to read a book all about how my twenties are ESSENTIAL for setting myself up for the rest of my life?!?* I was already drowning in panic and overwhelm. I didn't need more. And also, *I don't agree.* Let's normalize getting married at thirty-six and starting your ideal career in your forties. Fuck all this pressure. Our own unique timeline is valid! Be the tortoise!

Instead, I think we need to get back to basics and remember that just being alive *is enough.* Getting by, having a few good friends, breathing deeply, and looking at a pretty tree . . . *that's enough.* It is OK to *just be a human.* It's OK *to not be impressive.* Our pressure to be impressive with our career is just as toxic as any other old-fashioned pressure to be, say: married by twenty or have an eighteen-inch corseted waist. It's all ridiculous. Just let us *breathe.* Let us take our time.

That's how I felt about my boring office job. I realized that I needed to be OK being unimpressive and unremarkable. And in theory, as long as I didn't mess up *too* badly, I could stay in a job like this forever. I could survive. And that was important for me to know. I didn't have to impress anybody at this office. Nobody knew I sang, or that people used to tell me I was going to be on Broadway. I was *unimpressive* actually and very mediocre at my job. I didn't have to make people laugh. I didn't have to be very pretty. I *just* had to answer the phone, use the copy machine, and (poorly) proofread their press releases. I was unremarkable, and it was relieving.

But I really did miss acting, and I'd never actually *tried* it without a debilitating obsession with food and weight. And now that the obsession had subsided a bit, I thought maybe I could try again? So, I stayed at this receptionist job for a year exactly, and then I left to go play a "factory girl" in another musical in Philadelphia. I moved to Philly for a few months, but this time I *didn't* live with my parents in the suburbs. Instead, I sublet a room in a hot attic in a South Philly row home with a bunch of other local actors, and I got into drinking bourbon like an old man.

But this acting job *finally* allowed me to join the actors' union. Once you're in the union you get paid more for acting work *and* you can get into Broadway auditions and have a designated audition slot without having to stand in line at 5:45 a.m. I thought: *OK, maybe this is now or never. I am going to join the actors' union and give acting one more final go.*

HOW TO FEEL

It seemed like a miracle, but I . . . wasn't obsessed with food anymore. I didn't *think* about food that much, unless I was hungry. It all seemed nearly impossible after my life of food obsession and bingeing. But it was happening. The F*ck It Diet had been good for me. I'd gone through a yearlong food bender and no formal exercise (except walking in a city), but now, a year and a half in, my appetite felt . . . *easy*. Really. It was easy.

Wild.

I wasn't as thin as I was on the Paleo diet or my French wine diet, but in general, I had settled at a weight that helped me trust that my body had my back. My health wasn't worse; in fact, it was a little better. I was getting my period. I was sleeping better. And I was crying *way* less. I had more energy, and I was just generally more at peace.

At this point, *The F*ck It Diet* blog was still *very* small-time, but people were definitely reading and sharing my posts. More people than had *ever* read *Non-Quick Oatmeal*, or anything else I'd ever written. I started getting emails from people telling me that reading *The F*ck It Diet* blog changed their lives. *Wait . . .*

really? People were emailing me to tell me that thanks to my blog, *they too* had decided to stop dieting, and to stop micromanaging their weight, and their lifelong "food addiction" went away too. Eating really was healing. My problem, and their problem, was *not* in fact a food addiction or emotional eating like we'd always thought. It was *dieting*. Dieting was the thing that exacerbated *all of it*.

I had really started writing about this just for *me*. It was like I was writing instructions to *myself* on how to get out of the hole I was in. But it turns out that it resonated with people. Wow. It also happened to be great accountability for *me*, so I kept writing. It was keeping me on track *and* it was forcing me to keep explaining and discovering the different pieces of the puzzle.

I thought maybe it was an ideal side job: flexible, creative, and based on something I really cared about. Plus, I *loved* writing. I always had. So, I started getting really into learning about online business again. If people were loving *The F*ck It Diet*, I wanted to figure out how to give people what they wanted in a way that felt sustainable for me. I wrote and wrote about how to re-feed yourself, but what I realized people *really* wanted was a way to move past the *emotional and mental* fears that come along with eating more and gaining weight. And I was still trying to figure that out too.

Even though my food obsession went away, I still felt fixated on my weight. I knew I didn't want to be, but I was. I wrote about it in my *Artist's Way* Morning Pages. I talked myself through my self-judgment. I wrote about it on *The F*ck It Diet* blog. I was very *aware* of the thoughts and feelings that were happening and aware that I didn't want them, but I still had them.

Then I stumbled on something on the internet, an acupressure method that was supposed to help release emotion. It was called EFT, which stands for Emotional Freedom Technique, but is sometimes just referred to as Tapping, because that's what it is: tapping on acupressure points. I'd actually first seen it back in college when I was a raw vegan *and* learning about how *my mind could heal anythingggg*. My mom and I cracked ourselves up following the instructions and tapping the top of our heads, our faces, and under our armpits, while saying a dramatic mantra over and over. Very plainly: EFT was *weird*. It *looked* weird, it felt weird, and back then, I filed it away as another odd thing I'd tried in my quest for spontaneous miraculous healing.

What I didn't know is that EFT is actually evidence-based for helping to process anxiety and trauma. And what I'd never considered before is that being taught to hate your body *is a trauma*. Going on diet after diet is a trauma. And until you address the trauma that's stuck in your body, it won't feel safe to let your obsession with your body *go*, because hating your body and trying to change your body was the thing that previously made you feel safe. Not to mention that eating disorders *often* arise as a symptom of *other* traumas. That's what we call *compounding-fuckin-traumas*.

So, treating trauma is actually one of the *best* ways you can address disordered eating and eating disorders. That being said, a lot of trauma requires outside guidance to help you process, so if you feel like any emotional work is too overwhelming, please get support from a trauma-informed therapist!

But back then, without knowing any of that, I tried this weird tapping on my discomfort with my body. The way it works is you lean into the emotional discomfort while you do the tapping points all over your face and upper body. You say, "Even though I _____ [insert negative emotional experience] _____, I choose to love and accept myself." Yes, *barf* on the wholesome train, but it was actually . . . life changing for me.

The difference between this and other mantra-based woo-woo stuff I'd dabbled in is that this is actually *acknowledging* pain. Which is so important. "Even though I *feel this pain*, I also choose to accept myself." It acknowledges pain at the same time it offers something supportive to coexist alongside it. And the actual "tapping" on the different points on your body seems to anchor you *in* your body and almost get the emotion and pain *moving* so you can actually feel it, and allow it to process, as opposed to ignoring it and pretending it doesn't exist.

A huge problem with saying positive mantras like a glazed-over cult member with a perma-smile is toxic positivity. Trying to *override* pain and negative beliefs with positive beliefs doesn't work. You end up denying the pain you already feel and try to slap a positivity band-aid on it. So, inherently, there is a dissonance and emotional conflict, because on the inside there is pain, and on the outside there is this fake "everything is beautiful and perfect" facade, and the pain isn't allowed to air out and heal. You start feeling like a fraud, and you feel frustrated that even though you "think" all these positive things, you're still in pain on the inside.

A few months later, I noticed I wasn't thinking about my body anymore. It took that long to notice, because it's hard to notice what you *aren't* doing anymore. It *seemed* like the tapping had released some old dark stuff that had been keeping me fixated on my body.

It's really important to note that this is *not* the only way to feel and process emotion and trauma. I feel no particular allegiance to EFT, except for the fact that it was the first thing I tried to help me address unresolved emotions. EFT is *not* the only way to process your "stuff." There are other ways. There are other evidence-based ways. This is one of them, but not the only one. Thinking that it is "the only way" is an example of cultlike, extremist thinking. *This is the only way to heal.* Well, it's not!

What I've realized since is that any modality that helps you process old emotions and unprocessed trauma is guiding you back into your body to *feel*. We spend so much time avoiding our bodies, and avoiding *what it feels like* in our bodies, but that's actually how we remain traumatized in the first place. The way to heal trauma is to come back into our bodies. We think we can intellectualize our way to healing, but we can't. We *have* to be in the body to heal the body. We have to be in the body to *feel* and process old stuff.

All those years in high school and college, when I thought I could just tense up, and run faster, and eat less, and finally lose weight and miraculously be healed, I was actually doing everything I could *not to feel*. I was never present in my body. I didn't know how. I didn't know how *important it was*. Everything I did in my pursuit of healing was actually a way to avoid the discomfort of having emotions and being alive. But in order to emotionally heal and process trauma, we have to be willing to pause, and breathe, and feel. We have to come back into our bodies to feel what's there, waiting to be felt.

HOW TO BE EXTREME
ABOUT EVERYTHING

It's worth asking: Is The F*ck It Diet extremism, all by itself? Is it not just more of the same? Isn't it its own extreme ideology? Here is the good news and the bad news: *Anything can be twisted into extremist cultlike thinking.* Anything! At any point! By anyone! So, do people turn TFID into an extremist belief system in their own mind? Sure. Yes. Unfortunately, it's what humans *do*. We gather beliefs, and we form an identity with them. And depending on how susceptible we are to extremism, we sometimes turn it into an informal cult, just like I did with raw veganism. There was no *leader* I was following and giving money to (except Sarma, I guess . . .), but I turned it into my little obsessive, fearful religion.

A lot of people think The F*ck It Diet sounds too extreme. "Can't we just be *balanced*??"

Well, I *get that*. But taking away food rules, and eating a lot of food after years of dieting, is actually a way for the body to restore balance. So, when the pendulum swings to the *other* side, that's part of the body trying to restore balance. Saying "just be balanced" is in fact unhelpful advice, because after years of restriction, part of balance is actually the overcorrection. It's terrifying, yes. And it's terrifying because we have learned that hunger is terrifying. But it's just the way it is. If sleeping for ten hours straight for months, after years of sleep deprivation, sounds extreme, then yes! It's extreme. But it's also just . . . necessary.

Saying "just be balanced" *also* isn't addressing diet culture and our years of physical and mental restriction. It isn't addressing psychological guilt around food and weight.

It also sounds extreme because it isn't beating around the bush like a lot of other "non-diet" messages out there. A lot of the messages out there that are teaching people to "stop dieting" are half-assed because they're afraid of scaring people. "You don't need to diet! You just need to be balanced! You just need to listen really closely to your hunger! You just need to eat small respectable portions! You just need to exercise!" Well, what if what I need, *Amanda*, is a lot of fucking food? Because I just spent every ounce of my being trying (and failing) to starve myself for ten years straight? What if my soul is fucking *starving*, even if I don't look starving?

Another thing to consider is that the antidote to our culture's cult that's made us all obsessed with food and weight . . . maybe *has* to be a little extreme? But the good news is that the extremity of The F*ck It Diet is a phase. In fact, right now as I write this, I am eating a reheated bowl of some grass-fed beef, brown rice, and vegetable casserole that my mom made for us last night, because I am hungry—and I need to eat. And food? It isn't that deep.

The F*ck It Diet *sounds* extreme because it is completely counter to our cultural conditioning. But it is more about unlearning our programming than anything else, and a phase of overcorrection. The goal is to reach a balance that happens naturally. Not a forced balance, but *genuine* balance. Balance that happens by healing the physical yo-yo between restricting and extreme eating or bingeing in response, and by healing the emotional and mental reasons a person might turn to food too. Balance that happens by trusting that, left to their own devices, our bodies do not want to self-destruct.

I want people to stop needing it once the healing phase is over. Then, people can just eat, and *live their lives.*

But, sometimes, people still treat me like a cult leader. Someone who has all the answers. Someone who can save them. So, my question became . . . how *do* you teach something without becoming an accidental cult leader? How can I make sure to *never become a cult leader, even by accident*? You could say that all it takes is "good intentions," but I don't know if that's specific enough. The biggest difference, to me, between a teacher and a cult leader, is that a cult is exploitative and takes away the follower's power and autonomy and instills fear. *Teachers* genuinely want to . . . *teach*, and empower their students by pointing people back to themselves. Cult leaders *retain* that power and claim to have all the answers.

The tricky thing for *me* is that a lot of people who *love* The F*ck It Diet think that I have all the answers. I don't! I don't! I really don't! But I'd like to take this opportunity to say that everything *anyone* says (your teachers, your therapist, your religious leaders, your favorite podcaster) should be weighed against your own unique needs, unique experience, and intuition about what is best for you.

HOW TO NOT BE A CULT LEADER

- Always empower people with information instead of disempowering or exploiting and fearmongering.
- The goal is to get people to *not* need you anymore, not to keep them forever dependent on you.
- Give them back the reins to their life, instead of having them give over the reins to you.
- No claiming to have *all* the answers, and deferring to people's experience and unique path.
- No brainwashing people by making them believe they are broken and that only you can save them.

Hey . . . I could make muchhhhh more *money* if I became a cult leader, finally fulfilling my dream of becoming rich on the internet. But, you know, it also takes a lot of energy to be a cult leader, and I'd rather just float in a pool.

HOW TO FIGURE OUT WHAT'S DEPLETING YOU

I'd been on The F*ck It Diet for *two years at this point*, and I had a new lease on life. I'd quit acting at the beginning of The F*ck It Diet so I could heal in peace, but after my four-month rebirth in a South Philly attic, while playing a factory girl in the musical *Parade*, I was finally ready to do all the things I was too insecure and tired to do a few years before. I decided to start going to *lots* of different classes and auditions, and I was going to try to find an acting agent who didn't want to go back to medical school. I finally had *space* in my brain. And I decided I finally was going to go for it. And *if* in a year or two I hadn't gotten anywhere, or wasn't enjoying myself, then I could do something else, knowing I'd actually tried. At this point I *wasn't* fully convinced that being an actor was what I was supposed to be doing, but in order to find out, I felt like I had to really give it my all, one last time.

So, for those next two years, I tried to do *everything*. Ev-

erything. I was trying to be an actor the straightforward way, by going to auditions, but I was *also* trying to be an actor and performer the *less* straightforward way: writing my own content, performing my own stuff, writing comedy, being part of other people's projects. I started writing my own shows and writing my own weird comedy songs and performing them. I performed them at Caroline's comedy club in NYC. I wrote an absurd solo show and I got a residency at a comedy theater to develop and perform the piece.

I was constantly auditioning, I was coaching kids on acting to make money, and I was taking a million different acting and audition classes and voice lessons. I was doing acting agent showcases. I was taking the express subway up and down Manhattan multiple times a day. I was writing and performing a one-woman musical standup show in people's *living rooms* (why) and at NYC and Philly music and comedy venues. I was performing improv in bar basements at midnight and practicing improv at my teammate's apartment in Queens. And I started a podcast for The F*ck It Diet. I was still writing *The F*ck It Diet* blog and had started to write *The F*ck It Diet* book. I was creating my TFID workshops. I was *marketing* my workshops. I was running my workshops and honing the way I taught and explained everything. Then I'd revamp them and run them again.

The whole two years, I was *high* on creativity, but I was also reaching my limit. I was burning the candle at both ends and I was starting to get *very* burnt out. I was literally trying to make eight different careers work at once. And the longer I tried to keep doing all these things, the more overwhelmed I was getting. *How am I going to become an actress, keep growing my solo* *show, keeping growing my kids' acting coaching, keep growing The F*ck It Diet?* How?

I was also doing a lot of personal development writing exercises. Some were from *The Artist's Way* and some from other books. One of the notable writing exercises was: "What do you *not* want to admit to yourself?" I avoided answering that for a while, because every time I read the question, I'd hear a tiny, meek little voice saying: *I . . . don't really want to be an actor. The constant auditions are too exhausting to be sustainable.* I ignored it. I mean, I'd ignored it for years, hadn't I? What's another year?!

But eventually I had to take stock. *Everything* I did with acting in New York felt like a closed door. No matter how well the auditions went or how well the classes went, even when people metaphorically peered through their windows and gave me a thumbs up, nothing was growing. Nothing was changing. Nothing was getting easier. Meanwhile, *everything* I did with The F*ck It Diet was opening doors left and right. And that comparison is what helped me see the difference.

I had been forcing myself to be an actress, partially because I loved acting, but even *more* because it's what I thought I was *supposed to do.* I was *supposed to live up to this expectation. I was supposed to figure it out. I mean, it's supposed to be hard, isn't it??* But it was draining my life force. I think that's what happens to us when we keep expecting ourselves to be something we maybe just aren't meant to be. It'll keep depleting us—because it's actually not meant for us.

I was expecting myself to be something I maybe just . . . wasn't meant to be. And I was really tired. I was working seven days a week, at all hours. And every single day, there was always an audition (or four) that I was supposed to be going to, and I never *ever* wanted to. It was draining. *Really* draining.

Then I read *The Life-Changing Magic of Tidying Up*. This was my accidental and unlikely gateway into *rest*. I didn't know it yet, because at first, I thought I was just decluttering physical *stuff*. The book encourages you to get rid of everything that doesn't "spark joy."

It's important to note that this kind of extreme decluttering *does* require enough financial stability to trust that you will be able to replace the things you get rid of, if you make a mistake. Hoarding is a natural response to scarcity. But hoarding is also saying *I don't trust that it's safe to get rid of this ugly shirt that I fucking hate.* And what good does that do?

So, I started decluttering everything. *Only* the things that you truly love (or I guess: truly need) are allowed to stay in your home and in your life. This whole method spoke to the part of me that had a life filled with things that didn't spark joy, and the part of me that wanted a life that *did* spark joy. It also spoke to the big part of me that was absolutely, undeniably exhausted.

All of this was right up my alley. It was dramatic. It was extreme. It was a little *mystical*, because you are also supposed to hold your clothes and items and communicate with them, and if they don't spark joy, you *thank* them for their service and the joy they brought, but "you have served your purpose, stupid shirt, thank you." The *big* takeaway from the book is that the things we are holding on to that *don't* spark joy anymore already sparked their joy. They *already* brought you the joy they were meant to bring. Now, it's time for them to go.

The combination of reading a book about decluttering *while*

I was burnt out is what led to my rest realization. I was reading about finding joy and seeking simplicity through decluttering *right at the time* that I was deeply physically and emotionally exhausted. It was the catalyst that made me realize that what I needed was just . . . LESS. I needed less to do. I needed time. I needed to turn my life on its head and *stop*. And rest.

Decluttering immediately felt like a metaphor to me. The symbolism was clear: What in your life is draining you, simply because you don't believe you're allowed to get rid of it? For *years*, I'd thought I wasn't allowed to get rid of acting, because I hoped it was *my destiny*. Because so many people told me how good I was. Because, in a lot of ways, I *did* love it. But as I decluttered old computer cords, old sheets that didn't even fit the bed I had, shoes I hadn't worn in years, and old papers that I never needed to keep, all of a sudden I found myself decluttering *all my audition dresses*. All the clothes that were supposed to make me look thinner, and demure, and . . . *whateverrrrr* in auditions. There was no question: they did not spark joy. At all. *I never want to go to another stupid class, or another stupid open call audition. I don't want to do this anymore.*

I'd never really considered what my lifelong subconscious guilt over my failed acting career had given me: *constant, chronic stress and guilt*. And constant self-scrutiny. Constant. I never even was able to identify it, it just *was*. I felt it all the time. I was *never* doing enough, I was never productive enough, I was never impressive or successful enough, I never looked good enough. I never ever felt like I was *allowed* to relax. Ever. And I was so . . . tired. All from subconscious beliefs and pressures that I didn't even realize were there. I was tired as fuck. Really.

So, what if I just . . . kept decluttering, and decluttered my whole life? What if I decluttered . . . all the audition classes I was taking? What if I decluttered acting altogether? What if I took the weight of that pressure and just let it float away? What if I just kept the thing that actually did bring me joy these days: running workshops and writing *The F*ck It Diet*?

I had run myself into the ground trying to make The F*ck It Diet a viable business, and over those two years of hustling, I'd learned a lot and made enough money to sustain myself for a little while. But I wasn't enjoying the hustle *at all*.

So, what if I . . . what if I took two years *off*? Not two years off from working, just off from *hustling*? And what if I moved out of one of the most expensive cities in the world and moved back down to Philadelphia and I paid way less to live by myself, and do the opposite of what I've been doing?

What if I took two years of . . . rest?

HOW TO FIGURE OUT
IF YOU'RE ALLOWED
TO BE TIRED

Even though four years earlier I'd had an epiphany about my food and weight obsession, I hadn't really stopped seeking. Ever. I'd never slowed down. I reversed my *direction*, but The F*ck It Diet was actually its own crisis. *Oh, my God, what now?! What am I going to do for a job? What am I going to do to stay alive? How am I going to heal this deep shit I'm in? Where am I going to live? How am I going to navigate this world while I heal? I need to buy all new clothes . . . can I even afford to buy all new clothes?*

Healing your relationship with food is *hard*. I needed to figure out how to heal really deep issues, and it took a lot of energy and vigilance and trust and surrender. Those first four years on The F*ck It Diet were absolutely life-changing, but they were not *restful*. Even though I deliberately rested *physically* from exercise in the beginning, my mind and emotions never, *ever* rested. And that's what I really needed at that point.

I *had* let myself off the hook from the ever-present pressure to be a thin, ethereal, wholly healed, glowing, perfect person, but there were so many pressures I still needed to untangle from. And this was my chance.

But really, I still didn't feel like I deserved to be exhausted. I really didn't. I had been *very* hard on myself for being exhausted for a long, long time. All those years when I was underfed. All those years when I thought I was lazy but just didn't have enough blood. *Just push through, Caroline. Stop being such a lazy wimp. Go for a run.* I wasn't doing any more than anyone else. In fact, looking at everyone else around me, most people were juggling *way* more. And I knew how lucky I was. I was in my twenties, living in New York City, trying to chase my dreams. *Cry me a river, little girl.*

So, I forced myself to push through my exhaustion until I literally couldn't ignore it any longer. I was extremely physically tired. More tired than seemed logical. There were times when I was in the middle of a conversation with someone and I had a hard time keeping my eyes open. Physically, something wasn't quite right. And it was hard to pinpoint, because so much of my physical health *was better* than it was before, thanks to my better relationship with food. But something was still off. I also started feeling depleted dread looking at my full schedule of running around New York, trying to make eight different careers happen. And going to one more class or one more audition started requiring me to summon more energy than I had.

Why can't I motivate myself? Why can't I just hack this life thing?

Something responded, *Because you're exhausted. And you keep forcing yourself to do things that are keeping you exhausted and depleted. Whether you think you deserve to be or not, you're burnt out.*

The oddest experience of all was that I'd started getting liver pain every time I had alcohol, even just one glass of wine. I expected that to go away eventually, but it didn't. I also started getting very frequent low-grade fevers, once or twice a week. At first I thought: *Wow, I keep almost getting sick, but my body keeps fighting it off!* But it kept happening, and I finally realized that something wasn't right.

I wasn't sure whether my exhaustion was just from all the years of pushing myself into being an actor and a performer and chronic *stress*. Or if I was exhausted because something *else* was physically going on in my body. Was it circumstantial? Or physical? Or both? I didn't know, but either way, I knew I needed rest.

I always compared myself to other people to justify why I *shouldn't* be tired, but really, what good did that do me? Exhaustion isn't a pissing contest. We can all be exhausted for different reasons. And most of us *are* exhausted, for one reason or another. Life is exhausting. And we do *not* live in a culture that supports and allows for *healing* from that exhaustion. We live in a culture that sees hyper-productivity and exhaustion as a badge of honor. We live in a culture that expects us to be able to work 9 to 5, five days a week, fifty weeks out of the year. And often way *more*. But did you know that the forty-hour workweek is actually *too long* for a lot of people? An article in atSpoke looked at different studies on work hours, productivity, happiness, and health, and stated, "There are a few studies that have shown employees are happier, healthier, and more productive when they work less than forty hours a week." In 2004, the CDC found that people who work overtime, or more than forty hours a week, are *less* healthy and *less* productive than those who don't. In the book *Laziness Does Not Exist*, Dr. Devon Price said that "researchers consistently find that in office jobs, people are capable of being productive for only about three hours a day, on average." Meaning, what *most* of us are expected to do, and expecting *ourselves* to do, leads directly to burnout. And none of us understand why, because we are trying to follow the norms of our culture. Just like with dieting and diet culture, we are all under the impression that we are broken. *We are doing it wrong! We keep eating too much! We keep feeling tired and lazy!* But in reality, we are just operating under ridiculous expectations. We are not *designed* to work constantly and never get a break. Under those conditions, we are designed to *fall apart*.

But still, we live in a culture that tells us we are not doing enough. We live in a culture where most of us feel constant guilt and worry, every day, that we aren't working hard enough. In the United States, two million hourly workers are at or *below* minimum wage, and *twenty million* hourly workers are earning "near-minimum" wage. Most of them will have to work multiple jobs, which puts them *way over* forty hours a week, just to barely make ends meet. By default, this is keeping people in constant survival mode, just because we refuse to raise the minimum wage. Most people also don't have paid sick leave, maternity leave, or bereavement leave. We aren't *allowed* to stop. We aren't allowed to heal. Even if we wanted to, most of us can't afford it.

Honestly, because of all this, a lot of our collective exhaustion is unavoidable. And even with better working conditions, there's no way to avoid the hardship and trauma that comes along with being a human. But *some* of our exhaustion *is* avoidable, and it's mostly the unexamined cultural, subconscious expectations lurking in the background. The stuff we are putting on *ourselves*. The stuff we don't even realize that we learned. Think about all the time and money we spend on . . . say, beauty, and weight loss, and skin care, and buying the latest fashion trends. If you genuinely enjoy it, that's one thing. But for most of us, we feel like it's not even a choice. We *have to*. We *have* to stay looking young. We *have* to run every day. *We have* to buy the newest cropped flared pant. But do we? Do we even realize what's our choice and what's pushed on us? What are the things we've taken on that we don't *need* to take on? What's the stuff that we don't realize we are using as weapons against ourselves? The world is cruel enough—why are we internalizing and perpetuating that cruelty on ourselves?

No matter what, you are allowed to be exhausted. And you are allowed to rest. And you're allowed to stop doing things you only do because you didn't realize you had a choice.

Even though I ended up overhauling *almost* my entire life, *you* being exhausted *doesn't mean* you have to quit your life. At all. It doesn't mean you have to stop doing anything you like to do! I am *not* suggesting that you do what I did. It is *not* the only way to rest. Realizing you are burnt out *just means* it's time to take stock of the things that are exhausting you, so you have more awareness. And *maybe*, with that awareness, you'll end up doing something about the pieces that *are* within your control.

A lot of people are tired for some deep reason that they

can't quite pinpoint. If that's you, it might be validating to realize: *Hey, I'm tired. And **this** is why. And in the very least, I can be compassionate with myself while I figure out how to keep going in a sustainable way.*

I'm going to go through *some* things that can and will exhaust us. As you read through, notice any of the things that may be at play in your life. If and when multiple things on the list apply to you, these probably have become compounding stressors.

AN INCOMPLETE LIST OF EXHAUSTING THINGS

THINGS BEYOND OUR IMMEDIATE CONTROL

Poverty and Financial Stress

This exhaustion is not *just* from the physical exhaustion of, say, working multiple jobs to feed your kids but it's also from the chronic stress it breeds. Worrying about how to make ends meet, and *if* you'll make ends meet, is traumatic and *exhausting* in every sense. We do *not* have equal access to education and job training. We *don't* all get the same head start. And the minimum wage in the United States is unlivable. There is no equal access to good-paying jobs. Therefore: *systemic exhaustion.*

Oppression, Stigma, and Marginalization (Racism, Weight Stigma, Ableism, Homophobia, Etc.)

Being ostracized, stigmatized, or treated poorly is exhausting. I don't mean that lightly. What I mean is that it's dehumanizing and traumatizing, and trauma is exhausting. In fact, *perceived* stigma alone is a chronic stress that can be very bad for our *physical health*, not just our mental health. What that means is that if you've been treated poorly enough times, it's a trauma, and you start to expect it. And even just the anticipatory stress hormones can run down your health and lead to chronic health problems. This isn't something you can blame on the individual: *Hey! Just stop being stressed by your oppression!* No. The oppression is the problem.

Health Problems

Chronic health problems usually cause actual physical exhaustion. But, on top of *that*, worrying about health problems, worrying about paying for the treatment of health problems, and blaming yourself for health problems, are all really difficult, scary, and exhausting.

Living in a country where you could go bankrupt from having a health problem? Barbaric. And as much as our culture makes it seem like we have ultimate control over our health if we just eat well and exercise . . . we don't. Sorry! That's just way too simplistic. Tell that to someone who has struggled with health their whole life. Sure, tweaks in lifestyle *can* absolutely improve our health, but they don't always. And as I've also explained earlier, sometimes the prescription for your health problems can create even *more* exhaustion, stress, and health problems. How fun.

THINGS WE CAN *SOMETIMES* DO SOMETHING ABOUT

PTSD and Unresolved Trauma

Like I mentioned earlier, trauma is unresolved and unprocessed survival energy, stuck in our system, keeping us in the fight or flight state. Poverty, racism, and chronic health problems often *become* traumas. So, what I'm going to say here also applies to those above. But, even without compounding and intersecting oppression, *most of us* are holding on to *some* trauma. Trauma expert Peter A. Levine wrote in *Waking the Tiger*, "What most people don't know is that many seemingly benign situations can be traumatic."

I have never been involved in what people *tend* to think of as a traumatic experience (an attack or big accident), but I still had some unresolved trauma from experiences that were fully innocuous on the outside, like . . . teeth surgery. And . . . singing in front of people. And years of panic over my weight and dieting.

Resolving trauma is possible, but it's not always easy or straightforward, and it usually requires professional support, money, time, patience, and *energy*. Which is why I've put it in the "things we can *sometimes* do something about" category.

Mental Health Struggles

Mental health issues are depleting. And . . . honestly, there are so many different causes of mental health issues. Some are chemical and inherent and genetic. Some are learned beliefs and behaviors. Some are circumstantial. Some are *because* of unresolved trauma. And all require and deserve support. And again, it's not easy, or cheap, or straightforward.

Being Stuck in Unhealthy, Toxic, or Abusive Circumstances

This would include: toxic work environments and toxic families and toxic or overbearing religions. These are things we don't consciously *choose*. We don't say, "Hey, I am going to choose a toxic family!" But without support and examination we also may stay in the toxic environment. It's easier said than done, but removing yourself from a toxic environment, when possible, is what we need and deserve.

THINGS WE DO HAVE CONTROL OVER
(ONCE WE LEARN ABOUT THEM)

Unresolved Emotions

In my experience, there's overlap here with unresolved trauma, but plainly: most of us did *not* learn to allow, trust, feel, and process our emotions. In fact, more likely, we learned to fear our emotions and suppress them, or we learned that feeling or showing emotions is *weak*. So, most of us spend our whole lives trying to avoid them and deny them, numb them, and push them away. This backfires, and not only is it bad for our mental health, but it can actually make us *physically* sick. And constantly numbing and running from your emotions will always be: *exhausting*.

Toxic Beliefs and Cultural Expectations

The guilt. The shoulds. The comparing ourselves to other people. The forcing ourselves to stay in jobs or relationships that we don't love, but that we don't think we deserve to leave. Beating ourselves up. Feeling like we aren't doing enough. Feeling like we don't look good enough. Feeling like we're not impressive enough. The constant *seeking*. The constant attempts at self-improvement. The constant attempts to fit in to our society so we can be accepted and treated better. The constant feeling that *something else is supposed to be happening. Something better. I'm supposed to be further along. I'm supposed to be doing more.* These are the expectations that are put on us by our culture, about what it means to be happy and successful, that we then take on and perpetuate on ourselves, usually without even realizing it.

The subconscious guilt that stems from these expectations becomes like a computer program running in the background, always draining your battery. You're not using the program. You're not even benefiting from it. It's just *there*, using up energy, draining you, and making all the other applications run slower. And I wanted to close and delete those fucking apps.

This is where I wanted to do the majority of my healing. This was the piece of my life I'd finally become aware of. And this was the piece I was finally ready to do something about. And this is the piece that *you* can do something about, even *with* other compounding exhausting factors and oppressions and traumas. You can delete those apps that are sucking your energy.

We need to *know* that we are allowed to be tired, and to acknowledge the legitimacy of *unavoidable* exhaustion. Even if we don't know what to *do* about the unavoidable exhaustion, acknowledging the toll it takes on our energy is important.

And sure, you *could* ignore the exhaustion and push through for the rest of your life. Lots of people do that. And some people like it that way. Some people don't see any other way. Some people think it's harder to unpack all of this rather than just keep pushing through. That's fine. I have some friends who feel like they *thrive* on stress, and hey, maybe they do! I'm not going to tell anyone how to live.

But maybe you're like me, and you're finally realizing that stress and exhaustion are eroding you from the inside out.

HOW TO RECONCILE THE PRIVILEGE OF REST

Without defining it more specifically, I know that *rest* just sounds like a nice little activity for trust fund babies or stressed executives. *Oh, poor thing, do you need to go take a vacation and sit by the pool? I hope you feel better with some good sleep and a month off! Your CEO position will be waiting for you when you are ready to return!* But that's not what rest is. At least, it's not how I'm defining rest.

To me, rest isn't about vacations, per *se*. (Though vacations are great and important.) Rest is a state of mind. Rest is a shift in perspective. It's a shift in the way we treat ourselves. It is a *deliberate* deprogramming from the cult of productivity. It encourages us to remember: *I deserve rest. I deserve to recharge. I deserve to take little moments of peace. My worth does not come from constant productivity.*

Rest as a state of mind is a resistance to the impossible expectations put on us to be everything to everybody, and to do it all, and have it all. It's a shifted worldview that gives us the permission to do what we *need* for our own physical and mental health. It encourages you to remember that you *deserve* to rest, and even if accessing physical rest is hard or nearly impossible, you still *deserve* it. You deserve to let yourself off the hook. You deserve to create boundaries that allow you to take the rest you need. You deserve little moments of quiet. Because what I've found, for myself and for other people, is that most of us don't even think we deserve it. We feel *guilty* for feeling tired or wanting to do less. So, we never do. And when we do, we are stressed about it. And that's not rest.

Rest as a state of mind is a resistance to the incessant productivity culture we live in. It is an invitation to say *fuck it* to all of the shoulds and expectations that won't stop telling you you're not doing enough, or that you aren't doing life right. Rest reminds you that even if your boss thinks you should be available at 9:45 p.m. to answer emails, he *isn't* inherently right just because he is your boss. This is *not* "the way it has to be." You deserve to rest, and maybe, just mayyyyybe, you have a toxic work dynamic. Rest as a state of mind is meant to empower you to remember that you are *not* a machine, and we should never be expected to be constantly productive, with no opportunity to recharge.

Rest as a state of mind does *not* rely on you being able to afford an all-inclusive resort for a month. That kind of intervention isn't accessible to the majority of people, and so what good is it to most of us reading this book? No good. Instead, rest can *just* be a shift in perspective: a shift in the way you buy into the system. A shift in the way you treat yourself. And if *all* you can practically take is a little moment to rest for five minutes, it's about taking that little moment.

Whether it feels accessible to us or not, we *need rest*. In fact, the *more* compounding stressors you have, the more you need and deserve rest as recharge and restoration of your body and spirit. Rest is *the only way to heal burnout*. The only way! In order to heal, in order to be with yourself, in order to gather strength, we need rest. It's good for us. It's good for our immune system. We can think more clearly and be better friends and family members, and have a better impact and a better life, if we are able to approach our work rested. (Plus, there's a reason why withholding food and rest is used to break people's resistance down during cult indoctrination. It *works*.)

The system has chewed us up and spit us out. The system is cruel and unfeeling and unconcerned with our own happiness or our own healing. When we buy into it, and don't question the way things are, we perpetuate it.

Don't buy the lie that only wealthy people are allowed to rest. Don't buy the lie that you're only allowed to rest once you achieve *x* or make a certain amount of money. Don't buy the lie that you have to bleed for a cruel system. You *deserve* rest—because most of us can't keep going at the rate we're going. And *yes*, big picture, we need a more forgiving and supportive system in place, a higher minimum wage, and a social safety net that can mitigate the compounding exhausting trauma of not being able to make ends meet. *But* in the meantime, you need ways to bring rest into your life. And you need it now. Just the fact that rest only feels accessible or *allowed* for those who need it least is the reason we all have to take the rest we can. It's the reason that we need rest as a state of mind. In a culture where rest seems frivolous and irresponsible and impossible, deliberate rest is a radical act.

Don't get it twisted, I was *not* thinking that big back then. My two years of rest was 100 percent self-preservation, because I simply . . . wasn't OK. There was nothing noble about what I was doing, I was just trying to figure out if I could ever feel OK again. But I've come to realize that rest is healing and necessary for everyone, even *more* so for people far more oppressed and exhausted than me. The Nap Ministry is a movement founded by Tricia Hersey that encourages Black women to use rest as a way to resist the system and to heal ancestral trauma and exhaustion. The Nap Ministry is calling for rest as a radical form of resistance. Their focus on resisting systemic racial injustice and exploitation is a wonderful example of rest being used to step out of the grind system that has historically and systemically exploited people of color.

Again, there are so many causes of physical exhaustion: poverty, racism, health problems, our health care *system*, and unresolved trauma. The way our country (and world) is set up allows for the exploitation of the working class. It relies on it. It relies on overworking the people who are in the most vulnerable positions. And it does *not* benefit the people running the show if their little worker bees are allowed or encouraged to rest, or to take significant restorative vacations, or make a living wage. Billionaires just don't seem to want to have to become embarrassingly unimpressive multimillionaires. So, nothing changes. But rest as a *state of mind* reminds you that you deserve rest, even if the world we live in is unsupportive.

If we *really* cared about people's health, and mental health, like we claim to, we would care about the systemic issues that keep people exploited, exhausted, and chronically stressed and ill. This book alone is not equipped to fix our system or heal our unavoidable exhaustion at the hands of an oppressive system. All it can do is invite you to remember not to buy into it. All I can do is remind you not to burn yourself out, on top of everything else. We need change, but along the way, we need you rested. So, in between working for a better future, rest.

Extended periods of physical rest may feel like an inaccessible luxury, but rest as a *state of mind* is accessible to everyone. Emotional and mental rest is where we have to focus our energy. What are your *beliefs* about yourself, or about the way it has to be, that are keeping you exhausted and depleted and exploited? *That's* what we have got to figure out.

HOW TO CLAIM REST

The first thing I did that spring of 2016 was make a plan to move to Philadelphia. Living in New York made perfect sense when my goal was Broadway. But now, by the magic of the internet and The F*ck It Diet, I was able to work from home. So, *why* am I working from home in an apartment that literally is on the ramp to a highway, with windows that look out at the walls of another apartment building, when I could live *alone* and have windows that actually let in light?

I love New York . . . so much. I wasn't leaving because I didn't love it. I was just tired. If I'd been rich, I could have stayed and done my two years of rest in New York. But I was not, so I had to go. I was moving to Philadelphia, I was going to live alone, and my apartment was going to have a *washing machine*. An in-apartment washing machine is a rare luxury in New York.

The weekend after I made my decision to rest for two years, and at least *temporarily* stop drinking to give my liver a break, I had a Memorial Day weekend trip I'd already committed to.

This trip was actually the *exact kind of thing* I wanted to stop automatically saying yes to doing during my two years of rest.

Trips like this were exhausting: sharing a bed in a questionable Airbnb. Drinking day after day. Trying to find golfers to date. None of it was restful to me. I was *tired*. I was tired of seeking Broadway, I was tired of seeking beauty, and I was tired of seeking husbands.

But I'd already said yes, *before* I landed on my rest plan. So, I either had to *not go* after I'd already paid for the Airbnb, which seemed a little dramatic, or I had to tell my friends: "Look, I . . . am very burnt out. And I need to stop drinking for a bit, so, just don't count on me to be fun this weekend." Thankfully, they were totally fine with me not drinking, because I don't have asshole friends.

I *really* needed a break from alcohol. That was clear as day to me. And if I ever forgot it, the pain in my right side reminded me. I'd *definitely* used alcohol as a social lubricant and a salve for my undiagnosed anxiety for a while, but at *this* point, my issue with alcohol wasn't actually emotional. I didn't use alcohol as a kneejerk reaction to numb myself anymore, probably because I had a better relationship with my emotions and with food. At this point, my issue with alcohol was *physical*.

The other big thing I knew about alcohol was that it royally fucked with my sleep. And if what I *really* wanted was *rest*, maybe laying off alcohol for a bit would improve my sleep and allow me to feel *rested? Maybe?! MAYBE?!* So, I cut it out, 99 percent, for those two years. I'd have a glass of wine on the rarest occasion, but for the most part, I didn't drink.

I *now* will sometimes have one or two drinks with friends here and there, but it's not my go-to anymore. And when I drink more than one drink, it has a *notable* effect on my sleep,

and anxiety the following day, and it definitely runs me down
and affects my immune system—especially if I have a period
of more socializing with alcohol. And because of all that, it
doesn't have a big place in my life anymore just because . . . *I
want to feel good.*

My break from alcohol was a big part of *my* rest, and the
experience was very eye-opening. It quickly revealed how much
our culture relies on alcohol in social contexts, and how uncomfortable people get when you're not drinking. I am *not* anti-
alcohol or even anti-alcohol culture. It's fun in social situations
if your body can handle it and if you don't use it as a primary
coping mechanism. But think: we live in *such* a pro-alcohol culture that it's considered weirder *not* to drink than to keep up a
dysfunctional relationship with alcohol. I had to be very careful
to turn down drinks in a *casual way* that wouldn't bum people
out or hide that I wasn't drinking at a wedding just so I didn't
make *other people* feel uncomfortable. In fact, when possible, I'd
usually just pretend to be drinking so people would leave me
alone about it. Back when I depended on alcohol a lot more,
I used to feel this way too when other people weren't drinking. (This was back when I was trying to make "functional alcoholic" a quirky part of my personality.) It made me anxious
when people weren't drinking. So, it's not that I don't *get it*, I
just see the alcohol mixed messages now with fresh eyes. *Wow,
we are all expected to drink . . . a lot.*

We tend to glorify people's ability to drink a lot. Holding
our alcohol is a badge of honor. We vilify and demonize mar-
ijuana and other drugs, we stigmatize psychiatric medication,
and lots of us are uncomfortable with feeling our emotions, and

up until very recently, good old *therapy* was taboo, but not getting shitfaced every night! *No feeling emotions! No therapy! Just pretend that whiskey is a part of your personality!* Again, I get it. It's fun. It's an escape. It's a part of *many* traditional cultures, and I actually think alcohol *can* be used in a healthy and joyful way, but more often it isn't. In fact, more than thirty-seven million adults in the United States reported binge drinking about once a week. Alcohol is *many* people's primary coping mechanism, and in many ways, it's glorified in our culture, but it's still the fourth leading cause of death in the United States. And if we are going to talk about exhaustion in our burnt-out, pro-alcohol culture, in the short term, alcohol *actively* disrupts our circadian rhythm and our sleep, especially during the second half of the night. Long-term, the health consequences are much higher. And if we use it primarily for a distraction from our emotions, those unhealed and unprocessed emotions will also keep us burnt out until we address them.

However, I also don't necessarily think that the black-and-white *binary* of having to label yourself an alcoholic or *not* an alcoholic is particularly helpful for everyone. There's allowed to be nuance. You're allowed to reevaluate your relationship with alcohol without cutting it out 100 percent or labeling yourself an alcoholic. For instance, for me, I knew that my issue with alcohol was not an alcohol addiction. I was just . . . tired, and I knew that alcohol wasn't helping.

So, that Memorial weekend trip, at the very start of my rest, was the first big weekend I *purposely* didn't drink. I just needed a break. And on the second night of the trip, I lost steam around 9:30 p.m. because my exhaustion wasn't being masked by alcohol. *OK . . . this bar isn't fun anymore for me. Good night! Have fun! Meet your husbands!* Back at the Airbnb, I made my herbal tea for my liver and sat on the bed to write a blog post: "WHY I'M GOING ON TWO YEARS OF REST." I was writing it mostly for myself, but also for the people who followed *The F*ck It Diet*, who had been curious about what I meant when I kept saying, "I'm going on Two Years of Rest" on Instagram.

Writing it was *so* helpful, and it reminded me why I left the bar that night, and why I wasn't out living carefree la-di-da. It helped me identify the *reasons* I was burnt out and at my wits' end with the way I was operating. I was able to explain clearly, to myself, *why* I needed a change. And, in the months following, I was able to refer back to it. It was . . . *A Declaration of Exhaustion*, if you will.

What I was learning, the more I thought and wrote about my exhaustion and need for rest, was that I needed a break from the way I was doing *everything*. I needed to change the way I was socializing *and* working *and* the way I was thinking. I needed to simplify. I needed less on my plate. And I had needed it for a long time. *That* was the reason for the two years of rest. I needed to stop distracting myself with nonstop activity. I needed to stop drinking for a bit so I could listen to my exhaustion better and not mask it with alcohol. I needed to stop taking jobs I didn't actually want. I needed to give myself unconditional permission to say *no* to things that I did not have the energy for.

We all have different ways we need to rest. In fact, this trip was a perfect example of that. This weekend would have been a *wonderful way to rest* for a lot of other people. Going on a fun trip with your friends? Sitting at a marina drinking a glass of rosé? A version of this would be *very* restful to me now, but not then. I was just too burnt out at the time to go for a party weekend. But *rest* will mean different things to different people. And it will mean different things during different *phases* of your life, depending on the cause of your own personal burnout. Everyone will need different versions of rest, depending on which parts of you are depleted.

We all have different situations, and different cultural expectations that we may have taken on. Some people feel burnt out *from* their social life. Some people feel burnt out from their work and need *more* social time. Maybe you're a mom who feels burnt out by the expectations and pressure on what *being a good mom* looks like. Maybe you're still stuck in the diet cycle, constantly undereating or overexercising. Maybe you're a workaholic who never feels like you are allowed to take time off.

Are you trying to keep up appearances with your neighbors or old high school friends? Are you staying in a relationship because you're afraid of what it means about you if you end it and are single again? Are you spending your energy trying to conform to an archetype that doesn't really serve you? Have you been exhausting yourself searching for a miracle cure? Are you in a career that inherently stresses you out? Are you exhausted because you live in a system that continually oppresses you?

If you are tired or feel burnt out, I recommend you write out all the reasons *why*. Write your Declaration of Exhaustion. And then use it as a way to start identifying the cultural beliefs that may be perpetuating your exhaustion.

"Hello, cruel world, I've realized that I've been taking on

too much, and so I will be prioritizing resting, and this is why: [fill in the blank]."

Why are you tired? What do you need a break from? What pressure do you need a break from? Explain it to yourself. It helps.

That night when I left my friends out at a bar, while I was sitting in the Airbnb bed writing about being tired, my friend Annie met her now husband. (Yes, he is a golfer.) *You see?* We all have our own paths. Some of us meet our partners at midnight at an outdoor bar. And some of us have to write a Rest Manifesto from an Airbnb bed sitting on a musty comforter from 1982. It's all *good*!

HOW TO BE OK
DYING ALONE

During the time when I was subletting an attic room in Philadelphia and drinking a lot of bourbon, I ended up dating *a lot of people* in a *very short* period of time, because I was finally around people my own age instead of three-year-old children with my same name. I went on dates with a lot of people *I* didn't like enough, I went on dates with a lot of people who didn't like *me* enough, I had a six-month relationship that ended miserably, and then I had a melodramatic fling that ended up breaking my heart, and I was heartbroken for a *year*.

Heartbreak is, obviously, fucking *exhausting*. It takes a toll on you mentally, emotionally, and physically. And during that heartbroken year, I lost *a lot of weight* and became really thin, completely accidentally. I didn't even notice until people pointed it out. And then, when I finally felt better and less heartbroken, the weight came back. *Huh.* It was clear as day: *weight loss is not always a good sign. In fact, sometimes it's a sign of deep distress.* And my sign of *improved* physical and emotional health? *Weight gain.*

Meeting people in real life is *way* more fun than any online dating I've ever done, but my *God*, even casual dating is
absolutely *exhausting*. The drinking. The late nights. The constant going out. The constant mind games everyone is playing. I
think it's brutal. I know it's alllll supposed to be worth it in the
end, but *what if you've been doing it for a long time and it hasn't
been worth it yet? How do you force yourself to continue?* That is a
question nobody can answer for me. Maybe dating just doesn't
fit with my personality.

Even when dating is fun, it still takes an exorbitant amount
of time and emotional energy. And when we're single, or have
been single for a while, we are expected to get to know people
nonstop, over and over, because of this looming unspoken (and
sometimes spoken) threat of dying alone. And when it *doesn't*
work out, we are just expected to keep doing it *over and over
and over again*. And it took me a while to understand how truly
exhausting this dynamic had become for me.

This was still one of the cultural expectations that had *really* been doing a number on me. I always had the feeling that
something was very wrong with me for being single. I knew
logically that wasn't true. I always *chose* to be single over dating
people I didn't want to be with. But I still felt this constant low-
grade pressure that *something else was supposed to be happening*.
It wasn't fully conscious, but it was always there, humming in
the background: a gnawing feeling that I needed to be *doing
things differently, being more open, going out more, going to the
right places, finding the right extracurriculars, and going on more
online dates* . . . the list went on and on. And it never felt like I
was doing enough.

My issue, I *thought*, was that I didn't like people *often* enough. So, I spent a lot of time trying to troubleshoot that flaw. A hairdresser once told me that she didn't even like her husband until their third date. *What?! I have to give people that long to know if I like them?* So, as a diligent little troubleshooter, I thought, *OK, maybe I need to give people at least . . . three chances before I'm allowed to decide I don't like them.* I went through a *very* rough phase where I forced myself to go on multiple dates with nice people who I didn't actually like, just in case it was going to *grow*. It didn't. It never did. All it did was exhaust me and make me dread dating even more than I already did. But I kept doing it! I kept trying to *force* myself out of my comfort zone, because I thought my comfort zone was the problem.

I also just didn't have many straight men in my social circles. I went to an all girls' school and then majored in musical theater and then babysat and sat in my room worrying about whether my meals were low-carb enough. So, for me, it was an *access problem*. And my personality type is "I am emotionally incapable of flirting with strangers at the grocery store."

I lived in New York City for ten years, and one thing I have learned is that even when you live in New York, life is not like *Sex and the City*. I went out to dinner all the time with my friends. I went to bars all the time. *Nothing.* I even ran into Aiden (John Corbett) one time in Central Park while I was babysitting, and all he did was assure me that I didn't need to be afraid of the raccoon who was walking around the playground where I was taking little Caroline. Anyway, yeah. Life is not like *Sex and the City*.

Who *did* I like? Oh . . . you know: people who didn't like

me back, baristas who are just flirting with you because it's their job, or people in college who I *thought* liked me but ended up dating my friend Jeff instead, or people I met through improv who usually were hiding a serious girlfriend or fiancée.

In my twenties, the world was also changing, and online dating was starting to replace in-person pickups in bars . . . so, the logical solution was to join the world and turn to online dating too. So, I did. And I . . . *hate it*. I don't know if I can articulate fully *how much* I hate it. But everything about online dating is draining. All of it. The swiping drains me. The messaging strangers drains me. The meeting up with strangers drains me. I can't *believe* how draining it is, and I can't believe that some people think it's . . . fun?!? My little sister thinks it's fun. And I can't even wrap my head around it.

I've spent a long time trying to figure out what's *different* about the way I interact with dating. What. Is. WRONG with me?! Why do some people enjoy it so much, and I feel nauseous having a vapid small talk chat with some rando on Hinge? Why are people hopping from boyfriend to boyfriend, and I'm just sitting here squinting my eyes trying to understand how I'm supposed to be interested in dating a stranger?

To me, online dating feels backward. I'm on a date with you, but I don't . . . know you. Therefore, I don't like you. Yet? But now there is this pressure that we need to figure out if we like each other quickly, because we are on this date. Am I supposed to fall for you like . . . right *now?* Like on this first date? Or on the second date? *Should I already be liking you? Or . . . do I have time?* How much of a chance are you supposed to give someone? Even now that I don't force myself to give three date chances, I still feel like . . . WHEN AM I ALLOWED TO GO HOME?

I've been craving some kind of revelation. Some kind of explanation for *why*. And *what to do about it*. I've even tried to coax out any buried lesbianness or bisexuality in order to discover my *true self* and finally feel *relief* that I'd figured out the problem. But that isn't actually my solution. My true self is straight. I just require a sort of casual social group situation love incubator that I don't have any access to. Look: *I JUST need to get to know you slowly, and then have you not act too overtly like you like me, even though you really do, and then I SEE how much you care in small subtle ways, and then I'll fall in love with you, and THEN we can go on a date.* ALL I NEED is a simple rom-com setup and seven months to let our love slowly grow before our first date! And so, I am single. Some call this *demi*-sexual. I call it: rom-com-sexual. Or: I work from home and it is what it is.

Those few times I was actually in more normal co-ed social situations, where I got to know people slowly and casually, I actually met guys, *liked* them, and dated them in a fun, low-stakes way. *WOA! Is this what normal people get to do all the TIME?!* Those experiences were always nice and heartening. *OK, it's all just circumstantial. Right? RIGHT?! So how do I manipulate my circumstances?*

I also have to grapple with the fact that there *are* a lot of really nice guys who have liked me a lot. And honestly, not *all* of the improv comedians I met were sneaky cheating assholes. Some were actually great, and they really liked me. I just . . .

didn't like them back. And I don't know what I could have done about it, except beat myself up over it. So, I beat myself up over it. *What is wrong with me?*

I don't know if *anything is* wrong with me. All I knew back *then*, in 2016, on the precipice of my two years of rest, was that I was tired. So, instead of going back into my normal nervousness that I should start online dating again, I realized: *this isn't right.* The kind of energy that this has taken up in my subconscious . . . isn't right. This can't be healthy. And now that I was in decluttering mode, and I'd decided to declutter the things that exhausted me, it became immediately clear that one of the biggest things that exhausted me, besides constantly forcing myself to be an actor, was constantly forcing myself to date. And to *seek out* dates. And to go on dates with people I didn't want to go out with. And feeling guilty and antsy if I wasn't. And judging myself for being single. So, I had to declutter it. I had to declutter dating.

I was twenty-eight, and that meant that at the end of my two years, I'd be thirty. And our culture is weird about women turning thirty. Everywhere you look, our culture is whispering, *You're getting olderrrrrrrr.* And lots of people subconsciously measure their lives against other people's. "Am I far enough along?" "Am I on track?" "Am I being impressive enough to start getting wrinkles?" "Is it safe to age?" It's a legitimate fear, considering how much women are valued for their youth. In fact, I just popped onto Twitter to procrastinate writing this paragraph, and the first thing I saw was that Emma Watson (Hermione Granger, beautiful, rich, movie star, model, and UN ambassador) told *Vogue* she realized she felt "stressed and anxious" to be nearing thirty and not be married and have a baby. Because, beyond all her accomplishments, that's what women are told makes them admirable and on track.

Hey, if Emma Watson can't help but feel stressed and anxious over this cultural marker of success, I can't help it either. But instead of rushing to accomplish more, or quickly going on thirty first dates, I was going to try to combat the cultural panic of nearing thirty with the exact opposite energy. To combat my lifelong guilt that I was supposed to be in love, I was *giving up*. I was quitting all pressure to seek out dating for at least two years, if not more. So, that meant that I would spend my last two years before turning thirty purposely *not* dating. I mean, I wasn't going to turn *down* someone great if they *happened* to come my way, but I was going to quit the madness, stop the worry and guilt, and chill the fuck out. And I didn't need to be *any further along* when my official rest ended at thirty. I didn't have to go on *one* date, or ever go out. I was going to rest. I was going to lie down. I was going to find a pool and float in it.

(Oh, do you think I'm going to tell you that, paradox of paradoxes, I quit dating and four months later, I met my husband? Well, I didn't.)

HOW TO BE ADDICTED
TO BUSYNESS

A lot of us are addicted to busyness. And I honestly didn't know "busyness" was a real word, but my computer is not autocorrecting it, so I guess it *is* a real word. We have an *addiction to being busy*. Not all of us, but a lot of us.

We use busyness as a wonderful, horrible distraction from life, and pain, and emotions, and things we don't want to face. It's a distraction from learning to be with ourselves. And it's sneaky, because it is a very socially acceptable addiction. We wear it as a badge of honor. *I am soooo busy. I have soooooo much to do.* It is a close relative of workaholism, another socially acceptable addiction. Another close cousin is perfectionism and addiction to "control." They're *behavioral* addictions, meaning the "high" is coming from the behavior, as opposed to a substance.

Our problem with busyness and productivity is twofold: First, it's a distraction from deeper things. And second, we've *learned* it's a responsible and noble distraction. So, we think it's inherently healthy, even when it isn't. Which may lead to it going unexamined for a very long time.

Busyness, workaholism, and perfectionism are also not-so-distant relatives of eating disorders, disordered eating, and weight obsession through micromanaging food and engaging in compulsive exercise. And I want to remind you that binge eating, emotional eating, and compulsive eating are all directly *exacerbated* by dieting, as well as rules and guilt around food. Which means that a lot of what we think of as being "out of control around food" is actually being perpetuated by attempts at weight control and food perfectionism in the first place. When we think of "coping mechanisms," we often think about compulsive eating, but we don't usually think about how our relationship with productivity, busyness, working, dieting, control, and perfectionism *affects* our relationship with food (and lots of other things too).

So *why* are we addicted to busyness? It's the same reason we are addicted to any behavior. It's a distraction. It's a distraction from emotions. It's a distraction from unresolved trauma. It's a distraction from feeling lost or discontent. And it's also something we have been conditioned to believe is responsible and important. And if you are constantly being impressive and responsible with your busyness, there isn't any *time* for reflection, there's just constant activity, sleep (if you can), then rinse and repeat.

It's also one of our newer cult mentalities. Derek Thompson's article "Workism Is Making Americans Miserable" asserts that for the college-educated elite, working has turned into "a kind of religion, promising identity, transcendence, and community." And even though traditional religious faith has declined, still: "everybody worships something," be it food purity and exercise or working yourself to exhaustion. The problem with this setup is that it's leading to *mass* anxiety and burnout.

There is nothing inherently *wrong* with being busy—it's a normal part of life. Life gets busy. Not to mention that productivity *can* be really joyful for people, especially if they're doing things they love, or just . . . doing things that need to be done. Being busy is morally neutral. And life getting busy is totally normal. It's just that, unchecked, it can run away with us. Unchecked, maybe we start to forget that busyness requires recharging in order to be sustainable.

Being productive can be really good for our mental health, but the issue comes once it becomes a compulsion. It's the same thing with exercise. Exercise is *great* for our physical and mental health, but not when it's a compulsion that begins to rule our lives. So, the question is . . . are you *using* busyness as a way to distract yourself from things that need attention? If someone took your busyness away, what would happen? If the answer is that you would be casually bummed—that's a good sign. *Hey, why did you take away all the things I love to do?* But if we are *terrified* of slowing down, it's probably *not* because we have a "passion for busyness," it's more likely because we are using busyness as a badge of honor, or a distraction, or we're avoiding something deeper.

We all have different *paces* we feel comfortable with, too. Some people *need* a slower pace. Some people *thrive* with a faster pace. Yes, there can still be avoidance going on for the inherently fast-paced people, but some people just *love doing things*. Not everyone wants to live a quiet, slow-paced life. Neither is wrong.

The thing to examine is . . . are we using busyness as a method for avoidance? Lots of us are.

The other problem is what we *associate* with busyness, and what we associate with rest. We associate busyness and constant productivity with being responsible and morally *good*. We associate rest with laziness and being morally *bad*. We think rest can't *do anything for us*. It's a sign of weakness. It's a sign we are irresponsible. Because that's what our productivity culture cult taught us.

So, this comes back to the same thing again: what have we *learned*? What have we *learned* that we are operating under, and what is it really doing for us? Because *really*, rest and downtime and stillness are healing. Living in a constant state of stress and adrenaline and activity usually ends up, best-case scenario: burning people out. Worst-case scenario: making us sick. Or coexisting with other addictions that help us to avoid whatever we're trying to avoid. Many people who are addicted to busyness may also be addicted to other behaviors or substances to do the same thing: *distract and avoid*.

And . . . what *are* we avoiding? Do we even know? Some of us might. Or we might have an idea. Maybe processing grief. Maybe processing known trauma. Maybe facing insecurity or emotions we were taught weren't safe to feel. Or maybe . . . we don't know at all. Maybe we have so successfully avoided it that we have absolutely no idea. Maybe we need to find a therapist to help us start to figure it out. And maybe we need more downtime to see what starts to reveal itself.

I can't believe I keep putting myself in a position where I'm telling everyone to deal with all these really hard things. *Deal with your crippling self-hatred and learn to eat more, you hungry fool! Learn to deal with your childhood trauma and stop numbing yourself with overexercise and bringing home work.* I don't know how I found myself in this position. I'd rather just tell you weird stories. And I just want to be able to tell you that you are allowed to *relax*, but the truth is, the reason we aren't letting ourselves relax is that we don't think we are allowed to, *or* because we are running from something. And it's not easy. But someone has to say it. And I guess, *ugh*, today, that someone is me.

So let me say it all again: you *are* allowed to relax. You are allowed to rest. Downtime is good for your brain. It's good for your body. It's good for your nervous system. Even if it *wasn't* good for you, you'd still be allowed to do it, because your *worth* is not dependent on your productivity or responsibility.

If you start to take some downtime and feel impending terror, there are probably some underlying things to deal with and heal from. And it might take time, effort, and lots and lots of support. But you can do it. I know you can.

HOW TO SORT OF DO A BAD JOB AT RESTING

The reason I was doing this whole *purposeful* rest experiment was, I knew I *was not good at rest!* I was not good at letting myself off the hook and letting myself relax. I needed *to practice rest.* And I was going to mess up, and then I'd need to practice some more. That's why I decided I needed two years, because I figured it would take time to actually figure it out and untangle the practical and emotional mess I was in.

Why two years? Why not one? Why not five? I didn't really know. I just knew I needed a significant buffer period, and two years sounded like a long enough period of time to *truly* be radical and give me time to work out the kinks. One year didn't feel long enough, and *longer* than two felt like more of a commitment than I was able to emotionally make. I didn't *know.* I was flying by the seat of my pants. I also knew that the details didn't *really* matter. I just needed a change, and I needed time to let the change sink in. I needed rest as a state of mind, and I needed it for a while.

I also thought it sounded funny. "I am on two years of rest."

Like a more absurd version of taking a sabbatical. It made me laugh . . . but it was also true.

What were those two years going to *look like*? I wasn't really sure, actually. I only knew *why* I needed a change. I didn't know what it would be like, exactly. It's not like I was going to live at a monastery or an ashram. I was still going to be living in the real world, in a major city. I was just going to be like . . . a *casual* monk in the real world. A casual, female monk, with a bob haircut and bangs that I kept cutting too short. *Why don't I learn! Don't cut them that short!* I was *still* going to be working and running The F*ck It Diet and trying to write a book. I just needed way less on my plate. I needed to practice rest. My main goal was to become *super* aware every time I got stressed, and then examine *why* I was stressed. And, spoiler alert: it was *always* about stupid, arbitrary, learned cultural shit. And I wanted to *stop that*.

The good news is, I felt a very marked relief once I decluttered "I should be going to auditions every morning" off my life to-do list. And "I need to become a successful actress" off my plate. I also felt so free once I got "spend your free time on dating apps and going on first dates with strangers so you can fall in love before *it's too late*" off my life plate. I decluttered my own arbitrary pressures, and it felt . . . amazing. I had a sense of calm that I had never, ever felt before. *Wow . . . I can wake up and not dread my life??* The relief I felt was proof enough that it was the right move, at least at this phase. I was able to work from home or from cafes. I wrote. I felt calm. I felt happy. The constant dread, the guilt, the resistance to my daily life—*it was gone*. Like a puff of smoke. *Is this what life could have been if I hadn't forced myself to audition all the time?*

I don't *know* if it's what life could have been. Honestly, probably not. Because if we don't try things out, we don't learn. I think it's ridiculous to expect ourselves to avoid the learning curve, or to avoid hard times or life-path mistakes. They're not even *really* mistakes, when you zoom out and look at the big picture. Would I have had the same *understanding* of cultural expectations if I hadn't been so ruled by them for so long? No! Would I have felt relief crossing those big life goals off my to-do list if I hadn't *tried?* Would I ever have been OK moving away from acting if I hadn't given it a real go? No. I wouldn't have. Not to mention, *would I ever have written my first book* and had the view I have on diets and diet culture, and the life and career I have now, if *not* for my decade-long diet self-torture? *No.*

The hard times can lead to perspective. They can lead to growth. They are often very important parts of the journey. The *other* important part of the journey is taking stock every now and again: *Is this working for me anymore? Is this still what I want? Can I tweak my approach and get some relief, or do I need to change course completely?* There is no way to know what to do, or what you need, until you . . . do *something*. It's not wasted time, it's learning.

Again . . . you don't have to quit your life to heal your burnout. We have to focus on what we *do* have control over: our *mentality* around rest. We need to declutter our guilt and unexamined *shoulds*.

I'd been allowing guilt to inform too many of my choices and to affect too much of how I felt. I had to spend time figuring out *where* was I exhausting myself with guilt and internal pressure. I was trying to let myself off the hook, in every way, in order to better identify where I *wasn't* letting myself off the hook. I needed to figure out how much of my anxiety and exhaustion was being perpetuated by my *own* beliefs and my own choices, and if there was anything I could do about it.

For example, if someone invited me to something, and I didn't want to go (for *whateverrrr* reason!), how much *guilt* do I feel for not going? How much stress do I feel by not participating in life the way people expect me to? Can I just allow myself to do my thing, without being an asshole to myself?

And what if it was a work opportunity? How comfortable was I turning down work opportunities to protect my desire for a slower work life? Would I automatically say yes? Would I say no and feel guilty? Did I think I needed an airtight "reason" or "excuse"??? How comfortable could I be *not* filling every waking moment with busyness? Or would I be comfortable just allowing myself to say . . . "thank you for the opportunity, but I'm not available"? How much resistance did I *have* to doing less? That was my question. I didn't know how easy it would be when things inevitably came up, so I had to see.

However, as soon as I moved to Philadelphia, a weird thing happened . . . I immediately got called in to audition for a few different musicals in Philly. I considered whether I actually *wanted* to audition for them. I was moving to Philly partially because life would be easier, slower, and cheaper, but I also knew that I was already a part of the theater community in

Philly and could potentially do some acting *sometimes? Maybe? Without* the grind of nonstop daily auditions in New York that I despised?

So, I auditioned, with the new, low stakes of basically having already quit acting. I didn't *need* the jobs. And I didn't even know if I wanted them. And so, of course, I booked all three of them. *Ughhhh. Where was this back when I wanted to do this?!?* All of a sudden, I had almost a *full* year of nonstop professional theater acting. *Wtf.* I already quit!

What I *really* wanted was to quit the desperate and exhausting *seeking*. I loved acting. I *hateddd* the grind of nonstop auditions. So, maybe this was ideal. I could just do these three shows I'd booked and let that be enough, without panicking about how I was going to keep up momentum and get *more* acting jobs, because that was the part I hated. I didn't need to get anywhere anymore. And that was a relief.

I also started looking at little houses, amazed that Philadelphia had real estate affordable enough to *maybe* buy, if I found something small. I assumed I would take at *least* a year before I was ready to seriously look. I wanted to just know what was out there. But, of course, I fell in love with the very first place I looked at that fell within my reasonable budget. *Fell in love.* So, I very quickly looked at about fifteen other comparable places, just to see: *Is this house really that great? Or are there plenty others out there just like it at a similar price point?* There were not plenty others. So . . . I bought it. I am sitting in it right now. It is very small, and my kitchen is the basement, but . . . love is love.

Within six months of me deciding to rest for two years, I was acting full-time *and* buying a house. I was also running

F*ck It Diet workshops and trying to finish writing *The F*ck It Diet* book. It was way more than I'd expected to be doing, especially during that first year of rest. But the reason why I said *yes* to those acting jobs and to buying that little house? Because . . . it mattered to me. I enjoyed it. They . . . "sparked joy," so they got to stay.

This is *also* why "rest as a state of mind" is all we can actually count on giving ourselves. Panicking that life got busy wasn't going to help anything . . . that's just more unnecessary stress on top of everything else. Yes, I was doing a lot, but I still knew that rest was my priority. I was saying *no* to lots and lots and LOTS of things. Things that stressed me out. Things that brought little joy. I had simplified in lots of ways. What I was *really* doing was saying no to the things that were depleting me and saying yes to the things that were exciting to me. And when I could: I rested.

HOW TO TAKE THINGS OFF YOUR (FIGURATIVE) PLATE

When I was able to reflect on those fifteen years of searching for a miracle cure, and dealing with health issues, and broken teeth, and incessant dieting and exercise, I was able to acknowledge how much *energy* that had taken up. How scary it was while it was happening. How desperate I felt. How *depleting* it had been. How incapable I was of living in the moment. I was able to understand a big piece of my exhaustion. Once I did that, I was able to be a lot nicer to myself about my exhaustion. No, I'm not "lazy," my exhaustion makes sense.

I made the decision to really *chill* on the only part I really had control over: the miracle cure quest. I needed to take "find miracle cure" off my plate, so to speak. I couldn't take my health issues off my plate (and believe me, I'd tried), but I *could* have awareness around the dynamics at play and declutter one piece of my exhaustion: *the feeling that I should be spending every moment figuring it out.* And that shift brought a lot of relief.

What other things are we forcing ourselves to do that we *do not need* to do? Where are the *shoulds* keeping us stuck doing things we don't need to do? What can you take off your plate? And I don't mean your dinner plate. Keep everything on your dinner plate. What can you take off your metaphorical *life* plate? How can you ease up on yourself? What would bring you *relief*, if you could just erase it from your life to-do list?

We have learned that we must be productive at all times. We feel nervous to relax. It feels *unsafe* to relax. This is partially a response to an unsafe world, to living without a safety net, and to an economic system where if you pause for just a moment, you worry you won't be able to pay rent. *But* this world has also led to *beliefs* about productivity that do not serve us: *I am never allowed to relax. It is never safe to relax. I am not doing life right.* Again, in an exhausting world, what good is it to perpetuate even more exhaustion on ourselves? Yes, life is scary and uncertain, but it *is* safe to relax and rest, even in an uncertain world. And we deserve it. (In fact, you could make the argument that it's less safe to never relax, because stress is a major determinant of health.)

What good is constantly feeling like you *should be doing something else*? Should you? Maybe. But maybe *not*. Maybe you should be taking that stupid arbitrary *thing* off your metaphorical plate. Maybe you should be taking the rest you can.

The good thing is that you get to decide what is depleting you. Some people feel pressure and overwhelm at the expectation to learn a new skill, like making a sourdough starter (yes, I'm writing this during the 2020 quarantine). And some people absolutely *love cooking and baking*. Some people are *thrilled* when they can find the time and opportunity to bake, and cook, and learn how to make new recipes, and to ferment their own sourdough starter. *To them*, it is rejuvenating. Learning to do something old-timey and impressive brings *joy*. To me? It's a burden. I'd rather go for a walk. I just want to get by and spend the least amount of time in the kitchen as possible, while still eating well-ish. We all crave something different. That's why we have to decide for *ourselves* what we need a break from.

Sometimes rest looks like taking time *to* exercise. Sometimes rest looks like taking time *off* exercise. It's about what *you* are burnt out from. The great thing is . . . there is nothing that needs to be decided on and stuck to. What you need is also allowed to change with time. It's allowed to change day by day and year by year. And it *will* change.

What *kind* of rest do you need? What kind of exhaustion do you have? Physical? Have you been *physically* doing too much? Overpacked schedule? Not sleeping enough? Overexercising? Having you been high on busyness? You may need to cross things off your to-do list and purposely seek out quiet time and nothingness.

Career exhaustion? Do you need better boundaries with yourself or your email inbox or your coworkers? Do you need more downtime? More time to socialize? More time to prioritize personal relationships? Do you need to look for a new job or company that's more aligned with your needs?

Social exhaustion? Have you been *over*socializing? Are you an introvert who needs to let yourself have more time to recharge?

Dating exhaustion? Have you been burning yourself out

with toxic relationships? Or just . . . too much dating? Do you need *a break for fuck's sake*? Or do you want to finally *prioritize* dating? I don't know what you need!

Parenting exhaustion? Do you need to let yourself off the hook with the expectations of parenting? With comparing your parenting to the way other people are parenting? Do you need to ask for help and childcare so you can have self-care time?

Distraction exhaustion? Have you been distracting yourself from emotions or trauma or self-reflection through busyness? Have you been filling your time up so you don't have to *deal*? That works for a little bit, but it will always end up being extremely depleting. In this case, rest might look something like therapy and taking time to learn how to be with discomfort and emotions.

Diet culture exhaustion? Have you been dieting and hating your body for years? Have you been forcing yourself to do exercise you don't love out of fear of gaining weight? Have you become afraid of different foods? Do you waste a lot of time overthinking the food you put in your mouth?

General cultural exhaustion? Have you been putting arbitrary pressure on yourself? Have you been putting pressure on yourself to live up to some cultural ideal that has ended up depleting you? Are you thinking you should be married? Have kids? Be richer? Be thinner? Be . . . *different? Be better? Be more impressive?* In this case, our stressful cultural beliefs about what we are "supposed" to be doing are what need to be decluttered and taken off our plates.

There is no right way to rest. There is no one-size-fits-all rest. There is no one thing that you should or shouldn't do. The question is: are you burnt out? Yes? OK, *why* are you burnt out? Once you identify that, are there any little things you can do about it? Is there any little thing you can let *go* of? Even just pressure?

HOW TO HAVE
BOUNDARIES

If rest had been forced on me—*quarantine 2020 style*—back when I was really tired and *craved* the world coming to a halt, it wouldn't have had the same impact. The *choosing* of it was such an essential part. It was about learning to give it to *yourself* in a world that doesn't give it to you. Forced rest, of any kind, is just another kind of mentally exhausting tribulation.

I had to choose rest. And keep choosing it. And when the world wanted to tear me from my rest by giving me the acting jobs I'd always wished for before, I needed to remember to choose it *again*, and create better boundaries during my off-time. Most importantly, I had to work through my *resistance* to relaxation and doing less.

Again, with rest as a state of mind, rest is not necessarily about how much you do. I did a *lot* during my two years of rest. I didn't lock myself away in a tower and keep my eye mask on all day. I was still working. I just gave myself permission *not* to do everything. And once I gave myself that permission,

I ended up being able to gravitate toward things that really interested me, really mattered to me, and didn't deplete me so much.

I did those three acting jobs that first year. And every moment that I wasn't working, I was trying to do as little as possible. *This is my period of rest.* Doing those three shows was more than I'd intended to take on, but they were also wonderful. I made lifelong friends in one of them. I originated a role in another one. And I won a Barrymore Award (a Philadelphia theater award) for the third one. It was joyful. It was fun. But it was exhausting, and during the following summer, when those shows were over, I *reassessed*: Do I want to keep this up? The answer was: no, not now. Now it's time for even *more* rest.

The second year of my rest, *all I did* was focus on finishing *The F*ck It Diet* book, and running workshops for The F*ck It Diet. I taught intuition a lot during that year too. I had an intuition intensive *and* a free little workshop called "Intuition for Lazy People." I was teaching that intuition happens in the downtime. During *quiet* time. It was the perfect focus for me while I was seeking out and needing downtime. When things were quiet, and I took lots of time to lie down and rest, I *heard* my intuition. I felt it. It was *very* clear to me. And thankfully, what it was saying was: *yes, this rest is what I need.*

But the truth is, it's a lot easier to say *no* to social engagements when you are *actually* busy, like I was that first year. People understand it more. But when you're *purposely* not doing much, to combat the *past* years of physical and mental exhaustion . . . people don't understand. People *won't* understand everything you need to do for yourself. And that's OK. That's part of the adjustment. That's part of the questioning *why we are doing the things we are doing.* Am I doing things just because other people don't understand? Am I doing things so people approve of me and the life I'm living? Or am I making choices to take care of myself and where I am right now?

People were fascinated by my intentional rest, and I think it's because most people feel like . . . *I want that! I need that too!* But lots were also confused and judgmental. I understand that, to a lot of people, the idea that I was burnt out was ridiculous. "*Why* are you so tired? What do you even *do*? You don't have any kids! You don't even have to go to a 9 to 5?! What was so exhausting to you? Were you deployed in combat or something?"

Based on our cultural understanding of how much we are expected to be able to handle with no consequence, my exhaustion didn't make any sense. "What's your job? You write, like, a blog, right?" But I knew why. And I tried to explain to some people, but expecting people to understand the subtle toll that *never thinking I was allowed to relax and spending the past fifteen years performing and hating my face and body and also thinking that dieting and plastic surgery were going to fix everything and trying to force myself to constantly fall in love with people* took on me . . . it just wasn't straightforward or easily explainable.

We also have such a poor cultural understanding of burnout, both how it manifests *and* how common it is. You don't need to work eighty hours a week to get burnt out. You can get burnt out from a standard forty-hour workweek, *and* you don't even *have* to be "overworking" to get burnt out. Even just monotonous and mundane work can lead to burnout. Burnout often manifests with anxiety and depression symptoms, including: fatigue, lack of purpose, detachment, a cynical outlook, and emotional numbness. Not to mention physical symptoms like headaches, trouble sleeping, and lowered immunity. But because we don't tend to understand the way burnout manifests, and how common it is, it all usually flies under the radar. We rarely think burnout is the culprit, and so we just keep grinding.

Based on our current understanding of burnout, my exhaustion sounded laughable. *Okayyyyy, princess, go lie down.* And at a certain point, it was easier to realize that people *weren't* going to get it, and just . . . make sure I found a way to have boundaries to protect my rest.

As nice as the flexibility of working from home is, when you work from home or have your own online business . . . the boundaries between work and life get very blurred. So, even though it *seemed* like I was able to do whatever I wanted, and "barely working," at the same time, I was *always* working. I always *could* be working. And therefore, maybe I always should be working?

I would have to troubleshoot tech problems with workshop signups on family vacations, during my cousin's wedding, during the holidays, and on weekends and late at night. I had a lot of flexibility, but I was also *always* working. I was *always* responding to emails, always worrying about tech glitches, and I was a one-woman band. I didn't have a team of troubleshooters and marketing geniuses helping all of it run smoothly. I wasn't making that kind of money, it was *just me* teaching myself how to use different platforms and answering alllll customer service questions, and hopping on the computer at 11:45 p.m. to fix problems.

Plainly, I had serious work boundary problems. One of the things I really needed to do to support my own rest was to hire a virtual assistant to respond to and filter business emails for me, and to help me troubleshoot back-end problems that popped up. So, if someone emailed me saying, "Help! I didn't get a confirmation email," I could forward it to her and have her take over during business hours, as opposed to getting out my computer and logging on and spending a half hour or more figuring out what the problem was while I was supposed to be having dinner.

I needed a virtual assistant. It was time. I'd done enough panicking over tiny things that I could afford someone else to troubleshoot. And it is affordable, because they are part-time, working hourly, and they have many other clients they do the same things for. In fact, if I'd known how affordable getting part-time online help was, I would have done it sooner. This was a rest necessity. At least I knew I didn't have to be the one to fix everything. Also, the emails I got (ones begging for help, ones telling me how stupid I am, ones raving about TFID, and all across the spectrum) would be going to her, not me. So, I could *choose* to look at them, but they weren't constantly flooding my personal inbox. That was a boundary I needed.

Another thing I adopted, that I still do to this day, was something I like to call "nighttime nothings"—a few hours every night before bed when I don't have to do *anything* except sit on my couch and enjoy my life. A time when I purposely *do not work*. I do not check email. I watch TV. I text my friends. I eat dinner and snacks. And they are some of the best hours of the day.

In the beginning of my online business journey a few years before, I worked at night *a lot*. I also took every single opportunity. I tried everything. I said yes, and panicked later. I said yes and figured it out later. I read every email. I responded to every email. I worked with people one on one. I was on everyone and anyone's podcast. I did everything I could. But now, as my online platform was growing, so were the work and collaboration opportunities. *More* people were asking me to collaborate. To speak. To coach people one on one. And I . . . didn't want to. I was burnt out, but *now* I was deliberately resting. I had to be OK turning down job opportunities, and trusting that this wasn't my *only* chance. The same reason you should turn down a date with someone you are not interested in just because of a low-grade sense of panic and desperation. *This is not your only chance. There are more chances.* Desperation leads to more exhaustion. I wanted to *trust* that even if I rested and did way less for two years, life would still be waiting for me if and when I was ready to say yes.

One of the other *not* so great things that reminded me that I *needed* rest was that I really didn't feel great. I was *really* tired. Really tired. I got horrible headaches all the time. I got low-grade fevers all the time. I *couldn't* really do much more than I was doing. I couldn't take on too much. I needed to just do the bare minimum to get by and focus on rest. I was actually using *that* as a boundary with people when I needed to. *I don't feel well.* I'm resting.

Believe me, we shouldn't need to get burnt out and physically *ill* in order to justify our rest. That should *not* have had to be the case. We should be able to do less and *prevent* running ourselves down. But this was the reality I was dealing with.

HOW TO HEAL CHRONIC EXHAUSTION

I was the girl who explained why dieting is bad for you, but now I really wasn't feeling well. *Oh, no.* And I'd already tried to heal myself with diets. Over and over again. For years.

The F*ck It Diet is *not* a cure-all for health problems. And I've never claimed it is. I was always upfront about my health when I wrote about The F*ck It Diet. It really helped some things: more regular cycle, better sleep, better mental health, but not everything. Nothing is a cure-all. The F*ck It Diet is only meant to help you heal your *relationship* with food, which tends to be supportive to your overall health, long-term. But I still felt nervous to be writing about food and weight and health, and not *feeling* healthy. It was a weird situation to be in, and I worried that if I was fully *open* about how I was feeling those days that people would blame it on the fact that I was The F*ck It Diet girl.

Everyone assumes that The F*ck It Diet is a steady diet of nonstop McDonald's and doughnuts and soda and potato chips. But it really isn't. That might be what the very beginning looks like, but the whole freaking *point* is that once you refeed yourself, you can finally hear what your body is asking for.

Once I'd healed my relationship to food, I actually ate really . . . "well." I hesitate to say this, because I know it's triggering to people who are healing their relationship to food. The natural response is: *Wait, should I be eating the way she is eating?* (No! You shouldn't eat how I or anyone else eats! Just heal your relationship to food!)

But, at this point in my journey, *years in*, I ate the way I always *hoped* I could eat as an intuitive eater. I loved both "healthy" food and cake. I loved salads and grilled cheese. I loved cappuccinos and kombucha and fish and bread and veggies and pasta. I ate well. I ate freely. It felt very unlikely that my health ailments were coming from the *quality* of the food I was eating. But just in case I was missing something, and out of fear of being screwed over by my own bias against diets, I went half a year eating gluten-free to see if it helped. It didn't. It didn't help a thing. So, I welcomed gluten back with open arms. *Come back to me, you sticky little wheat protein!*

I know some people really do find that certain foods contribute to flare-ups in their chronic health issues. That comes with its own struggles, especially if you have a history of disordered eating. But my situation seemed to be the opposite. No matter *what* I ate, I felt the same: *tired*.

So, my question was . . . What the *fuck* was going on with me *physically*? And *what* is causing what? Am I having weird health problems *because* I'm run down and exhausted? Or am I exhausted *because* of health problems? Or both? Or neither??? What's coming first, the chicken or the exhaustion?

One thing I knew for sure was that I couldn't count on figuring this out. I'd already spent a decade desperately seeking a cure, and what had that gotten me? It's not that I didn't care about my health. I did. I *really* did. It's not that I didn't *want* to figure out what was going on. I did. But I'd already run myself into the ground trying to heal in a million different ways. I had to approach this in a different way.

I had to be OK *not* figuring it out . . . ever. Maybe I'm just a mildly sick person? Maybe it's a temporary period? Or maybe it will be like this forever. And maybe I just have to accept it. I didn't *like* that, but . . . the only silver lining was that it gave me an excuse to rest. *Leave me alone, I'm apparently vaguely chronically ill. Oh, what's wrong with me? No clue. But I'll see you next year!*

I had to take off all pressure to "figure it out." That was *part* of the two-year incubation period. I didn't have to figure ANYTHING OUT. I WAS ALLOWED TO JUST EXIST. However, I felt pretty horrible. Fevers. Headaches. Liver pain. Exhaustion.

So, I turned to my old elusive friend, Mister *God*. Ugh, wait. He isn't even a man. I turned to *Doctor* God.

Hi God, remember me? Thank you for this weird life you've given me. What the *bleep* is going on with my health? And while you're leading me to my healing, do you want to spontaneously and miraculously heal my huge pores while you're at it? If not, maybe just point me in the right direction? Actually, sorry. I should stay on track: Please *just help me with my exhaustion and headaches and liver. What am I supposed to do? And* then, *if the skin is connected . . . great. If not, just . . . forget it, I guess.*

I forget about God/the Universe all the time. Sometimes for months or years at a time. Then, when I'm really confused and suffering, I remember. *Whoops. Hi God. Sorry sorry, here I am.*

I waited a few days, and eventually God emailed me back in my brain: *You need to go to the doctor.* Ahhhhh, that makes senssssse. Can't believe I didn't think of that. Good idea, God.

So, after my decade-long aversion to doctors and their drugs and their diets, I started going to doctors again. I ended up going to a *lot* of doctors. (And barely any of them were covered by my "bronze" insurance.) I went to mainstream doctors. I went to naturopathic doctors. I went to many, many expensive doctors, and told myself it was worth it if I could rule some things out. I went to them all. I told them I had headaches, exhaustion, lots of low-grade fevers, and this new liver pain.

Going to doctors for vague and unclear issues is . . . not fun. And it's not restful. And I'd already been *very* disheartened from years of unhelpful advice and treatments that led to a decade of madness and obsession with food and weight and health. Of *course*, with this issue, most doctors had no idea what was going on. One doctor listened to my symptoms and tested me for HIV. Thankfully, negative. Another naturopathic doctor tested me and said I had high mercury levels, and I had to take, like, clay and algae to bind to the metals. My mom had tested high for mercury a few years before, and because of that she had her mercury fillings removed. Mercury toxicity can also be passed on in utero, so . . . *okayyyy.*

Learning it was *mayyybe* mercury toxicity is not a relieving diagnosis. Mercury is extremely toxic, and really hard to heal from. It can cause horrible neurological symptoms, serious mental health issues, tremors, memory loss . . . it can cross your blood-brain barrier and make you go . . . actually insane (it's where the term "mad as a hatter" came from, because hat makers used to use mercury in the hat-making process). And it can kill you! *Great.* Doing great.

I started taking all kinds of binding agents that are supposed to pull it from your tissues and bind to heavy metals, and I did it for over a year. I don't know how to say whether it made any real headway on this, or if this *was* an underlying cause or just a piece of the puzzle, but chelating mercury is no joke. I sort of *lightly* tried it for a while, and got even *worse* headaches while I was doing this.

The fact that I was able to go to all these doctors and never have them tell me that I was probably tired because I needed to *lose weight* or *change my eating* was a glaring sign of thin privilege. If I had a naturally bigger body, I would have had a very different, and way more stressful, experience. (And, spoiler alert, it wasn't anything to do with weight or food!)

Also, the doctors I went to were not cheap. So, this is a literal financial *barrier* to healing. If I had had these problems but couldn't afford the visit? I'd either have gone into debt over it, or just not gone. And . . . the stress of being in debt? Affects your health. This is often a *cycle.* The cycle of poverty and stress and illness.

Eventually I went to *another* doctor, who a friend recommended to me. He is an MD, but also an acupuncturist and does integrative medicine as well. He told me that my exhaustion and liver pain were primarily from chronic Epstein-Barr. Epstein-Barr is *mono. UGH, MONO, stop ruining my life!* Yeah,

I'd had mono, and then I had basically been tired ever since. There are also some who say that chronic Epstein-Barr is at the *root* of some people's chronic fatigue syndrome. And—*it can also cause liver inflammation.*

I was bracing myself, because I expected him to tell me to go on some celery juice cleanse like the Medical Medium does, but he didn't. He gave me parasite drugs, because I also had parasites (*ew*). And for the Epstein-Barr? I honestly don't even understand what he gave me. It was some kind of low-dose immunotherapy, just drops to take. And very quickly, most of my headaches went away, my *extreme* exhaustion went away, and my liver pain was *mostly* gone.

Just like that, near the *end* of my two years of rest, a piece of my physical exhaustion was so much better. I sometimes have exhaustion flare-ups, but for the *most* part, it's a lot better. Eventually, at a follow-up appointment, I said, *OK, miracle worker, can you cure my fucking skin and hormones?!?!* Well, I didn't say that. I said, "So, my cycle is sometimes normal, and sometimes very irregular, and I just get spotting. *Why?*"

And he said, "Eh, you just have low progesterone. It's just the way you are, and it's not that big of a deal, especially if you're not trying to get pregnant right now, and it's not causing too much discomfort. If it's ever low for a few months at a time, we can always give you progesterone to bring on a period. But I'd prefer not to put you on the pill because it tends to make things worse long-term."

This was the first time *ever* that someone, let alone a doctor, communicated to me: *This is just the way you are, you can just . . . let it be. You don't have to rabidly search for the cure. You're not that broken and it's not that bad.* It was . . . a bizarre and relieving prospect. I can just . . . chill? And not go madly searching for a cure?

Now . . . on the flip side, I don't know that I 100 percent *agree* with him. You could look at it like, this is a convenient male perspective. *Eh, period problems! Whatever!* And the truth is, low progesterone sucks. Progesterone is a *calming* hormone. It helps you sleep. Besides irregular cycles, low progesterone is associated with: headaches, anxiety and depression, insomnia, and other symptoms of estrogen dominance. *And* the catch-22 with progesterone is that stress can *cause* low progesterone, and low progesterone can cause *stress.* Like so many things: *ugh.*

Yeah, it's at least partially genetic, but I know for a fact that *stress* is a direct correlation to when my cycle gets less regular. I'm still curious about it, and I'm still open to trying things to support my body where it needs support.

But *just the idea* that I could relax and let it be was revolutionary.

HOW TO LIVE

Decluttering changed my life. I know that sounds absurd, but it's true. The *spirit* of decluttering changed my life. I didn't stop at decluttering *things*. I started decluttering jobs, and aspects of my business I didn't really want to keep doing. I started decluttering the toxic expectations about what I was supposed to be doing or who I was supposed to be. And I unintentionally even decluttered some friends who, when I took a step back to think about it, were not actually good friends anymore. Hey, some friends are meant to be with you for a whole lifetime, and some people are just supposed to be in your life for a time.

I tidied up my stuff, my stupid clothes, my jobs, my beliefs, and my social life. And guess what! I had more space to think! I had more time to relax! It created a vacuum in my life where new things, new jobs, new beliefs, new friends, and new ideas could come in. There was more time to sleep, to write, to create, to laugh, and to figure out what I wanted to be doing with my time.

I constantly asked the question: "Is this serving me anymore? Do I even *like* this thing I have? Or this thing I do?" And when the answer is no, then the next question after "Oh, shit," is: "What am I going to do about it?"

Until a few years ago, I spent all my energy trying to get somewhere. To heal. To improve. To impress. So, I turned my entire life goal on its head. Before it was: *push yourself as hard as you can until you succeed succeed succeed and impress impress impress*. But rest was all about stopping the grind. It was about letting go of my previous goals and markers of success and happiness. It was about pivoting to a life (and a job, luckily) that was more enriching and replenishing and sustainable. It was about redefining what happiness looked like to me. And it . . . worked. It really did.

But happiness isn't static. Nothing is. You never arrive. There are always new things to be stressed about. There are always new things to overwhelm you and exhaust you. I don't say that to be pessimistic, it's just *true*. Great things can happen. Great things happen all the time. Life, even in all its cruelty, can be amazing. But no matter how great your life is, those great things will also happen alongside horrible, stressful, heartbreaking things. Life never promises ease, which is why you should take ease when you can. Rest when you can. And enjoy what you can, when you can.

The great thing is, once I let myself have a very significant period of rest, I started wanting to do things again. Fancy. *That*. I'm not as tired anymore, but I still *love* to rest, and I still prioritize it whenever I can.

Just like the beginning of The F*ck It Diet, the *intensity* of my "rest" was a phase. It didn't need to be some obsessive thing that I thought about nonstop for the rest of my life. I let it do its thing. I let it bring the healing it was meant to bring. And eventually I didn't need to think about it so much anymore.

Of course, as soon as I was *finally* ready to have a soft opening of my life, go to more restaurants and see more friends: the pandemic hit. *Ha.* You make plans, and God laughs and then doesn't email you back. It's just the way it is. So, I guess . . . life is about making the best of the situation you have. And then crying for a few days straight because of masks in a heat wave.

It was *essential* to allow my body time to heal and rejuvenate after years of adrenaline and guilt. But now, it's time to live. Well, when the world opens up again.

Until then, I'm resting. Wanna join?

ACKNOWLEDGMENTS

My mom is a big presence in this book, and I want to thank her for everything. Everything she did for me. Everything she worried about. All the time spent trying to help me. (The only thing I cannot forgive is the little-bangs incident.) Everything else: thank you.

My mom does not love being written about. But in order to write about what I went through, she had to be in it. We went through a lot. She will sometimes say to me, "Caroline, that was the craziest and most stressful time . . . those years when you were in high school." And they were. It was a lot for a (potentially) lead-poisoned mother and daughter to go through.

Mom, as weird and hard and stressful as it all was, even if there are things we would do differently, it is crystal clear how much you cared about me and my well-being, physically and mentally. And I am very, very lucky, and very thankful.

I want to thank my dad for always being supportive and generous, and for making me white-bread French toast when I was sick of Ezekiel toast as a kid. And for continually telling me that his friend told him that my second book should be called "F*ck You, Too/2."

(My parents do not *like* or understand why my book titles

have to have the word *f*ck* in them, but they've bucked up and supported me anyway.)

I want to thank my siblings, Shane and Margaret, who barely made it into the book, but who are the best siblings I could ever ask for. Thank you for being fun and funny, wise, and kind.

I want to thank my agent, Susan. You are *the best*. I am so lucky to have you. And all that time spent trying to manifest an amazing "theater" agent really paid off. Turns out the world doesn't always give you what you want but what you need.

I want to thank my editor, Rebecca, who left my publisher right as I finished up the book to go back to medical school. This is now *two* people that I've worked with whom I've sent running away from the arts and straight to medical school. Thank you for helping make this book what it needed to be. You're going to be an awesome, thoughtful doctor.

I want to thank my best friend, Annie, for being my friend since 2002, for being so easy-breezy, for sticking with me even when I was little miss doom and gloom. Annie's chapter was way longer originally, but I had to cut it way down because the book was too long. If the chapter doesn't really make sense . . . that's why.

I have so many people in my life that I want to thank just for being supportive friends: Melanie, Matt D 1, Matt D 2, Susan, Desiree, Elisa, Casey, Katie, Sam, Neal, Lexy, Emma, Alexis, and more. I'm so lucky to have you as friends.

Lastly, I want to thank my dog for reminding me to (and demanding that I) get off my phone and off my computer and pet her.

NOTES

INTRODUCTION: HOW TO BE FILLED WITH DREAD

xvi all kinds of oppression *affect our health*, more than anything we eat: L. Bacon and L. Aphramor, *Body Respect* (Dallas: BenBella, 2014).

xvi As if "lose weight" isn't already proven to backfire: F. Grodstein et al., "Three-Year Follow-up of Participants in a Commercial Weight Loss Program: Can You Keep It Off?," *Archives of Internal Medicine* 156, 12 (1996): 1302–6; D. Neumark-Sztainer et al., "Why Does Dieting Predict Weight Gain in Adolescents? Findings from Project EAT-II: A 5-Year Longitudinal Study," *Journal of the American Dietetic Association* 107, no. 3 (2007): 448–55.

xvi lead to weight cycling: L. Bacon and L. Aphramor, "Weight Science: Evaluating the Evidence for a Paradigm Shift," *Nutrition Journal* 10, 9 (2011), https://doi.org/10.1186/1475-2891-10-9.

xvi which often exacerbates chronic health issues: K. Strohacker and B. McFarlin, "Influence of Obesity, Physical Inactivity, and Weight Cycling on Chronic Inflammation," *Frontiers in Bioscience* (2010): E2:98–104.

HOW TO BE CULT SUSCEPTIBLE

8 "faith in science can serve the same mentally-stabilizing function as religious beliefs": J. Holmes, "Be Careful, Your Love of Science Looks

a Lot Like Religion," *Quartz,* August 11, 2015, https://qz.com/476722/be-careful-your-love-of-science-looks-a-lot-like-religion/.

HOW TO BECOME OBSESSED WITH FOOD

25   girls who diet are twelve times more likely to binge: D. Neumark-Sztainer, *"I'm, Like, SO Fat!"* (New York: Guilford, 2005).

25   attempts to diet actually feel like nonstop semi-famines: L. M. Kalm and R. D. Semba, "They Starved So That Others Be Better Fed: Remembering Ancel Keys and the Minnesota Experiment," *Journal of Nutrition* 135 (2005): 1347–52.

HOW TO FOCUS ON THE WRONG CURE

32   90 to 95 percent of people regain the weight they lose, *no matter what*: J. E. Brody, "Panel Criticizes Weight-Loss Programs," *New York Times,* April 2, 1992, https://www.nytimes.com/1992/04/02/us/panel-criticizes-weight-loss-programs.html/.

32   it's just a question of how quickly they gain it back . . . 23 percent of people gain *more* weight than they lost: T. Mann et al., "Medicare's Search for Effective Obesity Treatments: Diets Are Not the Answer," *American Psychologist* 62, no. 3 (2007): 220.

32   gaining weight and losing weight over and over . . . *exacerbates* insulin resistance, among other problems: J. P. Montani et a l., "Weight Cycling during Growth and Beyond as a Risk Factor for Later Cardiovascular Diseases: The 'Repeated Overshoot' Theory," *International Journal of Obesity* 30 (2006) (Suppl 4):S 58–66.

33   dieting is linked to *more* weight gain: L. O'Hara and J. Taylor, "What's Wrong with the 'War on Obesity?' A Narrative Review of the Weight-Centered Health Paradigm and Development of the 3C Framework to Build Critical Competency for a Paradigm Shift," *Sage Open* 8, no. 2 (2018), https://doi.org/10.1177/2158244018772888.

33   weight loss lead to people gaining *more* weight than they started with: K. H. Pietiläinen et al., "Does Dieting Make You Fat? A Twin Study," *International Journal of Obesity* 36, no. 3 (2012): 456–64.

33 weight cycling and exacerbated insulin resistance: "Methods for Voluntary Weight Loss and Control," NIH Technology Assessment Conference Panel, *Annals of Internal Medicine* 116, no. 11 (1992): 942–49, https://doi.org/10.7326/0003-4819-116-11-942.

34 dieting is a *huge* predictor of disordered eating behavior: K. M. Middlemass et al., "Food Insecurity and Dietary Restraint in a Diverse Urban Population," *Eating Disorders* (2020): 1–14, https://doi.org/10.1080/10640266.2020.1723343.

35 the *danger* of yo-yo dieting and weight cycling for insulin resistance: L. Bacon and L. Aphramor, "Weight Science: Evaluating the Evidence for a Paradigm Shift," *Nutrition Journal* 10, no. 9 (2011), https://doi.org/10.1186/1475-2891-10-9.

HOW TO BE OBSESSED WITH BEAUTY

69 constantly seeing images of "the thin beauty ideal . . .": G. López-Guimerà et al., "Influence of Mass Media on Body Image and Eating Disordered Attitudes and Behaviors in Females: A Review of Effects and Processes," *Media Psychology* 13, no. 4 (2010): 387–416.

69 Consuming the media that's been out there for the past century . . . affects our self-esteem and body image: H. S. Peek, "Distorted Reality: Reality Television and the Effects on Female Body Image," in *Child and Adolescent Psychiatry and the Media*, ed. C. K. Olson and E. V. Beresin (St. Louis: Elsevier, 2018), 11.

70 using social media for thirty minutes a day can change the way we view our bodies: R. M. Perloff, "Social Media Effects on Young Women's Body Image Concerns: Theoretical Perspectives and an Agenda for Research," *Sex Roles* 71 (2014): 363–77, https://doi.org/10.1007/s11199-014-0384-6.

72 "better looking girls tend to 'marry up'": N. Etcoff, *Survival of the Prettiest* (New York: Anchor, 2000), 65.

72 women with greater *intelligence* have no advantage on the marriage market: N. F. Marks, "Flying Solo at Midlife: Gender, Marital Status, and Psychological Well-Being," *Journal of Marriage and the Family* 58 (1996): 917–32.

73 When all you see on your TV and in magazines are skinny white
    people, who all have similar faces, we subconsciously wonder what's
    wrong with us: S. C. Want, K. Vickers, and J. Amos, "The Influence of
    Television Programs on Appearance Satisfaction: Making and Miti-
    gating Social Comparisons to *Friends*," *Sex Roles* 60 (2009): 642–55,
    https://doi.org/10.1007/s11199-008-9563-7.

74 by six years old, girls want a thinner figure, and it's highly influ-
    enced by *the images they see in the media*: H. K. Dohnt and M. Tigge-
    mann, "Body Image Concerns in Young Girls: The Role of Peers and
    Media Prior to Adolescence," *Journal of Youth and Adolescence* 35, 135
    (2006), https://doi.org/10.1007/s10964-005-9020-7.

HOW TO LOSE FEELING IN HALF OF YOUR FACE

79 trauma is less about *what happened* and more about *how your
    body processed it*. Or, rather, how your body *didn't* process it: P. A.
    Levine, *Waking the Tiger* (Berkeley, CA: North Atlantic Books, 1997),
    149.

81 if PTSD symptoms go unprocessed, they can eventually manifest
    as chronic fatigue, immune system problems, or endocrine problems: P.
    Payne, P. A. Levine, and M. A. Crane-Godreau, "Somatic Experiencing:
    Using Interoception and Proprioception as Core Elements of Trauma
    Therapy," *Frontiers in Psychology* 6, no. 93 (2015), https://doi.org/10.33
    89/fpsyg.2015.00093.

81 "trauma victims cannot recover until they befriend the sensations
    in their bodies": B. A. van der Kolk, *The Body Keeps the Score: Brain,
    Mind, and Body in the Healing of Trauma* (New York: Penguin Books,
    2014), 102.

HOW TO BE AN ACTUAL CHEESE GRATER IN A MUSICAL

86 Yaz was once considered "the most complained about drug on the
    internet," according to the internet: H. Grigg-Spall, "Just How Safe Is
    Yaz? Women Need to Know!," *Ms. Magazine*, February 9, 2012, http://

msmagazine.com/blog/2012/02/09/just-how-safe-is-yaz-women
-need-to-know/.

HOW TO NOT KNOW YOU HAVE AN EATING DISORDER

91 "Starvation can occur in people of any body shape and size. It doesn't just happen in people with lower body weight, although society and the medical profession may not understand this fact": J. L. Gaudiani, *Sick Enough: A Guide to the Medical Complications of Eating Disorders* (New York: Routledge, 2018).

92 in the body that will protect the highest adult weight in response to dieting: M. W. Schwartz, "An Inconvenient Truth about Obesity," *Molecular Metabolism* 1, nos. 1–2 (2012): 2.

92 calorie restriction makes food extra appealing, increases the brain's chemical reward for eating food, and makes us more fixated on food: E. Stice, K. Burger, and S. Yokum, "Caloric Deprivation Increases Responsivity of Attention and Reward Brain Regions to Intake, Anticipated Intake, and Images of Palatable Foods," *Neuroimage* 67 (2013): 322–30.

93 our hypothalamus adjusts our metabolism to generally keep us in our range: Schwartz, "An Inconvenient Truth about Obesity."

94 Clinicians are less likely to recommend that Black women receive professional help for the same disordered eating behaviors that white women have: K. H. Gordon et al., "The Impact of Client Race on Clinician Detection of Eating Disorders," *Behavior Therapy* 37, no. 4 (2006): 319–25, https://doi.org/10.1016/j.beth.2005.12.002.

HOW TO HEAL YOUR CREATIVE SOUL

192 the history of fatphobia and white supremacy: S. Strings, *Fearing the Black Body* (New York: NYU Press, 2019).

HOW TO BE A RECEPTIONIST WHO'S AFRAID OF THE PHONE

202 67 percent of millennials said they felt "extreme" pressure to succeed, compared to 40 percent of Gen Xers and 23 percent of boomers:

M. Curtin, "Why Millennials Should Stop Trying to Be Successful . . . Immediately," *Inc.*, April 27, 2016, https://www.inc.com/melanie -curtin/why-millennials-feel-more-pressure-to-succeed-than-any -other-generation.html.

203 the more time you spend on social media, the more depressed you tend to be: University of Pittsburgh Schools of the Health Sciences, "Social Media Use Associated with Depression among US Young Adults," *ScienceDaily*, March 22, 2016, www.sciencedaily.com/releases /2016/03/160322100401.htm.

HOW TO FIGURE OUT IF YOU'RE ALLOWED TO BE TIRED

225 employees are happier, healthier, and more productive when they work less than forty hours a week: J. Greene, "Is 40 Hours a Week Too Much? Here's What History and Science Say," atSpoke, https://www .atspoke.com/blog/hr/40-hour-work-week/.

225 people who work overtime, or more than forty hours a week, are *less* healthy and *less* productive than those who don't: C. Caruso et al., "Overtime and Extended Work Shifts: Recent Findings on Illnesses, Injuries, and Health Behaviors," CDC Workplace Safety and Health, April 2004, https://www.cdc.gov/niosh/docs/2004-143/pdfs/2004-143 .pdf.

225 "researchers consistently find that in office jobs, people are capable of being productive for only about three hours a day, on average": D. Price, *Laziness Does Not Exist* (New York: Atria Books, 2021), 82.

228 *perceived* stigma alone is a chronic stress that can be very bad for our *physical health*: E. A. Pascoe and L. Smart Richman, "Perceived Discrimination and Health: A Meta-Analytic Review," *Psychological Bulletin* 135, no. 4 (2009): 531–54, https://doi.org/10.1037/a00160 59.

HOW TO CLAIM REST

241 more than thirty-seven million adults in the United States reported binge drinking about once a week: Centers for Disease Control and

Prevention, "During Binges, U.S. Adults Have 17 Billion Drinks a Year," March 16, 2018, https://www.cdc.gov/media/releases/2018/p0 316-binge-drinking.html.

241 alcohol is the fourth leading cause of death in the United States: National Institute on Alcohol Abuse and Alcoholism, "Alcohol Facts and Statistics," accessed October 2020, https://www.niaaa.nih.gov /publications/brochures-and-fact-sheets/alcohol-facts-and-statistics.

ABOUT THE AUTHOR

Caroline Dooner is a humorist and a storyteller. She spent years as a performer and dieted like it was her job (because it kind of was). Since fixing her relationship with food, she's been sharing what she learned. She lives with her anxious bernedoodle in Pennsylvania, and they're just trying to live the simple life. She believes wholeheartedly in the healing powers of food and rest.